Objects of Desire

Objects of Desire

Consumer Behaviour in Shopping Centre Choices

Charles Dennis with
Andrew Newman and David Marsland

First published 2005 by
PALGRAVE MACMILLAN
Houndmills, Basingstoke, Hampshire RG21 6XS and
175 Fifth Avenue, New York, N. Y. 10010
Companies and representatives throughout the world

PALGRAVE MACMILLAN is the global academic imprint of the Palgrave Macmillan division of St. Martin's Press, LLC and of Palgrave Macmillan Ltd. Macmillan® is a registered trademark in the United States, United Kingdom and other countries. Palgrave is a registered trademark in the European Union and other countries.

ISBN 1–4039–0170–8

This book is printed on paper suitable for recycling and made from fully managed and sustained forest sources.

A catalogue record for this book is available from the British Library.

Library of Congress Cataloging-in-Publication Data
Dennis, Charles (Charles E.)
    Objects of desire : consumer behaviour in shopping centre choices / Charles Dennis.
        p. cm.
    Includes bibliographical references and index.
    ISBN 1–4039–0170–8 (cloth)
        1. Shopping centers–Marketing. 2. Consumer behaviour.
3. Consumers' preferences. I. Title.

HF5430.D46 2004
658.8'343–dc22   2004048878

10   9   8   7   6   5   4   3   2
14   13   12   11   10   09   08   07   06   05

Printed and bound in Great Britain by
Antony Rowe Ltd, Chippenham and Eastbourne

To my wife Mary for loving support (when I was around enough to appreciate it); to my daughters Trish and Juliet; my mother Joan; and to Ross and Janine.

Contents

List of Tables

List of Figures

Acknowledgements

The author thanks the many people who have helped bring this book to completion. In particular, thanks are due to the co-authors of the research papers on which many of the chapters were based including Professors David Marsland and John Murphy; Drs. Tony Cockett, Lisa Harris and Andrew Newman; Julia Hilton, Eleni Papamatthaiou, Tara Patel, Balraj Sandhu and Shahid Zaman. The author also thanks Capital Shopping Centres PLC and GlobeCast for assistance with funding. Thanks are also due to Professor Peter McGoldrick of UMIST for posing many searching questions on early versions of the results of Part II, anonymous reviewers of the various papers for constructive suggestions, Professors Ross Davies of the Oxford Institute of Retail Management, Clifford Guy of the Cardiff University of Wales and Heli Marjanen of Turku School of Business administration for providing much extra useful information and insights. Thanks are also due to Mary Dennis, Meera Doulub, Aniela Grundy, Chris Jackson, Ronny Nicholas, Tara Patel, Anthi Vakali and Shahid Zaman for assistance in data gathering and processing. The author also thanks the anonymous shopping centres for their co-operation and participation in the research.

Particular acknowledgements refer to Chapter 9. Firstly, I am grateful to co-author Dr Andrew Newman for agreeing to the use of this chapter in the book. The Mall Corporation provided the site for the trial and the provision of the Captive Audience Network (CAN) was project managed by How and Why Ltd. GlobeCast funded the project with a generous research grant. Thanks are also due to imedia inc., Easton Town Center and Michael Morrison for permission to use the photos in Figure 12.8.

List of Contributors

Dr Charles Dennis is a Chartered Marketer and a Senior Lecturer in Marketing and Retail Management at Brunel University, London, UK, where he heads up the 'Marketing' pathway of the University's BSc Business and Management degree. Originally a Chartered Chemical Engineer, he spent some years in engineering and technical posts, latterly with a 'marketing' emphasis. This was followed by seven years with 'Marketing Methods' as an Institute of Marketing approved consultant. Charles has been full-time in this current post since 1993. Charles has published internationally on consumer shopping behaviour, e-shopping and e-retailing. The books *Marketing the E-business* (Harris and Dennis) and *E-retailing* (Dennis, Fenech and Merrilees) were published in 2002 and 2004 respectively.

Professor David Marsland is professor of Health Informatics at Brunel University. UK. He is a London School of Economics (LSE)-trained sociologist who has specialised in the study of youth, welfare and research methods. His latest book, *Welfare or Welfare State?*, was published by Macmillan in March 1996. In 1991 he was the first winner of the Thatcher award for contributions to the analysis of freedom. Professor Marsland has lectured to a wide international audience and is a well-known broadcaster and journalist.

Dr. Andrew Newman lectures in retail operations and customer behaviour on the MBA and corporate programmes at Manchester Business School. He has attracted considerable research funds for the University of Manchester by way of government funding and collaborative ventures with various commercial partners. These include KTP/DTI projects that focus on retail sourcing and knowledge management, the reengineering of a fashion retailer's supply chain systems, and EPSRC funded work that explored the planning of retail store layouts and customer movement patterns. Andrew is also co-investigator for an EPSRC retail network that commenced in November 2003. His doctoral students research in areas of business process reengineering, retailer branding and loyalty, the internationalisation of retailing and retail consumer behaviour. He also publishes in journals and appears frequently in the media as an expert in retail customer behaviour. Andrew's latest book is entitled: Retailing: Environment and Operations and published by Thomson Learning. Before entering academic life, Andrew spent 23 years working for British Airways in areas marketing and customer services.

Part I
Introduction and Background

Introduction

What determines where people shop? Why would shoppers visit one shopping centre rather than another? Answers to such questions can be of crucial importance in the development and management of shopping centres. Developers, backers, planners and Government will wish to make reliable estimates of the viability of proposed new centres. Developers wish to plan, build and/or improve shopping centres so as to maximise profitable retail sales. These are some of the purely practical reasons for investigating shopping preferences. From a broader perspective there is a need to understand shopping as a fundamental aspect of modern society.

There are many methods available that aid decision making in choosing sites for shopping centres and predicting shopping levels. Despite considerable academic research and presumably substantial resources available from developers, this nevertheless appears to be still an inexact science, emphasising the need for a deeper study of the question at the heart of this book: 'Why do people shop where they do?' A survey of shopping centres twelve months after opening by Kirkup & Rafiq (1994a) found that occupancy levels (by number of units, excluding 'anchor' stores) varied from below 50 percent to over 80 percent. It is reasonable to suppose that those with lower occupancy levels were performing considerably below the levels predicted before development.

For example, the Catwalk Centre (a UK shopping centre – not its real name) can be considered as under performing. This centre is in a provincial town, has a department store anchor and a high proportion of fashion-related merchandise. Excluding the anchor store, the occupancy rate climbed to 65 percent within 15 months of opening but dropped shortly afterwards with the loss of a number of stores. Three

3

years after the centre opened, 55 percent of tenants had been trading for less than 12 months. Kirkup and Rafiq (1994b) commented:

> In terms of occupancy levels and tenant closures it is clear that factors were at play which countered the centre's attractions in terms of a major anchor store, car park and a large catchment population. Undoubtedly the recession had a major impact .... However, given the relative success of some other schemes, which opened in the same year, one might also question the influence of other factors.

The poor performance of the Catwalk Centre illustrates the need for more research into what make shopping centres successful. As Kirkup and Rafiq (1993) pointed out, referring to UK shopping centres:

> A number of clearly successful centres imply that others may not have followed best practice in research, design and marketing. Similarly, it is expected that developers and backers would wish to be able to predict the higher levels with improved accuracy and select those for development and improved demand forecasting is needed in the future.

Research in this area is helpful not only in the planning of new centres but also potentially in the improvement of existing centres. The attributes affecting shopping levels can be identified more precisely by using the methods described in this book. Using these techniques, managers of new or existing centres will be able to improve or modify their offering and increase business.

Kirkup and Rafiq (1993 and 1994a) analysed common attributes of some of the most successful UK shopping centres. In effect, they provided some of the answers to the key question of 'what determines where people shop' – for example, the choice of well-known stores, car parking and easy access to large anchor stores.

For most of the shopping population of the UK, though, there are other centres within easy reach offering the same facilities. For example, the Catwalk Centre is the second enclosed and managed centre to have opened in the town (Kirkup and Rafiq 1994b). So how do people decide which to use? Is travel time/distance the main criterion? Do perceptions of 'image' influence shoppers' attitudes to individual town centres or shopping centres? This is what Marjanen (1993, page 10, citing Jones and Simmons, 1990) calls the 'mystery of consumer behaviour' because 'we are not able to explain **why people shop where they do'**.

This work has set out to investigate the relationship between the 'image' or 'attractiveness' of (UK) shopping centres and individual shopper behaviour. It is not an attempt to re-write the extensive literature on spatial interaction and discrete choice models nor to produce a 'grand' or 'comprehensive' overall 'model' of shopper behaviour such as attempted by Huff (1963) and developed further by many other researchers. Rather, the aim is to provide methods that may be of use as a part of or in combination with existing theoretical models. The methods could be used for example in the Huff model in order to estimate parameters, following procedures described by Ghosh and McLafferty (1987), or in the multiplicative competitive interaction model (MCI) (Nakanishi and Cooper 1974, Achabal et al, 1982) or more recent forecasting models. One specific finding is that the effect and shape of the distance/demand curve varies considerably. This explains much of the lack of success of existing models in predicting shopping centre sales values. Other useful outcomes concern the effects of pleasure and experience on shopping behaviour and how atmospheric variables might be modelled and adjusted.

The empirical work primarily concerns case studies of six UK shopping centres (fictional names are used to protect the guilty!). The centres, in ascending size order, were:

- The Metropolitan Centre, an in-town sub-regional centre
- The Delphi Centre, an in-town sub-regional centre
- The West London Shopping Centre, an in-town sub-regional centre
- The Jubilee Centre, an in-town regional centre
- The White Water Centre, an in-town, regional centre and
- The Blue Rose Centre, a large, out-of-town regional shopping centre.

The theory structure is made more coherent by a schematic diagram of the propositions that received support, with the chapter numbers marked on the paths. This diagram can be found in the final chapter, Chapter 13, Figure 13.1 page 243. The book proceeds as follows. After the introduction and background in Part I, Part II explores questions on why people shop where they do, considering the attributes of shopping centres and aspects of travel time/distance that affect shoppers' decisions about where to shop. Part III then addresses shoppers' decision-making processes. Finally, Part IV introduces issues concerning e-shopping and brings together the findings, to draw conclusions and comment on the implications.

Following this Introduction in Part I, Chapter 1 outlines the background to shopping centres in retail, marketing and historical contexts.

Part II starts with Chapter 2, which develops the research questions, hypotheses, methodology and questionnaire design for Part II. Chapter 3 then explores the attributes of shopping centres that affect shoppers' decisions concerning where to shop. Different attributes are significantly more critical for some shopping centres than others. Chapter 4 continues the theme of the image of shopping centres by considering the shopping centre as a brand. Even though the terminology of branding is little used for shopping centres, those that are more strongly 'branded' in the terms used here tend to be more successful.

Chapters 5 and 6 put the shopping centre into a spatial context, investigating the effects of shoppers' travel distance and time on shopping choices. Chapter 5 is the 'title' chapter: the shopping centre as an object of desire – attraction and distance in shopping centre choice. The chapter attempts to explain some of the discrepancies that researchers have reported in the balance of the effects of attractiveness with distance/time. Chapter 6 updates Central Place 'Theory' with a more practical and realistic view of the retail hierarchy and catchment boundaries that does not rely on the unsustainable assumptions of the original theory.

Chapter 7 considers marketing segmentation issues: differences in shopping centre choices and the implications for marketing mixes for different groups of customers. An essential aspect concerns the differences between segments defined by benefit or importance motivation.

Part III starts with Chapter 8, an attempt to explain some of the psychology of shoppers' choices by using or adapting classical Motivation theories. A hierarchy is confirmed in terms of some motivations being higher-level than others and having an equivalently greater effect on shopping centre success.

Chapter 9 takes an Environmental Psychology approach in attempting to explain processes in shoppers' choices of shopping locations. The findings include the significant, positive effect of a controllable atmospheric stimulus. Chapter 10 looks deeper into the 'why' of shopping with a preliminary attempt at an empirical approach to understanding shopping in Evolutionary Psychology terms. Shopping styles may be rooted in the lifestyles necessitated when our ancestors adapted to life in the African Savannah.

The final part, Part IV, starts with an investigation into shoppers' motivations for e-shopping rather than conventional shopping. Many of the motives applying to conventional shopping were found to be also valid for e-shopping. Chapter 12 compares e-shopping directly with shopping centres, eliciting preliminary findings on ways in which shopping centres need to improve their offers in order to compete with competition from e-retailers.

Finally, Chapter 13 draws together some of the main findings, summarising the propositions that have been supported.

Settled domesticity of the Neolithic era ... began around 8000 BC. ...
The people of the town of Catalhoyuk [founded around 7000 BC]
were traders too [as well as being hunters and farmers]. ... Polished
mirrors made from obsidian were shown to have been imported from
quarries 120 miles away in Cappadocia.

(Daily Mail, UK, 11 January 2000, commenting on Richard
Rudgleys's (2000) *The Secrets of the Stone Age*)

1
Background

Shopping is a primary human activity in which almost every individual in civilised society takes part .... Shopping may be either a chore, a social pleasure, a relaxation or a stimulus.

(Beddington, 1991)

Throughout the world, shopping for goods and services ... by the exchange of money or goods, has always been and still is an important part of ... daily life .... The underlying and basic desire ... is to create a pleasant environment – not only for ... buying ... but also to satisfy a social need.

(Redstone, 1973)

Since the beginning of history, retailers have sought to make shopping a pleasurable experience:

The Sumarian and Mesopotamian caravanners of 4000 years ago ... knew well the importance of creating just the right atmosphere for selling. No unit would depart from Damascus on its journey to Jeddah without ... magicians, snake charmers, story tellers, dancers, sword swallowers and craftsmen who theatrically fashioned goods in situ ....

(English Tourist Board, 1989, page 3)

In the UK (the English Tourist Board went on to point out) the Romans 'formalised and enhanced the market system that was already in place'. For instance at what is now Leadenhall street in London, Forshaw and Bergstrom (1983) stated that the Romans 'built a market place or forum, a large square 200 yards across'. This would have had traders around the periphery and an area in the centre for public leisure and socialising.

Medieval times saw the growth of markets in England and Wales with 2800 markets franchised between 1199 and 1480 (Gosling and Maitland, 1976). In the time of diarist Samuel Pepys's – the mid 1600s – Leadenhall market was still the most important of London's markets (and remains one of the best known meat and fish markets in the UK today).

Shopping for fashion and pleasure can be traced back to the sixteenth century in the UK. Financial trader Thomas Gresham built the Stock Exchange with atrium and a shopping gallery on the second and third floors in the City (financial district) of London in 1568. Queen Elizabeth I liked shopping there for fashionable clothing and named it the Royal Exchange. Following the Great Plague of 1665 and the Fire of London in the following year, the suburbs took on more importance. Covent Garden became London's most fashionable area, centred on Inigo Jones's piazza, a two level gallery of small shops (not today's building) which had opened in 1631 (Arburgham, 1979 and Forshaw and Bergstrom, 1983). Covent Garden and the new shopping galleries that appeared in London (including the rebuilt Royal Exchange), Paris, Antwerp, Prague and Amsterdam set the scene for stylish early modern shopping. Shopping galleries were 'covered shopping areas, purpose built and designed, and containing a large number of different shops lined along walkways' (Walsh, 2003). Shops selling high fashion to high society shoppers paid high rents in the Royal Exchange and London's four other shopping galleries. Despite the influence of USA designs, UK shopping centres stem from these early roots.

Retail in a marketing context

For centuries retailers have striven to understand and satisfy customer needs and wants and thus make a profit. Mui and Mui (1989) have demonstrated that many of the innovations previously attributed to Victorian entrepreneurs were actually in use in eighteenth-century England. As early as 1688 William Stout of Lancaster set up his shopkeeping business. Lacking efficient channels of distribution, he had to travel on horseback to London to seek out manufacturers and suppliers of general groceries and hardware, to Sheffield for ironware and to Bristol and the local customs port for sugar and tobacco. Stout may or may not have been unusual in making these long, dangerous journeys but he was not unique – he travelled in convoy with other shopkeepers. What was unusual was writing his autobiography (Marshall, 1967, cited by Mui and Mui, 1989). In reward for his efforts in obtaining the goods that his customers wanted, he was able to sell at an average mark-up of 100 percent. Thus, we can infer Stout's understanding of what is now known as the 'marketing concept' of creating customer satisfaction profitably. This concept was explicitly stated (though still not by that name) in the second half of the eighteenth century. Mui and Mui (1989) quote W C Trant's advertisement for condiments, olives, anchovies and truffles: 'The wish nearest to my heart ... is to give entire satisfaction to all persons who favour me with their order.'

Shopping has long been associated not only with the supply of basic needs, but also with image and fashion. Josiah Wedgwood (1730–95) claimed that 'fashion is infinitely superior to merit in many respects' (according to McKendrick and colleagues, 1982 cited by Mui and Mui, 1989). In order to establish his UK-based business as a mid-eighteenth century world market leader for quality china, he used public relations and networking to attract the leaders of fashion: 'the monarchy, the nobility and the art connoisseurs'.

The meaning of 'image'

This book seeks to investigate aspects of what determines where people shop (choices of shopping centres). Topics concern not just physical attributes but also less tangible atmospheric stimuli that, collectively with the tangibles, we refer to as 'image', and the processes by which images may be associated with shopper behaviour. In his seminal work, Boulding illustrated the meaning of 'image' by parallel with a furnace control device that, 'if not congruent with the desired state, takes corrective action'. A human functions in a similar way, although the mechanism is complicated by 'imagination':

> The process by which we obtain an image of value is not very different from ... an image of fact ... . The image of value is concerned with the rating of the various parts of our image of the world.
>
> (Boulding, 1956, page 11)

Authors on retail image have broadly followed Boulding's approach, viewing image in terms of the tangible and intangible perceptions of shoppers that influence spending behaviour. McGoldrick (1990; 2002) reviewed literature on image, citing Berry (1969); Houston and Nevin

(1980); and Lindquist (1974). Berry (1969) viewed image as 'the result of differential reinforcement in the context of a given stimulus or set of stimuli'. Lindquist (1974) considered image in terms of not just stimulus and reinforcement but also perceptions:

> The behaviour of a human is not directed by mere knowledge and information but is a product of the images that a [person] perceives .... We function or react not in response to what is true but to what we believe to be true.

Houston and Nevin (1980) defined image as:

> The complex of a consumer's perceptions of a store on functional attributes (e.g., assortment of goods offered, price level, physical layout, etc.) and emotional attributes (e.g., perceived clientele, atmosphere etc.). Research findings ... have shown that store image is significantly related to store choice.

McGoldrick (1990, page 125) pointed out that images are formed somewhat selectively 'from a combination of factual and emotional material'. Smith and Burns (1996) quoted a similar definition that they claim to be 'most accepted by scholars': 'a combination of tangible or functional factors that a consumer perceives to be present.'

Howard (1995, page 44) accepted this approach for shopping centres and stated that:

> Images are ... based on experience of the product and of its advertising, and its competitors, and influenced by the attitudes, expectations and circumstances of the consumer. Images can be formed very selectively from relatively few pieces of information ... . Explanations of relative success of particular [shopping] centres ... can be analysed in terms of image.

When image is defined in terms of a combination of tangible or functional attributes and intangible or emotional factors within a competitive context, the term becomes almost indistinguishable from 'branding':

> A brand is a product or service made distinctive by its positioning relative to the competition and by its personality. *Positioning* ... describes the brand by defining its competitive context ... .

Personality consists of a unique combination of functional attributes and symbolic values.

(Hankinson and Cowking, 1993)

For consistency with most of the retail literature, the term 'image' rather than 'brand' is usually used in this book – except where addressing specific marketing branding issues in Chapter 4 below. In summary, image can be considered to consist of the complete mix of cues which communicate with the customer and influence shopping behaviour: sensory, intangible, tangible, stores and all others. A large proportion of this book concerns the measurement of and the effects of the images of shopping centres.

Shopping centres

The shopping centre industry uses 'rules of thumb' for design, decor and image cues such as tenant placement (for examples, see Brown, 1992a and Beddington, 1991) but as Brown (1992a, page 178) pointed out:

They appear to be the outcome of a long and expensive trial and error process, *not* extensive empirical research (Beddington, 1982). As such, they are in danger of being elevated into unbreakable shopping centre axioms.

This book attempts to identify and quantify the effects of some of these atmosphere and image cues. Intuitively, we might consider that people like to shop – it is not just a chore – and like to have a choice of merchandise and to be able to choose from a wide range of shops – small as well as large. This is presumably one of the reasons behind the growth of 'shopping centres'. In retail marketing terms a shopping centre is considered to be 'a planned retail development comprising at least three shops, under one freehold, managed and marketed as a unit' with a minimum gross retail area of 5000 m^2 (based on Guy, 1994b). A shopping centre also includes 'some planned pedestrian area' additional to the shops and car park (Reynolds, 1993). For the purpose of this book, the pedestrian precinct of a shopping centre is covered from the weather – thus distinguishing the shopping centre from, for example, retail parks. UK Shopping centres usually include at least one large 'anchor' store (commonly a department store) and a number of smaller stores providing diversity.

The historical context of shopping centres

> Imagine elegant corridors lit by ... lamps reflected in mirrors and marble and by diffused light from glass roofs ... accommodating beautiful shops to satisfy the whims of the passer-by and ... protecting ... from the vagaries of the weather.
> (MacKeith, 1985, describing the Burlington Arcade opened in 1818)

Some early markets and bazaars were developed into sophisticated arcades. An arcade is a glass-covered passageway connecting two busy streets, lined on both sides with shops (Beddington, 1991). The first recorded arcade was the Passage Delorme in Paris, France, opened in 1809 (Geist, 1983). The Burlington Arcade in London, UK, opened in 1818 (MacKeith, 1985) and is still the busiest and most prosperous arcade in the UK. MacKeith was describing just such an arcade in the quote at the start of this section – a description that fits well to the image that many of today's shopping centres strive for.

The first true shopping centre is said to have been a 50 shop, three level enclosed arcade opened in 1829 in Providence, Rhode Island, USA (Dawson, 1983). This author considers that the European arcades of earlier date – or even shopping galleries such as the Royal Exchange – would also have a claim to the distinction. The first purpose built out-of-town shopping centre is reported as having been the Country Club Plaza, Kansas City, USA, opened in 1923 (McGoldrick and Thompson, 1992b, citing Sternlieb and Hughes, 1981). On the other hand, the Covent Garden piazza – then out-of-town – also has a claim – as early as 1631. The pattern of two-level, air-conditioned malls was set by the Southland Centre, Minneapolis, USA, opened in 1956 (Martin, 1982).

In this post-war period it was becoming clear to planners that people like to shop traffic-free. When a sewer burst in a Norwich, UK, street in 1965, it was closed for repairs. The expected drop in sales never happened and Norwich became the first city in the UK to eliminate traffic permanently from a central commercial street (Brambilla and Longo, 1977). The growth of shopping centres in the UK actually began in 1964 with the Bull Ring in Birmingham (Rebuilt in 2004) followed by other town centre schemes such as the Arndale Centre in Doncaster in 1968 (Davies and Bennison, 1979). In design terms, this has been described as the era of brutalist architecture and concrete 'raw from the shutter' (Scott, 1991).

The first **regional** shopping centre in the UK (i.e. with at least 50 000 m^2 gross retail area) was the Arndale Centre, Poole, opened in 1969 (Guy,

1994b). At the time of writing there are seven in-town regional shopping centres in the UK. The first new-town regional shopping centre from a current total of seven was Runcorn Shopping City in 1971.

According to Guy (1994a) the first **out-of-town** regional shopping centre in the UK was said to have been Brent Cross, Hendon, in 1976 but the description 'out-of-town' could be arguable in this case as Hendon is a very urban area. There is no accepted definition of the terms 'out-of-town' or 'edge-of-town' but McGoldrick (1992b, page 7), appears to accept Hillier Parker's view that out-of-town centres are 'developments which are not part of an existing centre of retail activity'.

All but one of the five subsequent UK out-of-town centres were **'super-regional'** – defined as having at least 100 000 m^2 gross retail area (Guy, 1994b). The first super-regional out-of-town shopping centre was the MetroCentre, near Gateshead, in 1986. One in-town centre is super-regional (the Arndale Centre, Manchester, 1976) and one new-town centre is super-regional (Milton Keynes, 1979). At the time of writing, new openings of super-regional centres have almost stopped across Western Europe; Russia is now the largest growth market (C B Hillier Parker, 2002).

Burke and Shackleton consider that increasing levels of crime and vandalism have reduced the attractiveness of traditional town centres, citing a study by Sheffield University, UK, reported in *The Times Higher Education Supplement*, 28 July 1995. Nevertheless, according to Hillier Parker (1993):

> The vast majority of shopping centre investment in the UK over the last three decades has been directed towards traditional town centre trading locations. Analogies with the blight of American cities are inaccurate and flawed.

The growth of out-of-town shopping has been slowed by planning restrictions (McGoldrick, 1992b; 2002). Current planning guidelines follow a 'sequential approach' with planning approvals favouring firstly town centre developments. Only if no suitable town centre site is available will suburban or edge-of-town sites be approved. Finally, out-of-town retail and leisure developments will only be approved if there is no suitable town centre, suburban or edge of town sites available (Revisions to Planning Policy Guidance Note PPG 6, 1993 and 1996, PPG13, 1994 and Draft Planning Policy Statement PPS 6, 2003.

In all there are approximately 225 shopping centres in the UK that comply with the definition in the 'Shopping centres' section of this chapter above – including more in-town ones than any other country (Allegra, 2002; Howard, 1997; OXIRM, 1993). The vast majority of both investment and shopping have been in-town and UK towns have in the main not yet suffered the blight that has affected United States cities (Fernie, 1995; Field C, 1997a). The Field survey reported 38 percent of adults visiting high street and town centre shops (excluding supermarkets), compared with 14 percent visiting out-of-town shopping centres. In terms of average number of visits per year the equivalent figures are 51 for high streets and town centres versus 26 for out-of-town shopping centres. According to Management Horizons (2004), Manchester, Glasgow, and London's Oxford Street are the UK's top shopping venues – well ahead of any purpose-built shopping centres. Of the Top 20 shopping centres in the UK (listed in Box 1.1), only eight (including the top 6, though) are out-of-town.

On the other hand, shoppers emphatically prefer to shop in an enclosed shopping centre when they have the chance. A survey of 4760 shoppers indicated that 61 percent preferred shopping centres compared to other locations such as retail parks and high streets

1. Bluewater	Greenhithe, Kent
2. MetroCentre	Gateshead
3. Merry Hill	Dudley
4. Meadowhall	Sheffield
5. Lakeside	Thurrock, Essex
6. Trafford Centre	Manchester
7. The Centre	Milton Keynes
8. Arndale Centre	Manchester
9. Eldon Square	Newcastle
10. Victoria Centre	Nottingham
11. Brent Cross	North London
12. Telford Centre	Telford, Shropshire
13. Cwmbran	Torfaen, Wales
14. West Quay	Southampton
15. Queensgate	Peterborough
16. Braehead	Glasgow
17. The Oracle	Reading
18. Arndale Centre	Luton
19. The Mall at Cribbs Causeway	Bristol
20. Clyde	Cydebank

Box 1.1   The Top 20 UK shopping centres
Source: Allegra (2002).

(Allegra, 2002). The main reasons stated for this preference concerned one-stop comparison-shopping and protection from the weather. A census of shopping centres and high streets in Melbourne, Australia indicated that shopping centres offered consumers greater 'spatial convenience' than high streets, in the form of one-stop shopping, greater selection of shopping services and extended trading hours (Reimers and Clulow, 2004).

Two of the best known UK out-of-town shopping centres (The MetroCentre and Lakeside) are understood to have attempted to be reclassified as 'in-town' for planning regulation purposes, on the grounds that residential and business development has been attracted to the area (Mintel, 1997). The trend for UK shopping centres to themselves become town centres may well be or become a reality rather than simply a planning device, based on the US experience. As long ago as the 1970s USA out-of-town regional shopping centres were reported to have the ability to draw other uses around them and become the hubs for community activities and business (Lion, 1976). These can become 'suburban growth poles' or 'minicities' with up to 50 000 residents like, for example Brae, California, USA, (Young, 1985)

The successful (managed) shopping centre takes on functions of or attempts to replicate (the best of) traditional town centres and high streets with which it competes for custom. Shopping centres also face competition from newer forms of retailing described by Fernie (1995) as 'the fourth wave', including factory outlets, warehouse clubs, 'big boxes', retail parks and 'power centres'. Power centres (in American terminology) are clusters of outlets not necessarily under single management, dominated by a few large stores known as 'power' tenants, located in close proximity out-of-town and containing few small shops (Bodkin and Lord, 1997). Such centres offer not just cheap prices but convenience – reported by Bodkin and Lord (1997) as the main reason for shopping at two USA power centres. Reynolds (1992 and 1993) pointed out the fast-growing extent of such competition. The number of retail parks had risen from one in 1982 to nearly 250 by 1992. Between 1971 and 1992 the number of out-of-town superstores (3000+ square metres sales area) increased from 21 to 719. By 2000 there were 960 (Lang and Rayner, 2001).

Faced with growing competition from retail parks and superstores, and continuing competition from traditional centres, shopping centres need to investigate and attempt to optimise the added value that centralised management can offer. A number of researchers have reported that most shopping centres have in the past insufficiently addressed marketing issues based on shoppers' images' of shopping centre strengths and weaknesses (Mintel, 1997; Turchiano, 1990).

Howard (1997) reported that UK shopping centres described as 'admirable' or 'excellent' have tended to be those where active marketing management is a feature. Fernie (1998) reported on the most successful UK retail locations in terms of sales turnover and profit. New out-of-town shopping centres are most successful but 'streets in the town centres of Glasgow and Newcastle are in the top 10'. As Fernie pointed out, shopping centres must compete with 'sound town centre management schemes' to attract investment and shoppers. For both town centres and shopping centres, the active management of attractiveness is critical to success.

In investigating 'image', this book helps to provide specific pointers as part of the proactive management and marketing of individual shopping centres, potentially improving the satisfaction of customers' needs in ways not readily identifiable using conventional methodologies. By better satisfying customers needs, the shopping centres may succeed in becoming or remaining social and community centres in a way that may be much more difficult for competitors such as retail parks or power centres.

In an article entitled 'Shopping as a way of life', Field M (1997) claimed that UK consumers 'want more than just products, they want the total experience.' Field identified the five hundred thousand square metre Mall of America in Minneapolis, USA, as a 'global benchmark ... where the prospect of log rides and Planet Hollywood attract around 40 million visitors a year'. Roy (1994) investigated motivational aspects of visits to USA shopping centres and concluded that there was a correlation between visit frequency and recreational shopping motivation. The USA 'total experience' may well be going too far for many non-USA shoppers but there is solid evidence that customers want 'more than just products'. Howard (1990) analysed what she described as 'ambient leisure' – creating a sense of leisure in shopping. There is considerable evidence of the importance of pleasure and atmosphere in shopping motivation. For example, in a postal survey with 503 respondents in Queensland, Australia, 38 percent of shoppers were classified as 'entertainment-seeking' (Sit et al, 2003). A mall intercept survey of 750 shoppers at three regional shopping centres in New Zealand that also examined actual sales figures and visitor numbers found that entertainment-based promotions were successful in attracting visitors (although those promotions on their own were not sufficient to increase spending – Parsons, 2003).

As evidence of the importance of social interaction, Harris et al (1997) demonstrated that (in the example of women's clothing) conversations between customers lead to higher levels of satisfaction (even more than the 'well documented benefits of conversations with sales staff'). Is this an indication that 'shopping as a social activity' could be a powerful selling tool in the shopping centre marketing mix?

Three further regional out-of town centres have opened at the time of writing, one of which is super-regional. Architecture and design ideas such as those of Field M (1997) are apparently influential, with Field drawing attention to Braehead Park's (Glasgow) 'three ice rinks, a maritime heritage centre, a hotel and ten restaurants' and Cribbs Causeway's (Bristol) 'ten screen cinema, bowling alley, a night-club [and] four restaurants'. The UK's largest and (according to Allegra, 2002) 'most admired' super-regional shopping centre to date is Bluewater (Greenhithe, Kent) with 149 000 square metres gross lettable area (GLA). Leisure and lifestyle features include over 50 eating places, a boating lake, climbing wall, cycles and tandems, golf putting, discovery trail, Land Rover adventure zone, cinemas and spas, set in 20 hectares (50 acres) of landscaped parkland with seven lakes. According to the Allegra (2002) survey, the average visit to Bluewater lasts over two and a half hours.

There has been a slowing down in the building of new shopping centres in the UK. Growth was three percent per year between 1990 and 1992 followed by 1.7 percent per year between 1993 and 1996 (Mintel, 1997). From 1996 onwards, new shopping centre openings have been mainly limited to those in the pipeline before 1996. Shopping centre expansion has continued flat across Western Europe, with the only significant increases in space since 1996 taking place in central and Eastern Europe. Nevertheless, the UK is experiencing substantial activity in the refurbishment of shopping centres and also an increase in downtown centres as towns are revitalised, with 0.8 million square metres of GLA in the pipeline in 2002 (C B Hillier Parker, 2002 – out of a total of 13.3 million square metres of shopping centre GLA – Frasquet et al, 2001). Lord (1985) drew attention to the ongoing need for shopping centre 'revitalisation', quoting Lieber's (1981) statement that shopping centres 10 years old are considered 'mature', those built 15 years ago 'old' and those aged 20 years 'ancient'. The findings from this book should be just as relevant to the revitalising and marketing of existing shopping centres as to planning new ones.

UK shopping centres account for 25 percent of retail sales (typical for Europe, but well below the USA's 51 percent). The UK has 13 million square metres of GLA in shopping centres – the highest in Europe (C B Hillier Parker, 2002). UK adults visit shopping centres an average of 21 times per year – third highest in Europe after Sweden and France – the average length of stay is 84 minutes (Cushman & Wakefield/ Healey & Baker, 2002). Most shoppers visited between three and five shops per visit (with women visiting more shops than men – Allegra, 2002).

Shopping centres are an essential part of UK life and shopping is an important social activity. Attractive shopping centres, town centres and high streets will be or become community centres, playing a role in the social structure of society.

In the UK, town centre and high street shopping retains an important place alongside edge-of-town and out-of-town. This book is therefore intended to be as applicable to in-town shopping centres as it is to out-of-town centres, with a majority of the case study locations being in-town.

The following part of this book, Part II explores questions on why people shop where they do, considering the attributes of shopping centres and aspects of travel time/distance that affect shoppers' decisions about where to shop. The next chapter, Chapter 2, develops the research questions, hypotheses, methodology and questionnaire design for Part II.

*The Sumarian and Mesopotamian caravanners of 4000 years ago ...
[created] the right atmosphere for selling. No unit would depart from
Damascus on its journey to Jeddah without ... magicians, snake
charmers, story tellers, dancers, sword swallowers and [artisans] who
theatrically fashioned goods in situ.*

(English Tourist Board, 1989, p. 3)

Part II

Why People Shop Where They Do: Shoppers' Responses to Attributes of Shopping Centres

2
Research Questions, Methodology and Questionnaire Design for Part II

Research questions and hypotheses

The aim of this book concerns the general question: 'why do people shop where they do (choices of shopping centres). Following the literature search outlined in Chapter 1 above, specific research questions can be posed:

(i) Which attributes of a shopping centre are most associated with shopper spending?

(ii) Can the attractiveness of a centre be measured in a way that has meaning and utility, for example in relation to shoppers' spending, the sales turnover or rental income of shopping centres?

(iii) Are the specific attributes most affecting shoppers' spending significantly different at various shopping centres?

(iv) Are the specific attributes affecting shoppers' spending significantly different for different segments of shoppers?

This chapter concerns the methodology adopted in attempting to answer these questions, relating to Part II of this book, i.e. Chapters 3 to 7 inclusive below.

Decisions consumers make on where to shop are affected not only by attributes specific to each centre, such as the choice of stores, but also by the distance or time of travel. According to spatial interaction theory (considered in more detail in Chapters 5 and 6 below), there is decay in shoppers' patronage of a centre with increasing travel distance or time. This decay in patronage can be described in terms of the 'distance exponent'. As argued in Chapter 5 below, the distance exponent can be considered as consisting of two components:

(a) The decay in the proportion of the population shopping at a centre with increasing travel distance or time and
(b) The decay in shoppers' assessments of the attractiveness of a centre with increasing distance or time.

Many authors – briefly summarised in Chapter 5 below – have studied Component (a). A number of researchers have drawn attention to the variable nature of this part of the distance exponent – possibly related to the size or attractiveness of the centre. Because of this link, the present study of attractiveness and image has also encompassed this variation in the distance exponent.

Component (b) has received less attention and indeed is difficult to study directly. In this work, an alternative proxy indicator has been investigated: 'Individual relative spending'. Again, because attractiveness can be postulated to be affected by distance, this research has also included the decay (or otherwise) of Individual relative spending with distance and travel time. To complete the picture in terms of the relationships between attractiveness and travel distance or time, two further questions, (v) and (vi) below have also been addressed.

(v) Can the variations in the distance exponent, Aspect (a), be quantified in terms of the measured attractiveness of centres?
(vi) What independent variable(s) influence Aspect (b), the decay (or otherwise) of individual relative spending with distance and travel time.

Accordingly, a study was designed aimed at answering the research questions as far as practicable.

Methodology

Research questions on shopping centre choice can well be studied by qualitative techniques focused on individual's perceptions of shopping centres and how these affect decisions on where to shop. Accordingly, in the preparatory work for this study, thirty unstructured, open-ended interviews were carried out with a convenience sample of shoppers. Central to this work, though, is the objective of testing hypotheses with a view to eliciting (so far as practicable) statistically significant answers to the research questions. Therefore, a structured question-naire, informed by the qualitative work, was utilised as the main instrument. Further qualitative techniques have been employed in the branding study in Chapter 4.

Selection of the sample of respondents was problematic. The aims might well have been framed in terms of the consumer population as a whole, in which case a postal survey of a random sample of population selected (for example) from the Electoral Roll would have been applicable. A mail procedure could have provided many more cases and been more representative of the population of an area. Such an attempt at random sampling would, though, have resulted in under-representing the users of the centres who shopped there most often. This study was aimed at shopping centre users, and the results intended to have implications for shopping centre managers – who presumably wish primarily to satisfy the wants of their most loyal customers. Therefore, the sample of respondents was intended to be as representative as practicable of shopping centre customers, rather than the population as a whole.

The desired sampling of shopping centre customers (omitting non-customers) was achieved by using a convenience mall intercept survey method. This method sampled shoppers approximately proportionally to their patronage of the centres studied (by visit time). It could be argued that shoppers with time to spare, such as the unemployed, were over sampled. In the event, the socio-demographic characteristics were reasonably representative of UK shopping centre customers. The number classified in the higher socio-economic groups of managerial, administrative, professional, supervisory or clerical (ABC1 on the UK JICTAR scale) was 59 percent. This compared, for example, with a figure of 63 percent for the Lakeside (UK) out-of-town regional centre (owner's proprietary survey of 2000 respondents carried out over two years) and 55 percent for the Treaty Centre, in-town, sub-regional (Hounslow, UK – from the centre 'Education pack' citing 'street surveys'). These figures allayed concerns of possible sampling bias towards the lower-spending consumers. The proportion in the younger age groups 16 to 44 years was 65 percent in this sample compared with 73 percent at Lakeside and 67 percent at the Treaty Centre. This sample was 69 percent females compared with 60 percent at Lakeside and 59 percent at the Treaty Centre. Again, the sampling might have been criticised on the grounds of over-sampling frequent shoppers who may have been lighter buyers travelling shorter distances. On the other hand, there is evidence that the higher-spending shoppers travelling longer distances stay in the centre longer, thus increasing the probability of inclusion in the sample and tending to offset the inclusion of lower-spending respondents (e.g. Lakeside Shopping Centre proprietary survey, November 1994 to February 1996). Despite its limitations, the intercept sample was considered on balance to be the most practicable approach to representative sampling for the centres' actual customers.

The main disadvantage of the mall interview method is that it is time-intensive, requiring a trained interviewer to administer a questionnaire with (in this case) 150 quantitative fields plus text data. Therefore, large samples were not practicable. A minimum total sample size of 200 was specified, with at least 50 at each of four centres, including a range of types of centre from in-town sub regional to large out-of-town regional. In the event, 230 responses were obtained. A further 57 responses were added from two additional centres, to make up the final 287 cases.

For the customer, there may be more than one centre near-by that rates highly on any desired attributes. The differences between centres – distinctiveness – may play a greater part in patronage decisions (Swinyard, 1992). Respondents were therefore asked to give a rating of the centre they were at and their most preferred alternative (which may have been liked more than the one they were at). The difference between these two ratings was used as a composite 'Rating/distinctiveness' measure. In addition, the specific criteria that might attract or repel shoppers were rated for 'Importance'. These two measures were multiplied to give a score for each criterion and each centre. The technique of multiplying rating by weighted importance may seem arbitrary as the function of the expectancy relationship (if any) could conceivably follow any form, and, indeed, other authors have challenged the technique. Bagozzi (1985), for example, developed a theoretical rationale for expectancy-value models, considering the many different mathematical approaches to combining 'beliefs' and 'evaluations'. Nevertheless, the simple multiplicative model is an accepted technique in marketing research. East (1997, page 112) points that this is consistent with the treatment of a product as 'a bundle of expected gains and losses'. This is the 'multi-attribute image model' of James and colleagues (1976) as used, for example, by Gentry and Burns (1977) in assessing attributes of US shopping centre attractiveness and more recently by Suarez et al (2004) for modelling patronage behaviour for Spanish shopping centres.

Shoppers' weightings of individual attributes have been reported to vary from one centre to another (Dellaert et al, 1998; Gautschi,

1981). Therefore, a further step was to multiply the resulting values by a 'weight' representing the degree of association of each attribute with respondents' relative spending at the centre studied, using a procedure similar to the 'Interbrand' or 'Brand Finance' approach to brand evaluation. Unlike those methods, the assignment of weights was not 'judgemental'. Rather, the weight represented a combination measure obtained by multiplying the strength ('elasticity' or regression coefficient) by the degree (R^2) of the association of the attribute with relative spending. The resulting values represented the respondents' satisfactions for each attribute. The attractiveness model for each centre was thus based in part upon the degree of association between the attributes and relative spending. A potential drawback is that there is some auto correlation and an association would be expected. Accordingly, an 'overall attractiveness' scale has been postulated, based on a composite of all of the critical attributes most associated with spending at all of the centres. Because significant variations were observed in which attributes were critical at each of the centres, the use of this more generalised attractiveness scale has reduced the auto correlation effect. Ideally, the weightings of attributes in the model would be universal for all shopping centres. This has not been practicable, but the spread of centres used represented the nearest alternative. Dellaert and associates (1998) confirmed that shoppers do not always weight attributes equally (or rationally), emphasising the need to study such weightings. Evans and colleagues (1996, page 180) state that the only way to examine image is to 'assess its effect on company profitability'. In the world of business, the term 'image' only has a real meaning as far as it is associated with commercial measures of success. That principal has been applied here in that those attributes that were most critical for a centre have been identified using their degree of association with shoppers' spending.

The resulting values represented the respondents' satisfactions for each attribute. The satisfactions for all attributes were then added to give each respondent's total satisfaction score for the centre studied. The average of the respondents' satisfaction scores represented a measured attractiveness for each centre. The scores were rescaled on a 0 to 100 scale, the 'Attractiveness index' for brand image values reported in the Results section of Chapter 4. This scale was such that a hypothetical centre scoring across the board '0s' for rating/distinctiveness (the lowest possible score) would have had a measured 'Attractiveness index' value of 0. On the other hand, a centre scoring across the board '8s' for rating/distinctiveness (the highest possible score) would have had a measured attractiveness value of 100.

Attribute evaluations were considered as interval rather than ordinal data (Oppewal and Timmermans, 1997). Accordingly, ordinary least squares regression analysis was used to investigate the associations between shopping centre attributes and shoppers' spending at the centre studied compared to a competing centre.

Respondents were asked how much they spent at the centre, and at the alternative centre, in an 'average' month. Much of the variation in shoppers' expenditures relates to person differences such as incomes, rather than attributes of the centres (McGoldrick and Thompson, 1992a). To counteract such influences, a composition variable 'relative spending', has been used. A value of 100 indicated all expenditures at (for example) the White Water Centre, none at the alternative centre; 50 represented half of expenditures at each centre. Travel distance and time have been scaled similarly. McGoldrick and Thompson (1992b, page 6) claimed that the relative measure 'provided the sharpest focus upon the competitive interaction between ... centres'.

As McGoldrick and Thompson (1992b) pointed out, preference does not always lead to behaviour. The Chartered Institute of Marketing (1997) concluded from Nishikawa's (1989) work that 'customers are only sincere when spending ... far less sincere when talking'. The authors have attempted to include stated behaviour as well as preferences by weighting some attributes more heavily than others. This model weighted attributes according to the degree of association with spending behaviour as measured by Pearson correlation coefficients (R) or rather the coefficients of determination, R^2 and the regression coefficients. This approach is broadly equivalent to Gautschi's (1981) 'elasticies of salient variables'.

The regression model linked shoppers' spending at a shopping centre with the attractiveness or image attributes and travel distance (or time). Regression models often suffer from problems with multicollinearity. The methodology here overcomes such problems by the use of the composite term for attractiveness or image, incorporating the relevant attributes, weighted according to their association with relative spending. The regressions therefore used at most two terms, travel time (or distance) and attractiveness. There was no significant association observed between these two terms.

As already mentioned, the main aim of this work has concerned identifying and quantifying the effect of specific attributes on the competitive success of shopping centres, leading to the modelling approach based on an external item analysis of individual attributes as described above. Nevertheless, within the general aim of answering 'why people shop where they do?' (choices of shopping centres), the constructs or factors making up shoppers' attitudes to shopping centres are relevant. Factor analysis has therefore been applied, with the objective of simplifying the attributes list and eliciting a smaller number of constructs. Various types of factor analysis and factor rotation have been investigated in order to select the procedure providing the greatest discrimination between the factors. Two factors were identified with confidence, and models of relative spending based on these factors have been derived. These factor analysis models performed nearly as well as the external item analysis models in terms of correlation with relative spending. The models contain three terms (two factors plus distance or time), rather than the two for the external item analyses, and therefore the 'p' values were slightly less significant. Nevertheless, there was no significant association between the three independent variables.

Summary of procedure

The centres were necessarily chosen on a 'convenience' basis, representing a spread of types of UK centre from sub-regional upwards. The managements kindly gave permission for the interviewing to take place, but have requested anonymity. The (renamed) centres (in ascending size order) were:

		Number of respondents
Metropolitan	In-town, sub-regional	51
Greenleys	In-town, sub-regional	28
Jubilee	In-town, sub-regional	56
The Woodlands	In-town, regional	29
White Water	In-town, regional	73
Blue Rose	Out-of-town, regional	50
Total		287

Conclusions relating to sub-cells of respondents have necessarily been restricted to those that can be demonstrated to be statistically significant, despite the small sample sizes.

Shoppers were interviewed during weekdays, 10.30 a.m. to 3.30 p.m. Respondents were asked for comparative ratings of two shopping centres, the centre where the interview took place and the one where they shopped most (or next most) for non-food shopping. The questionnaire was derived from McGoldrick's and Thompson's (1992a; b) and the pre-liminary unstructured interviews. In addition to 'Ratings', respondents were asked for the 'Importance' of each of the 38 attributes (such as 'Quality of stores' and 'Availability of toilets', following Hackett and Foxall, 1994). Other questions concerned estimated perceived travel dis-tance and time to both centres and stated details such as monthly spend-ing at each centre, age, location of residence, household income, occupation of the main earner in the household and type of transport.

The respondents' answers were processed to produce a satisfaction rating for each attribute variable. The results for Ratings were coded for analysis on a 1 to 5 scale, where 1 = very poor and 5 = very good. The difference between the values for the two centres represented a com-posite of both the rating of the centre studied and its distinctiveness. The numerical values were adjusted to be always positive (by the addi-tion of 4 to each) for convenience in further processing.

The five-point scale was the semantic differential approach proposed by Osgood et al (1957), commonly accepted in marketing research and used in a number of studies on the image of shopping centres (e.g. Gentry and Burns, 1977; McGoldrick and Thompson, 1992a; b). One of the benefits of the approach is that it is particularly good for brand image comparisons (Phipps and Simmons, 1996).

The usual use of five-point scales as numerical data would need an assumption that all respondents possess a common scale of measure-ment. This drawback has been largely overcome by relying on a com-parison with an alternative centre, rather than an absolute scale.

If the objective had been specifically to compare two centres (as in McGoldrick, 1992a; b, for example), the 'Rating/distinctiveness' measure would have been more clear-cut. One objective of this study, though, was to determine which attributes were most critical (most scope for improvement) at each centre studied. For this reason, re-spondents were required to compare the centre with their own choice of competing centre. Thus, the comparison genuinely reflected ratings of attributes in their competitive context. Competing centres were thus represented (so far as practicable) in the sample in proportion to their use by the customers of the centres studied. It would not have been possible (or, for this application, desirable) to have the same sample evaluate all centres. Analysis of a sub-set of results to compare a test centre with a specific competitor would be expected to improve the 'fit' of the model (and was observed so to do). Nevertheless, to best answer the research questions, the results have been reported based on the 'spread' of actual competitors.

Similarly, the Importance values were also recorded on a five-point scale where 1 = no relevance and 5 = extremely important. This would normally imply the assumption that all respondents value importance on the same scale. In order to eliminate the need for this assumption, an alternative scaling was investigated, standardising the scale such that the totals of each respondent's Importance scale values were equal. Results were calculated in parallel with results using the 'raw' 'importance' scores. The results from both approaches were similar, but the 'fit' of models based on the 'raw' importance scores was slightly better than of models based on the 'standardised' scores. In the interests of simplicity, only the results based on the 'raw' importance scores have been reported in this book.

East (1997), Westbrook (1980), Oppewal and Timmermans (1997) present evidence that supports the measurement of attractiveness or image by the addition of attribute satisfactions. Accordingly, the weighted attribute scores were added, giving the overall 'Attractiveness index' measured value – expressed on a 0 to 100 relative scale. The model used is of the compensatory type, which, according to Oppewal and Timmermans (1997) has been found to be as good as or superior to non-compensatory models.

In an alternative approach where straightforward ratings on a 1 to 5 scale were compared with patronage, a discriminant analysis would have been appropriate. Here, though, Attractiveness, Distance and the dependent variable Relative spending are measured on continuous scales. The Oppewal and Timmermans approach was followed in considering image evaluations as interval rather than ordinal data. This use does not require the assumption that the evaluations 1 to 5 were spaced evenly apart, only that a scale existed, i.e. that 'very good' could be rated numerically higher than 'good'. Non-linear models would have been used if necessary to accommodate uneven scales. In the event, the 'fit' of the linear models was at least as good as the non-linear ones.

Questionnaire design

Because the selected methodology called for a mall intercept survey, the instrument chosen was a structured questionnaire. More in-depth approaches would have been impractical in the mall setting.

The starting point for the questionnaire design was McGoldrick's (1992a; b) 27 image attributes:

Cleanliness   Parking facilities
Quality of stores   Toilet facilities

Lighting
Spaciousness
'In-place' to go
Availability of seats
Choice of major stores
Stores opening hours
Place to spend time
When weather is bad
For eating and drinking
General décor
Friendliness of atmosphere
Standard of security

Product selection in stores
General layout
Variety of stores
Air conditioning
Helpfulness of store staff
Place to take children
Access by bus
Access by car
Level of crowds
General price level
Undesirable characters

Following the thirty open-ended interviews, a further 11 attributes were added (to make up a total of 38 in all):

Other shoppers nice people
Good food shops or supermarket
Baby care facilities
Lively or exciting
Pleasant environment outside
Advertising and marketing activity

Shelter between car park
(bus station, etc) and shops
Get out easily to local shops
Get out easily to local cafes
Big shopping centre
Loyalty scheme/customer card

The final attributes list incorporated those that other academic researchers have demonstrated to be associated with greater patronage behaviour at shopping centres (e.g. LeHew et al, 2002; Finn and Louviere, 1996; Frasquet et al, 2001; Severin et al, 2001; Sit et al, 2003; Wong et al, 2001) plus those derived from Repertory Grid analysis (Timmermans et al, 1982), from trade sources (by Hackett and Foxall, 1994) and commercial research (Allegra, 2002).

McGoldrick's questionnaire was designed for use in the respondents' homes, by prior appointment. It ran to many pages long and would have been unsuitable in this form for use in the mall setting where a bulky questionnaire would have tended to put off the respondents. Therefore, the attributes and spaces for answers were laid out in a column format, giving as simple and concise impression as practicable. The questionnaire was introduced with:

'Hello, I am doing a survey for Brunel University, about the "image" of shopping centres. Have you a few minutes to help me with a few questions, please? (It will take about 10 minutes)'.

Respondents were asked at which shopping (or town) centre they spent most and next most. The designation letter (a) was used to signify the centre at which the interview took place, with (b) the main competing one. The image attribute questions then followed, starting with:

> When deciding which shopping centre or town centre you'll use (for example [the White Water Centre], how important is the quality of the stores? (That is, how 'up-market' the shops are).

The reply code for 'Importance' was entered in the 'I' column on the questionnaire:

1 No relevance
2 Only slight importance
3 Moderately important
4 Very important
5 Extremely important.

The question continued with:

> And how do you rate [the White Water Centre] on how 'up-market' the shops are?

The answer code for the centre evaluation was entered into the (a) column:

1 Very poor
2 Poor
3 Moderate
4 Good
5 Very good.

The final part of this question was:

> How would you rate [shopping centre (b)] on how 'up-market' the shops are?

The evaluation code for the main competing centre was entered in column (b). The process was continued for each of the attributes. Travel data gathered included the estimated travelling time (minutes) and distance (miles), the type of transport used and where travelled from (place name and post-code). Finally, respondents were asked for their overall image of both centres (marks out of 10), spending (non-food) in an average month at each centre, household income, sex, age band and occupation of the main earner in the household. When the structured questionnaire had been completed, respondents were given the opportunity to use their own words:

And finally, could you please tell me why you didn't shop at (b) today?

Investigating research questions

The regression models were used to determine the association between specific attributes of centres and shoppers' relative spending at those centres. Correlation of attribute values against individual spending at shopping centres produced a ranked attribute table and a weighted model of attractiveness. This methodology provided answers (for the specific centres, within limitations) to research question (i) and, by inference, threw light on question (ii). The part played by individual attribute associations was calculated in order to answer research question (iii). The regression models for different shopper segments were examined to answer research question (iv). The utility of the attractiveness measures was assessed in terms of the rental incomes, estimated sales turnovers, distance exponents and catchment boundaries of exemplar shopping centres, addressing research questions (ii), (v) and, in part, (vi).

This chapter has outlined the research questions addressed and the methodology adopted in the search for answers. The following chapter reports the main attributes that were found to be significant in shoppers' choices of shopping centres at the six individual centres, investigating research questions (i), (ii) and (iii).

London's First Shopping Centre?

When developers demolished a disused bank [between Aldgate and London Bridge in the City of London] the plan was to replace it with a ... shopping centre fit for the 21st century. ... [This turned out to be] a case of history repeating itself ... For archaeologists have discovered the lost remains of a forum ... 'It was a great shopping centre in the heart of London' said Dr Simon Thurley, Director of the Museum of London ... 'It was a one-stop shop where you bought your clothes, food and books.' ... The Romans had a [25000 square metres] meeting place, plus shops and a town hall.

Daily Mail, 5 February, 1999.

3

Why Do People Shop Where They Do? The Attributes of Shopping Centres that Determine Where Consumers Choose to Shop

This chapter is adapted from a paper delivered at the *International Conference on Recent Advances in Retailing and Services Science* (Dennis et al, 1999).[1]

Introduction

This chapter explores Research Questions (i) to (iii) inclusive (see Chapter 2 above):

(i)   Which attributes of a shopping centre are most associated with shopper spending?

(ii) Can the attractiveness of a centre be measured in a way that has meaning and utility, for example in relation to shoppers' spending, the sales turnover or rental income of shopping centres?

(iii) Are the specific attributes most affecting shopper spending significantly different at various shopping centres?

Two testable hypotheses can be proposed that will contribute towards answering Research Questions (ii) and (iii):

H1   'Relative spending' at shopping centres is significantly related to 'attractiveness'.

---

[1] Dennis C E, Marsland D and Cockett W (1999) 'Why people shop where they do? The use of image and attractiveness measurements in determining the critical attributes in consumers' choice of shopping centres', *6th International Conference on Recent Advances in Retailing and Services Science*, Puerto Rico, EIRASS.

H2 The critical attributes that affect shoppers' spending at shopping centres are significantly different for different shopping centres.

The methodology used for this chapter was as described in Chapter 2 above. Briefly, the survey results took the form of Rating/distinctiveness and Importance measures ascribed by respondents to various attributes at different UK shopping centres. A regression model was used to model relative spending according to these measures and shoppers' relative travel time or distance to the centres. Both the Rating/distinctiveness and travel terms were relative to competing centres.

Results

Table 3.1 lists the shopping centre attributes significantly ($p = 0.05$) associated with relative spending at the respective centres, ranked in order of the degree of association. The ranking of the Importance measures is included for comparison. The attributes that respondents considered most important are not the same as those most associated with spending. One observation from the Importance scores was that the results seemed to indicate that respondents did not see travel distance or time as particularly important. On the other hand, the regression results below demonstrate that travel does indeed play a strong role in shoppers' choices of shopping centres. A similar pattern was observed by Gentry and Burns (1977) who concluded that where consumers shopped was determined by perceived proximity but the shoppers failed to express that explicitly.

Table 3.1 is an external item analysis that ranks attributes in order of weight. A conventional item analysis (Oppenheim, 1992) would use correlation as the basic measure, but Table 3.2 goes a stage further in taking into account both the correlation with relative spending and the regression coefficient (elasticity) of each attribute on relative spending. The measure is the regression coefficient, weighted according to the coefficient of determination, R^2. Only attributes having a regression coefficient of at least double the standard error of the regression coefficient have been included in the table – significant at $p = 0.05$. The procedure was to use the R^2 value as a correction factor, having the effect of scaling down the weight of attributes that have less correlation with spending. Multiplying the R^2 value by the attribute regression coefficient gave the attribute weight. This quantity represents a combination of both the narrowness of spread of points on the scatter graphs and the steepness of the regression plots – an overall measure of 'association' between the attribute and spending.

Table 3.1 Attributes most associated with relative spending at each centre compared with respondents' main competing centre, ranked by attribute weight (regression coefficient weighted by coefficient of determination, R^2)

Rank by attribute weight		'Importance' rank (for comparison)	R^2	Regression Coefficient (B)	Attribute weight: $R^2 \times B \times 100$
(a) White Water					
1	Nice place to spend time	20	0.128	0.858	11.0
2	Cleanliness	1	0.104	1.04	10.8
3	Access by public transport	31	0.122	0.842	10.3
4	Travel distance	30=	0.222	−0.319	−7.1
5	Covered shopping	13	0.094	0.744	7.0
6	Availability of seats	26	0.084	0.662	5.6
7	Travelling time	22	0.161	−0.327	−5.3
(b) Blue Rose					
1	Nice place to spend time	21	0.094	0.674	6.3
2	'Quality' of the stores	25	0.075	0.678	5.0
3	Access to local cafes	40	0.045	1.08	4.9
4	Covered shopping	15	0.079	0.609	4.8
(c) Jubilee					
1	General layout	17	0.160	1.52	24.4

Table 3.1 Attributes most associated with relative spending at each centre compared with respondents' main competing centre, ranked by attribute weight (regression coefficient weighted by coefficient of determination, R^2) – *continued*

Rank by attribute weight		'Importance' rank (for comparison)	R^2	Regression Coefficient (B)	Attribute weight: $R^2 \times B \times 100$
(d) Metropolitan					
1	Baby care facilities	40	0.307	1.16	35.6
1	Baby care facilities	40	0.307	1.16	35.6
2	Helpfulness of the staff	5	0.209	1.36	28.4
1	Baby care facilities	40	0.307	1.16	35.6
2	Helpfulness of the staff	5	0.209	1.36	28.4
3	Availability of good toilets	2	0.200	0.967	19.3
4	Environment outside	21	0.167	1.08	18.0
5	In-place (stylish)	36	0.175	0.764	13.4
6	Relaxed atmosphere	28=	0.107	0.772	8.3
7	Eating and drinking	22	0.087	0.717	6.2
8	Value for money	3=	0.066	0.890	5.9
9	Cleanliness	1	0.080	0.732	5.8
10	Availability of seats	31	0.084	0.648	5.4

Note: The 'attribute weight' represents the regression coefficient weighted according to R^2, thus a term that reflects both the strength of association and the correlation.

Only attributes significantly associated with relative spending at p = 0.05 were included in Table 3.1. It is possible to take account of even 'minor' attributes in the model. The 'attractiveness' measure has been calculated for each shopper by the addition of the weighted 'importance × rating/distinctiveness' values for each relevant attribute. Attributes have been included in the model (rather than in the table) based on being at least marginally significantly associated with relative spending (p = 0.1), i.e. twice as likely to be associated as not. The confidence of any individual attribute may not be high, but the overall confidence of the model in (for example) Equation 3.1 is much higher.

Taking the example of the White Water Centre, a relationship can be demonstrated (by linear regression, SPSS) between relative spending, attractiveness (sum of attribute satisfactions) and travel distance (travel time could be used in place of travel distance but in case of the White Water Centre, distance gives the closer correlation). The greater the distance that respondents have to travel to the centre, compared with their main competing centre, the less they tend to spend. Conversely, an increase in attractiveness (for example arising from improvements to the 'Eating and drinking' facilities) would result in an increase in spend. Figure 3.1 indicates the relationship between relative spend and attractiveness for the White Water Centre with Figure 3.2 illustrating an improved correlation with a correction for respondents' travel distance. Time could be used in place of distance but in this case, distance

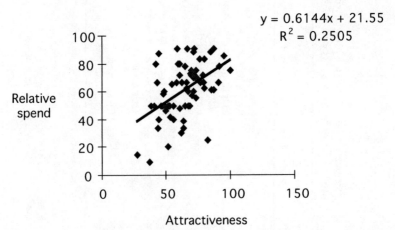

Figure 3.1 Scatter graph showing relative spend *vs.* attractiveness for the White Water Centre.

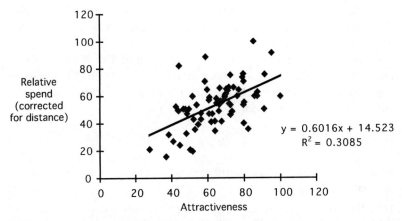

Figure 3.2 Scatter graph showing relative spend *vs.* attractiveness – with relative spend corrected for the distance effect – White Water Centre.

gives the better correlation. Equation 3.1 (produced by linear regression analysis using SPSS) describes the relationship:

$$\text{Relative spending} = 37 + 0.62 \times \text{Relative attractiveness} - 0.32 \times \text{Relative distance} \tag{3.1}$$

The Coefficient of determination, $R^2 = 0.48$, indicates that Relative attractiveness and Relative distance together were associated with 48 percent of the variation in Relative spending. The relationship was significant at $p = 0.0001$, indicating 99.999 percent confidence that a positive relationship between these variables exists.

The intercept, attractiveness coefficient and distance coefficients respectively for each of the four centres are reported in Table 3.2. The 'fit' of these models would normally be accepted as 'modest' (Bryman and Cramer, 1994). In the case of the Jubilee Centre (only), a slightly better fit would be obtained by substituting 'relative travel

Table 3.2 Models of individual relative spending

Centre	Intercept	Attractiveness coefficient	Distance coefficient	R^2	Significance level, p	Equation number
White Water	37.0	0.62	0.32	0.47	<0.0001	3.1
Blue Rose	32.2	0.53	0.31	0.19	<0.01	3.2
Jubilee	24.0	0.68	0.17	0.26	<0.001	3.3
Metropolitan	15.1	0.53	0	0.33	<0.001	3.4

time' for 'relative travel distance' (R^2 = 0.29 rather than 0.26). Nevertheless, 'distance' is used in all of the results here in the interest of consistency.

There were too few results for Greenleys and The Woodlands to report as individual centres. Nevertheless, results from those centres were useful in providing a better spread of centres for calculating the overall attribute weightings.

Discussion and hypothesis testing

Research question (i): Which attributes of a shopping centre are most associated with spending?

This book has set out to investigate why customers choose to shop at one shopping centre rather than another? The answers are far from clear cut or simple as the most critical attributes varied markedly from centre to centre. For the total sample of shoppers, the 'top ten' attributes on average, with weights expressed on a consistent scale are listed in Table 3.3. These are the attributes which are most associated with relative spending at the six shopping centres – all significant overall at p = 0.05.

Table 3.3   Attribute weights

Rank		Attribute weight
1	General layout	11.4
2	Access by car (roads)	7.8
3	Nice place to spend time	6.7
4	Cleanliness	6.0
5	Covered shopping	4.5
6	Quality of stores	3.9
7	Shoppers nice people	3.9
8	Availability of toilets	3.9
9	Friendly atmosphere	3.8
10	Helpfulness of staff	3.1

Notes: The 'top ten' attribute weights are listed. These were the attributes most associated with relative spend at the six shopping centres (all were significantly so at p = 0.05). These are not necessarily the attributes that the respondents considered most 'important' because the 'weight' also takes into account the degree and strength of the association of the respondents' rating of the attribute with relative spend. Hence 'weight' is intended to model the weight that the attribute carries in shopper spending decisions. In this table, less significant attributes have been omitted, but the numerical values are scaled such that if all attributes are included, the weights total 100.

Research question (ii)

H1 'Relative spending' at shopping centres is significantly related to 'attractiveness'

Using the scales of 'attractiveness' for the models specific to each centre, the significance 'p' values of the association with relative spending were all significant at p = 0.01. On that basis, therefore, H1 is supported. Nevertheless, the attractiveness measure for each centre is based in part upon the degree of association between the attributes and relative spending. The overall attractiveness scale largely corrects for the auto correlation effect. The revised p values incorporating the adjustment were:

- White Water Centre   0.0052
- Blue Rose Centre   0.091
- Jubilee Centre   0.040
- Metropolitan Centre   0.0006.

The models based on the overall attractiveness scale have an aggregate coefficient of determination of 0.23. Although this degree of fit would be described only as 'modest' (Bryman and Cramer, 1994), it was achieved in only two stages of regression, meaning that the degree of confidence in the relationship was relatively high (significant at p = 0.001). Therefore Hypothesis H1 is supported, shoppers' relative spending' at shopping centres is significantly related to the 'attractiveness' of the respective centres.

Research question (iii)

H2 The critical attributes that affect shoppers' spending at shopping centres are significantly different for different shopping centres.

The results in Table 3.1 indicated that attributes that were critical at one centre were not necessarily so at other centres. The differences were examined to determine whether any were large enough to support H2. Here, it must be noted that the attribute weights reported in Table 3.1 were based on the use of the R^2 value as a parameter. This is a valid approach, with the limitation that a simple ANOVA cannot be used to test for significant differences (Block, 1978). Therefore, the association of the attributes with relative spending was tested using a bootstrapping procedure to determine whether within reasonable limits of probability, the clustering of critical attributes could have arisen at random from a homogenous sample of shoppers. Ten samples of shoppers were selected at random from the complete data bank. If these had indicated the association of critical attributes to be distributed as widely as are the actual distributions of the centres, H0 would have been supported; i.e. there would have been insufficient evidence to justify H2. The spread of associations for the attributes have been examined using the 'one sample t-test' (Kinnear and Gray, 1997). The t-test p values are listed in Table 3.4.

Table 3.4   Significant differences in associations of specific attributes (from bootstrapping)

Attribute	Centre	P-value
Access by public transport	White Water	<0.0005
General layout	Jubilee	<0.0005
Helpfulness of the staff	Metropolitan	0.001
Availability of good toilets	Metropolitan	<0.0005
Eating and drinking	Metropolitan	0.025
Access to local cafes	Blue Rose	0.028
'In-place' to go	Jubilee	0.001

The p-values in Table 3.4 demonstrate that for each shopping centre studied, there are significant differences concerning the critical attributes of the centre that are associated with shoppers' spending. H2 is therefore supported: The critical attributes that affect shoppers' spending at shopping centres are significantly different for different shopping centres.

Did the differences in shoppers' behaviour arise from differences between the shoppers?

Could differences in compositions of the samples at the different centres account for the differences in critical attributes observed at the centres? Critical attributes have been calculated for shoppers segmented by sex, socio-economic group, age, income and type of transport. Of the seven critical attributes identified as significantly different between centres, four are not appreciably different between the other segments studied:

- Helpfulness of staff
- Access by public transport

- Access to local cafes and
- 'In-place' to go.

This means, for example, that the association with spending of 'help-fulness of staff' is very different between the Metropolitan Centre and The Woodlands, whilst not being appreciably different between females and males, nor the other socio-demographic segments. The above four attributes can thus be safely be included as critical attributes significantly different between shopping centres, free of influence from identified differences in the sample segments studied.

For those critical attributes that were significantly different between segments, there were no appreciable imbalances in the sample composition and sampling differences were not sufficient to affect the conclusion that the attributes were significantly different between centres. All seven critical attributes were safely identified as significantly different between centres, the differences not arising from any obvious differences between the shoppers. Differences between individual attributes associated with spending were larger between shopping centres than between identified shopper demographic segments.

The finding both compares and contrasts with work by Severin and colleagues (2001), who compared shopping centre attributes in Canada, USA, and Norway in order to assess spatial stability. They concluded that even though the magnitude of attribute parameters varied between centres, the attributes themselves remained stable. They considered that the variations in scale parameters were due to variations in random components. Therefore, they considered that strategies in one location should also work in another, although the scale of the effects might be different. For example, if the same strategy were applied in Edmonton (Canada) and Oslo (Norway), it should result in larger effects on shopper choices in Oslo. Partially contrasting with their conclusion, our results indicated that the variation in the effects of the parameters was significantly different between different UK shopping centres, and the differences were **not** accounted for by random effects. Rather than suggesting similar strategies for all centres (but expecting different scale outcomes) the results from this chapter indicated that different strategies should be appropriate for different shopping centres, addressing different critical attributes.

Implications

There are self-explanatory implications for UK shopping centres following from the 'top ten' attributes. Of these, only one, ('Quality of the stores') directly concerned shops – and arguably, even this has a 'service experience' aspect? Three related to structure or infrastructure and six were clearly 'service' or 'experience'. Shopping centre managers should focus at least as much on the 'nice time' and 'customer service' aspects as on more tangible 'shops' considerations.

There are specific marketing uses of the attribute differences for the individual centres listed in Table 3.4. For example, the model predicts that the Metropolitan Centre could increase sales turnover by at least a whole percentage point by a modest improvement in the toilet facilities. On the other hand, the Jubilee Centre would be expected to have more success by tackling the problem of its image as an 'in-place' to go, perhaps by adjustments to the tenant mix when possible, and/or the use of celebrity endorsements.

As an out-of-town centre, the Blue Rose Centre could have difficulty in providing access to genuine local cafés – but they could build their own near what could be, for example, a simulated village green next to the duck pond.

The management of the White Water Centre may well consider that public transport is an external factor beyond their control. Nevertheless, it could well be cost effective to subsidise a bus service and/or provide a bus stop on site.

Conclusions and limitations

This chapter has set out to study 'Why people shop where they do?' in terms of the attributes of shopping centres that distinguish between them. The 'convenience' sample cannot be truly representative of all shoppers, but even so, identified differences between shoppers do not account for the differences between behaviour at different shopping centres. As an exploratory study, the sample cell sizes (50 minimum for centres reported individually) are smaller than ideal for such studies; but the critical attribute differences between centres are statistically significant.

The conclusion is that people are attracted to different centres for different reasons. Of course, there are differences in clientele between the centres. For example, the Blue Rose Centre is the most 'up-market', a large survey indicating 24 percent of shoppers in the most affluent 'AB' category (owner's market research data). On the other hand, the Metropolitan Centre is the most 'down-market' with the owner's data indicating 20 percent AB. The attributes, though, which were significantly different between centres, did not appear to be significantly influenced by income or socio-economic group. Attributes such as 'helpfulness of staff' were significantly different between centres, but not significantly different between affluent and less affluent segments.

Differences between **shoppers** have been demonstrated **not** to account for the differences between centres. On the other hand, differences between centres and **competitors** do seem to be relevant. For all of the significantly different critical attributes, the centre where the interview was held performed relatively poorly compared to the competition (average rating values for the centre below the average value for the respondents' alternative shopping locations). The results can be interpreted as indicating that shoppers have different **expectations** of different shopping centres – largely formed on the basis of evaluations of competing centres with overlapping catchment areas – and these different expectations are reflected in their shopping behaviour. Specifically, shoppers spend more at centres which more closely match their requirements on specific named attributes, compared to competing centres.

The following chapter, Chapter 4, will develop the concepts of the image of shopping centres further, considering the shopping centre as a brand and proceeding to a more searching investigation of research question (ii).

The First Covered Shopping Centre?

Thomas Gresham [financial trader] built the Stock Exchange [shopping centre with an] atrium and shops on the 2ⁿᵈ and 3ʳᵈ floors. Queen Elizabeth liked it, bought all her hats there and named it the 'Royal Exchange'.

(Adam Hart-Davis, *What the Tudors did for us*, BBC2 (television),
7 October 2002)

4
The Shopping Centre as a Brand

This chapter is adapted from a paper that first appeared in the *International Review of Retail, Distribution and Consumer Research* (Dennis et al, 2002a).[1]

Introduction

In the context of shopping centres, the terms 'image' or 'attractiveness' tend to be more used than 'branding'. In this chapter, it is argued that techniques of measuring brand image and building brand value can help towards customer satisfaction and commercial success for shopping centres. The concept of 'branding' is well known for consumer products. Successful manufacturers have built up brand value through the development of a differentiated brand personality and a long-term reputation for quality backed up by advertising and other forms of brand support. Concentration in retailing has led to the balance of marketing 'power' shifting towards retailers, whose brand equity has overtaken that of even leading manufacturers (McGoldrick, 2002). Jary and Wileman (1998) questioned whether retail businesses are really brands. They concluded that retail brands are 'The Real Thing' although differing from product brands 'not least because of the difficulty of managing the multiplicity of attributes of a retail brand'. The larger retailers are building their brands – for example one study rated the leading multiple grocer Tesco in the top 10 (out of 115) major UK companies committed to building powerful brands (Brand

---

[1] Dennis C E, Murphy J, Marsland D, Cockett W and Patel T (2002a) 'Measuring image: shopping centre case studies', *International Review of Retail, Distribution and Consumer Research*, 12 (4): 353–373.

Finance, 1999). Retailers have become more aware of the value of branding and have (according to Davies, 1998) attempted to copy the images of manufacturers' brands in developing their own brands.

There is a strong link between retail concentration and the share of trade taken by retailer brands (Akehurst and Alexander, 1995). Just as consumers' preferences are moving towards fewer, larger retail stores, so they are also moving towards larger shopping centres. Between 1986 and 1999 the number of 'super-regional' shopping centres (over 100,000 m^2) in the UK rose from two to seven (based on Guy, 1994b). The number has only grown by one since 1999 as planning approval is almost impossible to obtain for new super-regional shopping centres in the UK, rather than on account of lack of demand. Shopping centres have been branded in practice – Arndale for example has been known as a shopping centre brand name since the opening of the UK's first regional centre (at Poole) in 1969.

Brand names affect perception (evidenced by the well known example that over half of consumers chose Diet Pepsi in blind tests, but when they knew the brand names, almost two thirds preferred Diet Coke – De Chernatony and McDonald, 1998). As Jobber (2001, p. 229) puts it: 'a rose by any other name would smell as sweet ... or would it?'. More than one of the shopping centres in our study was under the same ownership – but shoppers would probably not have known this. Many UK shopping centres do not make use of a name in branding to any extent. Exceptions include The Mall – applying consistency of branding across a portfolio of shopping centres and The Bentall Centre in Kingston on Thames, which benefits from association with a well-known department store having a long history and a reputation for quality. The Mall Corporation (a joint venture of Capital and Regional plc with funding partners) owns 21 UK shopping centres at the time of writing and plans to increase to 30 to 35 branded centres. For the future it might be expected that more shopping centres may follow the general retail trend and seek to build their brand images.

Others have studied the marketing of shopping destinations, including work by the Association of Town Centre Managers (e.g. 1994) and Warnaby and associates (e.g. Medway et al, 1999; Warnaby and Davies, 1997; Warnaby, 1998; Warnaby and Medway, 2000). Nevertheless there has been little research to date, in the UK, on the branding of shopping centres. According to Howard (1992), shopping centres had up till that time largely ignored centre branding considerations. In this chapter, the author reports a preliminary exploration of the potential using UK case studies. The aim is first to demonstrate that both qualitative and quantitative brand image measurement techniques can be of use for shopping centres and second to consider whether shopping centres might put brand-building techniques to use.

Why is the branding of shopping centres important? Aaker (1991) described one approach to brand equity based on the use of share price data. When the costs of an organisation's tangible assets, together with non-brand values such as technology are subtracted from the total share price value, brand equity can be estimated. Shopping centres may well not aspire to the brand equity levels of the food or clothing industries (which Aaker states to be around 60 percent of asset values). Nevertheless, the potential financial value for investors can be glimpsed from an annual report of Capital Shopping Centres PLC (CSC, 1996, p. 8):

> The MetroCentre achieved a 17.5 percent increase in asset value [based on independent valuation] from £354 million to £416 million reflecting the value of CSC's active management expertise in its first year of ownership ...

The substantial increase in asset valuation reflecting what CSC termed 'active management' arose mainly from a growth in rental values. A small but significant proportion of rents were sales-turnover-related, and in addition to this immediate effect on rents, rental values in the medium to long term tend to follow sales turnover. The increases in rental values were presumably linked to shoppers' and retailers' value of the 'attractiveness' of the MetroCentre. The example illustrates that there is a huge financial potential for less actively managed shopping centres to improve their attractiveness.

Active management and pro-active marketing are features of successful shopping centres (CSC, 1996; Howard, 1997; Mintel, 1997). Even so, UK shopping centres have been reported to lack marketing orientation (Kirkup and Rafiq, 1999, drawing support from Cooke, 1993), which Howard (1995) blamed on the industry's preoccupation with property investment rather than customer issues.

According to Randall (1997), branding is fundamental to the success of many organisations. The author believes that in the increasingly competitive climate branding will become even more relevant for shopping centres. This chapter, therefore, has set out to investigate the applicability of brand measurement techniques for shopping centres and to propose simple preliminary ideas for ways in which shopping centre managers might use standard brand-building tools.

What is meant by 'brand'? Hankinson and Cowking (1993, p. 1) defined the term as making a product or service distinctive by its 'personality' and 'positioning relative to the competition'. Personality 'consists of a unique combination of functional attributes and symbolic values' and positioning 'describes the brand by defining its competitive context', i.e. distinctiveness.

Personality

According to de Chernatony and McDonald (1998, p. 407), 'personality is a useful metaphor ... the brand is used to make a statement about the user'. De Chernatony and McDonald emphasised the importance of brand personality, particularly in cases where there are only minor variations in physical characteristics.

Distinctiveness

The need to distinguish from competitors is central to 'branding'. A number of authors have commented (directly or indirectly) on the distinctiveness of shopping centres (Burns and Warren, 1995; Howell and Rogers, 1980; SERPLAN, 1987). USA shopping centres have been reported as in decline (Carlson, 1991) ascribed to a lack of distinctiveness (Cavanaugh, 1996; Wakefield and Baker, 1998). Swinyard (1992, p.9) measured 'distinctiveness' and concluded that the successful retailer must 'distinguish itself from its competitors in appealing ways.' In Chapter 3 above it was demonstrated that differences between shopping centres play an essential part in patronage decisions.

Building successful brands

How can shopping centre brands be built? Jobber (1995; 2004, drawing support from King, 1991 and Doyle, 1989), lists factors that can be important in building successful brands:

(1) Being first
(2) Quality
(3) Positioning
(4) Repositioning
(5) Long-term perspective
(6) Internal marketing
(7) Credibility and
(8) Well-blended communications.

This chapter has used Hankinson's and Cowking's followed by Jobber's approaches in designing the framework: firstly, by considering the use of brand personality techniques in eliciting customers' understandings of shopping centres and secondly by investigating the distinctiveness of shopping centres relative to their competitors. Finally, the possible implications of building successful brands have been outlined.

Methodology and procedures

In measuring brand personality, researchers such as Aaker (1997) and Alt and Griggs (1988) have used psychometric approaches to demonstrate that brands can be described in terms similar to humans. Our approach has been to consider the 'personality' of a shopping centre using human type descriptors together with positioning relative to the competition in terms of the attributes or constructs making up a respondent's image of a shopping centre. Although the brand 'personality' of a shopping centre (if it has one) cannot be considered the same thing as its 'attractiveness', both aspects are part of the overall concept of branding. Indeed, looking for definitions of retail 'image', there are descriptors that fit both the concepts of symbolic or psychological values and measurements of perceptions of tangible, functional attributes (e.g. Martineau, 1958). 'Branding' spans the various concepts and terms such as the 'development and maintenance of sets of product attributes and values which are coherent, appropriate, distinctive, protectable and appealing to customers' (Murphy, 1998, p. 3). Rather than dividing the study along unclear semantic boundary lines of branding, image and attractiveness, in this chapter observations have been categorised into qualitative, semi-structured and quantitative work.

In the qualitative and semi-structured part of this chapter, summaries of the results of focus groups, personal constructs and semi-structured questionnaires have been reported. The analysis followed de Chernatony's and McDonald's (1998, p. 407) approach in 'gauging the image associated with a brand' with questions like 'if [the shopping centre] came to life, what sort of person would it be?' On the other hand, the quantified attribute approach has utilised the procedure of multiplying 'Importance' by 'Rating' (described in the 'Methodology' section of Chapter 2 above), a method that is 'particularly useful to marketers wishing to do brand comparisons' (Phipps and Simmons, 1996, p. 197). This has been combined with Butterfield and Haigh's (1998) assignment of weights to brand image attributes. In the 'Interbrand' or 'Brand Finance' approaches the assignment of weights is 'judgmental' (Birkin, 1994; Haigh, 2003; Murphy, 1989). In contrast, as an essential part of the procedure attribute weights have been **calculated** according to their degree of association with shopper spending. The Interbrand and Brand Finance methods are intended for brand valuation for accounting purposes rather than measuring image, but the principles serve well in our attributes-measurement approach.

The study was designed to explore the branding of exemplar shopping centres in three stages. The empirical work consisted of a series of linked investigations aimed at exploring the broad area of branding and attractiveness of shopping centres from different methodological perspectives. First, qualitative and semi-structured techniques were used to compare 'personality' differences between two shopping centres. Second, the distinctiveness relative to the competition of six shopping centres was evaluated using quantitative techniques. Finally, the utility of shopping centre image measurements was examined, considering sales turnover, rental incomes and catchment area boundaries as dependent variables.

Qualitative and semi-structured

The first stage in the qualitative study took the form of six focus groups. The respondents were shoppers familiar with two shopping centres, the Metropolitan Centre and The Woodlands (these are not the real names as the centres have requested anonymity). These initial groups comprised six to eight respondents each, many of who (for convenience) were university students in the West London (UK) area. Students' views may not be representative of all UK shoppers. Therefore a final focus group was carried out with 10 respondents including both sexes with a range of ages and socio-economic classifications. The respondents of this final focus group were not previously known to the interviewer or to each other.

A second stage comprised a 'Repertory Grid' to investigate shoppers' personal constructs in shopping at the two town centres that included the Metropolitan Centre and The Woodlands. The sample consisted of 20 participants, selected on a convenience basis from shoppers known to shop at the centres. As Oppewal and Timmermans (1999) pointed out, the technique avoids one of the drawbacks of attitude scales in that the respondents rather than the researcher can specify the items that shoppers like and dislike. The disadvantage is that the analysis process is lengthy and convoluted. In comparison with conventional in-depth interviews, the interpretation of the Repertory Grid (based on the work of Kelly, 1955; Fransella and Bannister, 1977) is more objective. Timmermans and associates (1982) used the technique to elicit the constructs which shoppers use in their choices of (Netherlands) shopping centres. A number of authors have used Repertory Grid in grocery shopping studies (for UK examples, see Hallsworth, 1988a; b; Mitchell and Kiral, 1999; Opacic and Potter, 1986). The repertory grid study will be reported more fully elsewhere but for a concise description of the techniques applied in a similar application, the reader is directed to Hallsworth (1988a).

The work with focus groups and Repertory Grid confirmed that shoppers were readily able to describe shopping centres in human personality terms. As a follow-up to the exploratory qualitative studies, a semi-structured questionnaire was carried out with a further 40 respondents. The respondents were selected on a convenience basis from shoppers known to shop at the centres. The semi-structured questionnaire was based on constructs derived from the focus groups and repertory grid and was designed to elicit 'personality' descriptions of the two centres.

Quantitative

The quantitative attribute measurement part of this study consisted of the empirical measurements of the attractiveness of shopping centres, together with shoppers' perceived travel distances and times, from shoppers' responses to structured questionnaires, as described in the Methodology section of Chapter 2. Briefly, the survey results took the form of Rating/distinctiveness and Importance measures ascribed by respondents to various attributes at different shopping centres. A regression model was used to model relative spending according to these measures and shoppers' relative travel time or distance to the centres. Both the Rating/distinctiveness and travel terms were relative to competing centres. The attributes were weighted in the model according to their degree of association with relative spending and the results were used to produce an Attractiveness measure for shopping centres on a 0 to 100 scale.

Mintel (1997) reported an attractiveness measurement scale for shopping centres and towns, based on counting shops, scoring multiples higher than others and certain specific named retailers higher still. This simple scale correlates well with both an equivalent scale from Management Horizons (1995) and with empirical measurements from questionnaire surveys (see Chapter 6 below). The author's 'Attractiveness index' represents actual measured values for respondents' assessments of the attractiveness of the centres. It would therefore be interesting to explore whether the measured values correspond with simple 'shop count' ratings such as the 'Mintel' score.

There is a complicating factor, though. Intuitively, it could be considered that in the case of some in-town shopping centres, shoppers' evaluations of centre attractiveness might be influenced by the attractiveness also of surrounding shops. For example, there are anecdotal reports that the attractiveness of shopping at the Bentall Centre, Kingston-on-Thames, UK, is considerably increased by being close to the John Lewis department store – an upmarket store that is located outside the covered, managed area of the Bentall Centre. Our survey interviewers reported that respondents at the in-town centres made decisions to shop in the shopping centre and the town – not just the shopping centre alone. Therefore the 'Mintel scores' for in-town shopping centres needed to be modified to include a correction for the town stores outside the shopping centre. The applicable correction turns out to be that the shops outside the shopping centre should count 50 percent of their Mintel score, those inside the shopping centre, 100 percent. The 50 percent value is not purely nominal but rather, gives the best fit with the measured 'Attractiveness index' of the centre: $R^2 = 0.92$. This 50 percent value gives a better fit than 48 percent ($R^2 = 0.90$) or 52 percent ($R^2 = 0.89$). The improvement to the fit of the model lends empirical support to the proposition that the attractiveness of an in-town shopping centre is inter-related to that of its surrounding town. The finding that the high street shops count only at 50 percent of the shopping centre ones is understandable in the light of research (a census of shopping centres in Melbourne, Australia) demonstrating that in addition to protection from the weather and many other benefits applicable to the planned management, shopping centres offered greater 'spatial convenience' than did high streets, i.e. higher on measures of (i) One-stop shopping; (ii) Selection of shopping choices; and (iii) Extended trading hours (Reimers and Clulow, 2004). Considerations such as these are of relevance not only to shopping centres but also potentially to the branding of towns.

On the basis of these results, in order to examine any relationship between measured attractiveness and, for example, shopping centre sales or rental values, the 'Attractiveness index' scores have been amended. This amendment took the form of a subtraction of the attractiveness of the out-of-centre shops. The correction was based on the Mintel shops count system, counting the out-of-centre shops at 50 percent of the in-centre ones. To facilitate these calculations, our attractiveness index has been rescaled arithmetically so as to use a scale numerically equivalent to the Mintel score. The conversion was achieved by utilising the linear regression model of 'Attractiveness index' *vs.* Mintel score to apply an arithmetic constant and a multiplication factor to the 'Attractiveness index' values. The resulting corrected scores are reported as the 'Brunel index' for brand image in the Results section below.

Results

Qualitative and semi-structured

The constructs that emerged from the focus groups are summarised in Table 4.1. These indicate consistent themes. The descriptions from the final (more representative) group included that if the Metropolitan Centre were an animal, it would be a 'cat or a dog – not exciting, just OK'. On the other hand, The Woodlands would be a 'tiger, lion or peacock: strong, vibrant, big and colourful'. If the Metropolitan Centre were a person, it would be 'dull, boring and old-fashioned – lower working class or elderly'. The Woodlands would be a 'trendy, prestigious, very smart person of good taste who enjoyed leisure'. The ten focus group respondents from the final group considered the Metropolitan Centre to be inferior to The Woodlands across a wide range of attributes, including choice of shops, eating places, crèche facilities and attractiveness in general.

Table 4.1 Focus group constructs

Metropolitan Centre: 'Good' constructs	*Focus group*
Access by all types of transport	B, D[1]
Car park	D, K[2]
Functional shopping, convenience, good for quick shop	C
Good for specific item	F
Value for money	K[2]
Shops like computer games and music attractive to teenagers	S

Metropolitan Centre: 'Bad' constructs	
Security	B, S
Teenagers	B, S
Lack of class shops	D
Centre too small	K[2]
Limited breadth of offering	C
Crowded	K[2]
Limited opening hours	K[2]
Not enough toilets	K[2]
Dark	F
Poor ambience, atmosphere	C

Table 4.1   Focus group constructs – *continued*

Poor surrounding facilities		C
No attractions or personality. Used to be good for families, now 'Poundsaver'		S

Metropolitan Centre: 'Personality'

Animal	Cat or dog (wide appeal/not exciting, just OK)	D, K^2
	Hedgehog, mole, rat	S
	Porcupine	B, C
Car	[Name omitted to avoid defamation] Does not work	S
Clothing	Crumpled suit	B
	Shell suit	C
Person	Dull, boring, old fashioned	K^2
	Lower working class or elderly	K^2
	Young, untidy male	S

The Woodlands: 'Good' constructs

Wide range of good quality shops for all the family	B
More variety, better quality bigger shops	F
Good security	B
Good décor and layout	F
Crèche	F

The Woodlands: 'Bad' constructs

Not enough car parking	B
Expensive parking	K^2
Town centre layout confusing	B
High prices	K^2

The Woodlands: 'Personality'

Animal	Tiger, lion, peacock (strong, vibrant, big, colourful)	K^2
	Lion	C
Car	Jaguar (flash, nice, clean)	S
Clothing	Designer suit	B, C
Person	Prestige, trendy, good taste, enjoys leisure, very smart	K^2

Notes:
[1] The initial letters are code identifiers for the focus groups
[2] Focus group K was the final, more representative, one.

The results of the Repertory Grid demonstrated many similarities between the two centres on shoppers' likes and dislikes. The main differences were in constructs that could be classified as 'Environment' and 'Socialising' for both of which the town centre which includes The Woodlands was more favourable than that of the Metropolitan Centre.

It is interesting to note that both relate more to 'experience' than to 'shopping'.

Exemplar results from the semi-structured questionnaire interviews of 40 respondents are given in Table 4.2. Respondents were asked: 'if the shopping centre were (for example) an animal, which one would you compare it with? Please explain why?'

Table 4.2   Exemplar results from semi-structured questionnaire interviews

	Highest ranked choice	*Typical comment*
Animal		
Metropolitan	Elephant 35%	Big, boring, not colourful
Woodlands	Peacock 80%	Colourful, elegant, attractive
Stone		
Metropolitan	Amethyst 30%	Reasonably nice, not glamorous/exciting
Woodlands	Diamond 55%	Class, luxury, quality
Hobby		
Metropolitan	Gardening 50%	Hard work but end result enjoyable
Woodlands	Horse racing 35%	Appeals to working and upper classes
Fruit		
Metropolitan	Banana 35%	Affordable but unattractive
Woodlands	Mango 45%	Unique, expensive taste
Car		
Metropolitan	[Name omitted] 55%	Working class, low profile image
Woodlands	BMW 70%	Class, status style
Newspaper		
Metropolitan	Mirror 65%	Working or middle class, mediocre
Woodlands	Guardian 40%	High standard, quality

Shoppers clearly considered that the 'personality' of a shopping centre is reflected in the type of person who uses the centre. Of course, few shoppers using the Metropolitan Centre would describe **themselves** in the terms used by the focus groups. Indeed, shoppers at the Metropolitan Centre usually stressed that they, personally, were not the typical Metropolitan Centre shopper – they were only there to buy a particular item or visit a specific shop.

Quantitative

The values for the 'Attractiveness index' brand image on the 1 to 100 scale are given in Table 4.3.

Table 4.3   Values for the 'Attractiveness index' brand image on the 1 to 100 scale

Centre	Attractiveness index
Blue Rose Centre	69.4
White Water Centre	64.9
The Woodlands	60.9
Jubilee Centre	55.5
Metropolitan Centre	52.4
Greenleys	51.3

The Woodlands – the centre with the 'strong and vibrant' personality – scored significantly higher than the 'dull and boring' Metropolitan Centre (at $p = 0.05$, 2 sample *t*-test).

As mentioned above, for convenience in comparison and prediction, the author's brand image measure has been re-scaled to use an equivalent numerical scale to the 'Mintel' score. The new attractiveness brand image scale was named the 'Brunel Index'. This Brunel Index, derived from the survey has been evaluated in terms of the degree of association with shopping centre sales turnover, rental income and catchment area boundaries.

First, Figure 4.1 illustrates the relationship between the measured brand image and the estimated sales turnover for the six centres. The sales value scale has been changed by an arithmetical factor in order to disguise commercially sensitive data. The sales turnover values are necessarily estimates and are of doubtful accuracy. These sales turnover estimates have been derived from the questionnaire responses for respondents' spending in the average month multiplied by visits per month data supplied by the centre managements. The respondents' recollections of spending and the managements' figures for visit rates must be of suspect accuracy. The estimates, though, were made before the Brunel Index was designed – and were not used in the development of the index.

Rental income is in some cases known with greater reliability than sales turnover. Figure 4.2 illustrates the relationship of attractiveness with rental income. The sources of the rental income figures are unreferenced as including them would compromise the centre owners' desires for anonymity, but the figures are taken from audited documents in the public domain. Three of the graph points in Figure 4.2 are measured Brunel Index values (rescaled to the same scale as the 'Mintel' scores). The other points are Mintel scores for centres not part of this empirical study. It is striking to note that the model based on

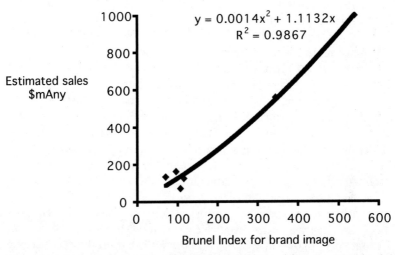

Figure 4.1 Estimated sales turnover of shopping centres *vs.* the Brunel index for brand image – Binomial plot forced through the origin.

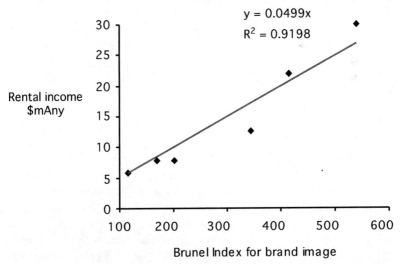

Figure 4.2 Rental income of shopping centres vs. the Brunel Index for brand image where known, otherwise Mintel score – corrected for towns – linear plot forced through the origin

the centres surveyed 'fits' predictions of rental values for centres **not** used in developing the model with a coefficient of determination of 0.98 (equivalent to the R^2 measure – Hoel and Jesson, 1982).

The Brunel Index brand image measure can be further validated by predicting the distance that a shopping centre's catchment extends and comparing the predictions with survey results. Spatial interaction ('gravitational') models of catchment area are based on the supposition that patronage of a town or shopping centre decreases with increasing distance from the centre – specifically that the patronage level divided by the distance raised to some power is a constant. The power to which the distance must be raised is defined as the 'distance exponent' – a parameter that is notoriously difficult to predict (a problem that will be considered further in Chapter 5 below).

In Chapter 5 below the relationship between the attractiveness of shopping centres and the distance exponent (with patronage based on visit rate per 1000 residents) has been investigated. In this chapter, the model from Chapter 5 has been used to compare predicted with observed values for two further centres. Data gathered from this questionnaire survey was not used, as to do so would involve an element of recursiveness (the distance decay data was used in generating the model). Published data is sparse but values derived from Howard (1993) and Victoria Centre (undated, approximately 1987) have been used respectively for comparison with predicted values: Meadowhall, Sheffield, predicted –1.66, actual –1.48; Victoria Centre, Nottingham, predicted –1.12, actual –0.97.

Predicted distance exponents have also been used to predict hinterland (catchment area) boundaries directly. Unfortunately, catchment area details for the Victoria Centre, Nottingham were not available. Instead, Northampton has been substituted, using data derived from Martin (1982). The Meadowhall data were again derived from Howard (1993). The measures of 'fit' of the predictions to the survey were: Northampton 0.82; Meadowhall 0.77. (Coefficients of determination of radii in the directions of towns – equivalent to the R^2 measure – Hoel and Jesson, 1982). The actual catchment boundaries are compared with the predictions in Figures 6.10 and 6.11 in Chapter 6 below, where the prediction of catchment boundaries is considered in more detail.

Implications and conclusions

Branding can be quantified by, for example, the procedure of multiplying 'Importance' by 'Rating' and by Butterfield and Haigh's (1998) assignment of weights to brand attributes (the Interbrand or Brand Finance method). The author has (in effect) combined these two approaches and modelled attribute weights from the association between shopping centre attractiveness attributes and shopper spending behaviour, developing the Brunel Index for brand image.

As far as can be determined from the data available, the Brunel Index for brand image does have meaning and utility. In the qualitative comparison of two centres, the centre attracting the more favourable descriptions was significantly higher rated than the other centre. The attractiveness measure has been successfully correlated with the estimated sales turnover of shopping centres. Furthermore, models have been developed and applied to data **not** used in generating the models to predict rental incomes, distance exponents and hinterland boundaries for shopping and town centres.

At the start of this chapter it was contended that 'Active management' and 'Pro-active marketing' are central to UK shopping centre success. The term 'branding' has been little used by academics or practitioners with respect to shopping centres. Nevertheless, this work has demonstrated that shopping centres can be described in brand personality terms. The Brunel Index for brand image has been demonstrated to measure and predict success for the exemplar samples of shopping centres. There is a direct parallel here with the studies of consumer products that have demonstrated that the most highly branded products are the most profitable ones and the ones with the highest market shares (e.g. Buzzell and Gale, 1987; Haigh, 2003; Knowles, 2003). As with other consumer products, so with shopping centres: active brand management could enhance commercial success.

What form should active brand management take? First, some pointers can be deduced from the table of attribute weights in Table 4.4 (reproduced from Table 3.3 in Chapter 3 above, for convenience). These are the attributes that carry most weight in the brand image model, ranked in order of their association with shoppers' relative spending. Of these main components of brand image, only one, (quality of the stores) directly concerns shops. Three relate to infrastructure and six appear to be 'service' or 'experience'. Monitoring and managing the service and experience elements is crucial to shopping centre brand image and success. Other attributes, such as size of the centre and range of stores are also important, but tend to be relatively similar between competing centres, and therefore do not appear in our list of 'critical' attributes – i.e. those having most weight in shoppers' choices of centres.

Table 4.4   Attribute weights from the quantitative survey

Rank	Attribute	Attribute weight
1	General layout	11.4
2	Access by car (roads)	7.8
3	Nice place to spend time	6.7
4	Cleanliness	6.0
5	Covered shopping	4.5
6	Quality of stores	3.9
7	Shoppers nice people	3.9
8	Availability of toilets	3.9
9	Friendly atmosphere	3.8
10	Helpfulness of staff	3.1

Note: The 'top ten' attribute weights from the quantitative survey are listed. These were the attributes most associated with relative spending at the six shopping centres (all were significantly so at $p = 0.05$). These are not necessarily the attributes that the respondents considered most 'important' because the 'weight' also takes into account the degree and strength of the association of the respondents' rating of the attribute with relative spending. Hence 'weight' is intended to model the weight that the attribute carries in shopper spending decisions. In this table, less significant attributes have been omitted, but the numerical values are scaled such that if all attributes are included, the weights total 100.

Second, brands can be built by planning and controlling aspects such as those listed by Jobber (referred to in the 'Introduction' section of this chapter above).

Being First: In the UK context, there may be a competitive advantage to be gained, not from being first as a shopping centre, but from being the first shopping centre (group?) to be truly branded, building the brand (for example) in line with these guidelines. In the UK at the time of writing, at least two shopping centre groups are making efforts to 'be first' in branding terms. British Land (owners of Meadowhall, Sheffield) are implementing many of the measures suggested here. The Mall Corporation (owners of The Mall, Ashley at Epsom and a score of others) are 're-branding' more conventionally by harmonising 'The Mall' brand across all centres in the group.

Quality: In shopping centres as in other consumer brands, better quality of the core product is associated with higher market share and profitability. Failure to get this right is a major reason for brand failure. Table 4.4 provides a checklist; for example, it is easy to observe less successful centres failing on basics such as cleanliness and toilets.

Positioning, repositioning and long-term perspective: Positioning in the marketplace involves the creation of a clear differential advantage in the minds of the shoppers, which can be achieved for example through brand name, image, service and design. A look at the dark colour scheme of the poorly branded Metropolitan Centre, compared with the light and airy atmosphere of The Woodlands demonstrates the relevance for shopping centres. Market research should be carried out to track changes in shopper requirements and reposition accordingly.

The MetroCentre at Gateshead, UK, for example, was the largest and most modern shopping centre in Europe when opened in the mid 1980s. By the time of the take-over by CSC in the mid 1990s, though, there was considerable scope for repositioning and a re-vamp of the image by CSC's 'active management'.

Internal marketing: Internal marketing is a building block in the process of satisfying external customers. Internal 'customer service' and 'marketing research' in the form of, for example, anonymous staff surveys, suggestions and complaints schemes can contribute to the differences in success of companies whose external mixes appear evenly matched. CSC, for example, have demonstrated a proactive approach to motivation and training – perhaps a contributory factor to the rapid improvement of results at the MetroCentre under CSC ownership. In the context of shopping centres, though, there is a further dimension to internal marketing – there are potential benefits from information sharing between centre management and retailers (See Chapter 7 below).

Credibility and well-blended communications: It is not enough just to offer a quality product; consumers must be aware of the benefits and values and have confidence in the brand. Marketers use stimuli to communicate brand personality and reinforce favourable attitudes; the Esso tiger, for example, symbolising grace and power. Our qualitative work has identified some of the cues that could be used in advertising to associate a shopping centre with a positive personality image – peacock, diamond, horse racing, BMW and so on.

In conclusion, this exploratory study has demonstrated that techniques of brand image measurement can be used for shopping centres. Those with the better brand images tend to have larger catchment areas, sales, and rental incomes. It would be natural to expect that, for a shopping centre owner, achieving higher rental incomes should lead to increased profits and shareholder returns. Evidence is lacking as to whether or not those centres scoring higher on the brand image measures have achieved their success by active brand management. Of the brand-building ideas discussed, only 'quality' could be considered to have been measured directly in this chapter. Nevertheless, it should be the case that applying brand-building techniques (successfully) would enhance brand image, and the author contends that the range of brand-management tools should be managed together to achieve congruence in the brand image. Therefore, active brand management could pay rewards in terms of customer numbers, sales turnover and rental income. The models outlined here can measure and predict the effects of changes to individual attributes on these dependent variables.

In conclusion, this chapter has produced a positive answer to Research Question (ii): the attractiveness of a centre can be measured in a way that has meaning and utility in relation to shoppers' spending, the estimated sales turnover and rental income of shopping centres. The following two chapters, Chapters 5 and 6, consider the attractiveness of shopping centres in conjunction with travel distance, time and catchment boundaries.

The Up-market Shopping Centre?

The shopping floors in ... [the shopping galleries] were ... large and spanned by a single roof, creating a single, cohesive space. ... [The shops sold] not only luxury, but also fashionable goods, restricting the retailers to haberdashers, stocking sellers, linen-drapers, seamstresses, goldsmiths, jewellers, milliners, silk merciers, ... stationers, booksellers, confectioners ... china ware, pictures, maps, prints [and so on]. ... The enclosed structure ... meant that social exclusion operated. ... Socialising was inherent within the activity of shopping ... making the galleries places simply to go in order to pass time and meet people.

(Claire Walsh on 'The shopping galleries of early modern London' (around 1668), in *A Nation of Shopkeepers*, Benson and Ugolini (eds), 2003).

5

The Shopping Centre as an Object of Desire: Attraction and Distance In Shopping Centre Choice

This chapter is adapted from a paper that first appeared in the *International Journal of New Product Development and Innovation Management* (Dennis et al, 2000a).[1]

Introduction

Chapters 3 and 4 above addressed the question of 'Why people shop where they do?' by considering the attributes and 'personality' of shopping centres. This chapter seeks to explore the effects of 'deterrence' or 'distance' in addition to 'attraction' in individual consumers' choices of shopping centres. Most of the shopping population of the UK will have more than one shopping centre within easy reach offering similar facilities. So how do people decide which to use? Is travel distance/time the main criterion? For some people and centres, the effects of travel time/distance appear to be dramatically different. In effect, the shape of the distance/demand curve can vary considerably. The finding may go some way towards explaining what is understood to be a noted lack of success of (some?) existing models in predicting shopping centre patronage.

This chapter uses the same dataset and initial data processing as Chapters 3 and 4 above. Chapter 3 reported the development of a simple model based on regression analysis linking shoppers' spending at a shopping centre with the image attributes of that centre and the travel distance. This chapter uses the same model in investigating the

---

[1] Dennis C E, Marsland D and Cockett W (2000a) 'Objects of desire: attraction and distance in shopping centre choice', *International Journal of New Product Development and Innovation Management*, 2(2): 43–60.

relationship between individual spending at one shopping centre compared with that at a competing centre. The relationship between individual relative spending and relative travel distance (or time) is studied. Tentative predictions are made for the two further shopping centres. The results of all six centres are used to investigate the association of individual spending with travel distance and explore a possible linkage with the effect of competing shopping centres.

Objects of desire

Every particle in the universe attracts every other with a force that varies directly as the product of the two masses and inversely as the square of the distance between them.

(Translated from Newton's 1687 Latin)

In the context of shopping location choice, Reilly (1929; 1931) used an analogy with gravitation as the basis of his 'law'. This forms the basis of many approaches to retail location, positing that the frequency with which residents trade with a town is directly proportional to the population of that town and inversely proportional to the square of the distance that they travel to the town. Spending can be considered as being positively related to some measure(s) of 'attractiveness' of the shopping location and negatively related to some measures(s) of unattractiveness or deterrence – such as 'distance'. Reilly considered 'population' to be a surrogate measure for attractiveness – but the 'population' measure cannot be applied to today's out-of-town shopping centres.

Reilly's law is a special case of the Luce (1959) choice axiom. This general axiom for human choice behaviour has been re-stated by Ghosh and McLafferty (1987) as holding that the probability of a consumer visiting a particular shopping centre is related to the 'utility' of that centre relative to competitors. The more generalised approach has proved useful in retail location studies. Firstly, 'attractiveness' (and deterrence) can be considered as a composite of numerous aspects of a shopping centre: choice of stores, car parking, layout, and toilets among many others. Secondly, and centrally to this chapter, the (inverse) effect of distance need not be limited to its 'square'. Re-phrasing, the 'distance exponent' does not necessarily have a value equal to the '–2' of Reilly's analogy with gravity.

Using an approach based on offsetting the utility of the estimated attractiveness of a shopping centre against the disutility of travel distance (or time), the probability of residents from various geographic zones trading with particular centres can be estimated. This is the basis of models such as Huff (1963 – see Ghosh and McLafferty, 1987), Lakshmanan and Hansen (1965 – illustrated in Davies, 1976) and Multiplicative Competitive Interaction (MCI – Nakanishi and Cooper, 1974; Achabal et al, 1982). This chapter does not seek to replace such models, but rather to study patterns in the relationships between shopper spending and travel distance – in effect exploring variations in the distance exponent. The findings might then be used to increase the precision of the more comprehensive models.

The conceptual basis of this chapter stems partly from the well-known retail 'gravitational' models, but more importantly from an exploration of a **dual** effect of distance originating from Catton (1966). Catton (page 144) considered 'attractiveness' as a function of 'proximity to the valuer'. He modified Hartmann's (1938) analogy to read:

> The desiring, or motivation, resulting from the attraction of a given goal is (directly?) proportional to its 'value' and will vary inversely with a power of the 'distance' ... between the valuer and [the object of desire].

Catton (page 245) attempted a theoretical analysis of a possible value for the distance exponent. The first effect of distance concerns travel – 'travel costs tend to be ... dependent on distance' – equivalent to Reilly's use of 'distance' in the normal linear sense. This first component should lead to a decline in usage with distance by retarding travel through increased cost. Secondly, 'Desiring or motivation' decreases with distance. In Hartmann's sociological view, the terms 'proximity' and 'distance' can refer to not only geographical distance but also to 'social distance' or 'value space'. For example, our desire to help a close relative or neighbour with a gift or loan may be much greater than our desire to help a needy individual from another culture in a far-off country. When a yacht skipper from the UK needed rescue in the South Atlantic Ocean, the Australian government put in place a navy rescue over a considerable geographical distance (Bullimore, 1997) – perhaps the cultural distance was not so great? Considerations such as these make up the second component, in which the attractiveness of an object of desire tends to decrease with distance.

Catton (page 255) suggests that combining the two components should lead to a value for the distance exponent of –1.5 (based on analogy with Kepler's third law of orbital motion, Blanco and

McCusky, 1961) compared with the value of –2 suggested by the gravitational analogy. For this chapter, some of Catton's results (visitation rates for USA national parks) have been re-evaluated, estimating distance exponents in various examples of –1.5, –1.7, –1.8 and –2.5.

On the basis even of Catton's own observations, the author believes that a theoretical claim for a constant value for the distance exponent (of –1.5) cannot be supported. Nevertheless, the distinction between two components has merit and forms the conceptual framework for this chapter. The first component can be viewed in the traditional way – the decay in the proportion of residents who trade with a centre with travel distance from the centre. The second component is less straightforward – the decay in individual desiring, perhaps related to what Catton terms the 'value space' distance.

As Scott (1970, page 169) pointed out, Reilly's own results from towns in Texas indicated that the distance exponent was not a constant (values ranged from 0 to –12.5, with the modal class –1.51 to –2.5 containing only one third of the values). Scott cited Illeris (1967) who compared theoretical catchment area boundaries of towns in Denmark with empirical results from surveys. For smaller towns the best value of the distance exponent was –3.0, compared with a value of –1.5 for the larger centres. The first component of the distance exponent can thus be seen to be a variable, which Scott considers 'related to the [attractiveness]' of the object of desire.

In retail location applications, Huff (1963) took a pragmatic approach, stating that the value of the exponent of distance must be determined empirically. Retail location researchers have followed the practice of assigning a value to the distance exponent based on the 'best fit' to the empirical data. For example, according to Jones and Simmons (1990, page 310) the distance exponent usually has values between –0.5 and –2.5 and is larger for convenience than for comparison goods. In one shopping area example (Lewisham – Rhodes and Whitaker, 1967) the value was determined as –1.7. Nevertheless, theoretical approaches have been 'less than successful in practical application' because of variation in the distance component (Rogers, 1984, page 320 citing Openshaw, 1973). Rogers pointed out that the measurement of the distance and attractiveness parameters in the Huff model has 'produced considerable controversy'. He drew attention to a number of theoretical approaches, citing Wilson (1971), Batty and Saether (1972) but agreed with Openshaw (1973) that the fit of the models 'was achieved by adjusting the distance component by the ... Fiddle Factor'.

Variations in the effect of distance were confirmed by Marjanen's (1993, 1995a and b, 1997, 1998, Boedeker and Marjanen, 1993) extensive longitudinal studies, tracking shopping patterns as out-of-town facilities developed in Finland. In a number of cases, Marjanen reported that there was no direct correlation between shopping behaviour and either travel distance or time. Although she did not state this explicitly, the finding refers to the **second** component of distance – the individual.

As has been made clear in this section above, there are many complex models available for predicting shopping behaviour. These tend to be 'unpopular among practitioners' (Breheny, 1988) who often find a relatively simple regression approach to be effective (Simkin, 1996; Coates et al, 1995). This is understandable since sales turnover is proportional to attractiveness (after allowing for the 'fiddled' distance factor – Openshaw, 1973; Rogers, 1984).

The conceptual framework of this chapter is firstly, to present an empirical method for measuring 'attractiveness' (valid for out-of-town shopping centres as well as in-town). Secondly, based on attractiveness measurements together with a measure of competing shopping centre influence, to present a structure for separately assessing the two components of the distance effect. The results should lead to realistic techniques for predicting distance components and, it is hoped, more precise modelling of shopping centre patronage. The basis is the simple proposition that sales turnover is proportional to attractiveness, after allowing for the distance factor, which can now be estimated realistically, rather than 'fiddled'.

The regression models reported in Chapter 3 above have indicated variations in the distance components for different centres and led to the generation of three hypotheses:

H1   'Individual relative spending' is significantly related to 'Relative travel distance' at some shopping centres but not at others.

What characteristics of shopping centres and their environments might underlie variations in the effect of 'distance' on 'spending'? Two alternative suggestions might be postulated. Firstly, the traditional observation relating the distance components to the size or attractiveness of the centre:

H2   Variations in the relationships between 'distance' and 'individual relative spending' are associated with the size or 'attractiveness' of shopping centres. Specifically, for the less attractive centres there is more association with distance and *vice versa*.

Alternatively, the variations in the degree of association might be related to competitive pressure:

H3 Variations in the relationship between distance and individual relative spending are associated with whether there are competing shopping centres within the catchment. Specifically, for centres subject to more competitive pressure, there is more association of spending with distance and *vice versa*.

A large sample of shopping centres would be required to test hypotheses H2 and H3. The current chapter nevertheless explores preliminary indications for H2 and H3, whilst seeking to test H1 more substantially.

Method

The quantitative attribute measurement part of this study consisted of the empirical measurements of the attractiveness of shopping centres, together with shoppers' perceived travel distances and times, from shoppers' responses to structured questionnaires, as described in the Methodology section of Chapter 2. Briefly, the survey results took the form of Rating/distinctiveness and Importance measures ascribed by respondents to various attributes at different shopping centres. A regression model was used to model relative spending according to these measures and shoppers' relative travel time or distance to the centres. Both the Rating/distinctiveness and travel terms were relative to competing centres. The attributes were weighted in the model according to their degree of association with relative spending and the results were used to produce an Attractiveness measure for shopping centres on a 0 to 100 scale.

Results for the four centres

Taking the example of the White Water Centre, a relationship can be demonstrated (by regression analysis) between relative spending, attractiveness and travel distance. (Travel time could be used in place of travel distance but in case of the White Water Centre, distance gives the closer correlation). The greater the distance that respondents have to travel to the centre, compared with their main competing centre, the less they tend to spend. Conversely, an increase in attractiveness (for example arising from improvements to the 'Eating and drinking' facilities) would result in an increase in spending. Equation 5.1 (Equation 3.1 from Chapter 3 above, reproduced here for convenience) attempts to describe this relationship.

$$\text{Relative spending} = 37 + 0.62 \times \text{Relative attractiveness} - 0.32 \times \text{Relative distance} \qquad (5.1)$$

The intercept, attractiveness coefficient and distance coefficients respectively for each of the four centres were reported in Table 3.2 in Chapter 3 above. The 'fit' of these models would normally be accepted as 'modest' (Bryman and Cramer, 1994, page 170). In the case of the Jubilee Centre (only), a slightly better fit would be obtained by substituting 'relative travel time' for 'relative travel distance' ($R^2 = 0.29$ rather than 0.26). Nevertheless, 'distance' is used in all of the results here in the interest of consistency.

It should be noted that the equations reported in Table 3.1 represent micro models for the **individual** shopper. This is equivalent to our second component of the distance effect: 'desiring or motivation' decreasing with distance.

Figure 5.1 illustrates the catchments of the four shopping centres relative to their competitors (names and orientations have been changed). These schematic diagrams illustrate the relevant cities, shopping centres and major roads. Shopping centres are indicated by circular symbols. On each diagram, the larger centres are shown with larger circles, but the diagrams are not to scale and sizes are not comparable between the four diagrams. The catchment radius data is derived from the questionnaire responses, the measure for each respondent being the perceived travel distance to the centre. Shoppers normally have a grasp of how far they travel and which route which offers the best combination of time and distance. There is reasonable agreement between shoppers perceived travel distances and those calculated from the 'Routemaster' (1998) program based on Automobile Association (AA) data.

The 'mean catchment' is defined as the radius that includes 90 percent of the respondents' perceived travel distances. The arcs on the diagrams are thus not true hinterland boundaries (for which more data would be required) but rather a locus of the mean radius. The 'competitor distances' to 'Substantial competitors' are road distances calculated by the 'Routemaster' program. Ideally, catchment might perhaps be better defined in terms of travel time rather than distance.

Unfortunately, there is a lack of an objective measure of travel time between competitors. Although the Routemaster gives reasonable agreement with shoppers' perceived travel **distances**, there is little agreement between Routemaster travel **times** and shoppers' perceived travel times. Specifically, shoppers perceive urban journeys as taking up to twice as long as predicted by Routemaster.

The association of spending with distance has been postulated in H3 as being related to the presence or otherwise of a competitor within the catchment. The measure used as a criterion was the 'competitor distance' as a proportion of the 'mean catchment'. From Figure 5.1, it can be seen that the White Water Centre has a substantial competitor just within its mean catchment, whereas the other centres do not. In the case of the Blue Rose Centre, Figure 5.1 (b), the 'Whitely Bay' and 'Eldon Square' shopping centres are too small to be considered as 'substantial competitors'.

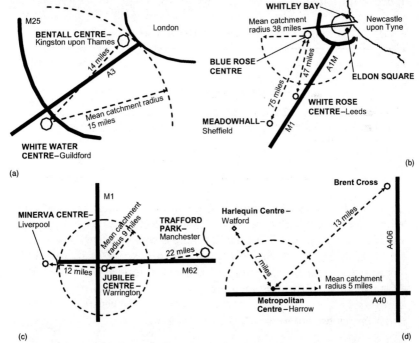

Figure 5.1 Schematic maps of the four shopping centres illustrating catchment and substantial competitors (the names and orientations have been changed). (a) White Water Centre, (b) Blue Rose Centre, (c) Jubilee Centre and (d) Metropolitan Centre.
Source: The author.

'Substantial competitor' can be defined for the purposes of this chapter as a shopping location used by over a quarter of respondents as a main or alternative centre. The size of competitor needed to achieve this degree of competition appears from the data in the questionnaire survey to be at least two-thirds of the size of the centre studied (see the 'Steps in the retail hierarchy' section in Chapter 6 below). This definition seems to be consistent with positions of centres in the retail hierarchy based on the limited data available (Martin's 1982 data for Northampton's catchment area).

The full results from the four centres have been used to produce a ranking of centres according to the degree and strength of association of individual customer spending with travel distance or time. The simple measure used here for the degree of association is the 'Confidence' (based on the regression coefficient and its standard deviation – Greensted et al, 1978). The rankings for association with distance or time are reported in Table 5.1.

Table 5.1　Rankings of association with travel distance or time

	Confidence % of association of spending with distance or time	Distance to nearest substantial competitor as % of mean catchment distance
1. White Water Centre	99.99+	93
2. Jubilee Centre	97.8	133
3. Blue Rose Centre	78.5	123
4. Metropolitan Centre	Not associated.	140

Table 5.1 indicates the gradual reduction in association of spending with travel distance or time as the distance to the nearest substantial competitor increases. It appears that there is some support for a postulation such as H3 relating the presence or absence of competitors within the catchment of a shopping centre to the degree of association of individual customer spending with travel time or distance. Conversely, these results do not support H2 as the centres are not in order (or reverse order) of size or attractiveness.

Predictions for two 'validation centres'

In order to test hypotheses H2 or H3, a study based on a large sample of shopping centres would be needed. Nevertheless, an indicator for the postulations might come from comparing results against predictions using data not used in producing the findings. The validation data available here consisted of the results from two further shopping centres, The Woodlands and Greenleys, with 29 and 28 respondents respectively.

It was necessary to determine in advance the catchment of The Woodlands and Greenleys without 'pre-judging' by using the questionnaire responses. The catchment distances determined from interviews with management are:

* The Woodlands   17 miles
* Greenleys   35 miles.

In order to identify competitors, maps showing shopping locations along with their 'attractiveness' would be useful. The 'Goad plan' (Goad Plans/OXIRM, 1991) indicates the locations of centres with 'Goad score' for each, described in more detail in Chapter 6 below. The scores represent the number of branches of major retailers (Reynolds and Schiller, 1992). The Goad plan lists town centres as well as shopping centres, and allowance must be made for developments since 1991. Subject to these restraints, the Goad plan can provide a usable preliminary guide to the locations of 'substantial competitors'. From the Goad plan, it is observed that there is a substantial competitor within the catchment of The Woodlands but not Greenleys. The predictions were therefore that travel distance and individual relative spending would be correlated at The Woodlands but not at Greenleys:

* The Woodlands   Significant at $p < 0.05$
* Greenleys   Not significant at $p < 0.05$.

Results for the two validation centres and combined results for all six centres

The observed results for association of 'Relative spending' with 'Relative travel distance were:

* The Woodlands   Significant at $p < 0.01$
* Greenleys   not significant at usual test levels.

The results for Greenleys and The Woodlands therefore provide support for the proposition that the degree of association between individual relative spending and distance is related to the presence or otherwise of a substantial competitor within the catchment.

Models for individual centres based on overall attribute weights

To some extent, in models relating relative spending to 'Attractiveness', a correlation would be expected. This 'autocorrelation' effect arises because relative spending determines (in part) the value of the attractiveness measure. The preliminary models such as those in Table 3.1 in Chapter 3 above must be viewed with caution, as the 'Relative attractiveness' components of the models are specific to the individual centres rather than based on a general, comparable scale.

For the purposes of comparing the attractiveness of centres and investigating any overall model, a 'standard' set of attribute weights has been used in Table 5.3 (rather than the attribute weights and 'Attractiveness' measures specific to the local centres, as used in Table 3.2 in Chapter 3 above, page 43). Because there is little consistency of attribute weights between centres and the basis is on only six centres, such modelling must be viewed with caution. Using the combined attribute weights for all six centres, the models have been re-calculated for each individual centre on a directly comparable basis – using the same 'attractiveness' scale for each. This is considered to be the closest approach that can be achieved on the available data to a 'universal' attractiveness scale, for UK shopping centres in general.

Table 5.2   Models of individual relative spending (reproduced from Table 3.1)

Centre	Intercept	Attractiveness coefficient	Distance coefficient	R^2	Significance level, p	Equation number
White Water	37.0	0.62	0.32	0.47	<0.0001	3.1/5.1
Blue Rose	32.2	0.53	0.31	0.19	<0.01	3.2/5.2
Jubilee	24.0	0.68	0.17	0.26	<0.001	3.3/5.3
Metropolitan	15.1	0.53	0	0.33	<0.001	3.4/5.4

For example, for The Woodlands:

$$\text{Relative spending} = 46.5 + 0.28 \times \text{Relative attractiveness} - 0.37 \times \text{Relative distance} \tag{5.10}$$

The overall 'fit' of the models is 0.23 (coefficient of determination), compared with 0.40 for the models specific to individual centres in Equations 5.1 to 5.4 in Table 5.2 above.

Table 5.3 Models of individual relative spending at each of the six shopping centres – based on overall attribute weights

	Distance to nearest substantial competitor (% of mean catchment)	Constant	Attractiveness coefficient or 'elasticity'	Distance coefficient or 'elasticity'	Equation number
Greenleys	145	–12.2	1.28	–0.023	5.5
Metropolitan	140	6.8	0.71	0	5.6
Jubilee	133	30.8	0.60	–0.17	5.7
Blue Rose	123	37.9	0.34	–0.10	5.8
White Water	93	43.5	0.56	–0.38	5.9
Woodlands	32	46.5	0.28	–0.37	5.10

From Table 5.3, it can be seen that where the distance to a competitor is low, then 'distance elasticity' tends to be high. In addition, where the 'distance elasticity' is high, the 'attractiveness elasticity' tends to be low. This might be anticipated, as when 'distance' is not the main criterion, it would be expected that 'attractiveness' would be. It is thus possible to postulate an overall model for individual relative spending at any of the shopping centres, based on non-linear curve fitting of the terms with competitor distance – see the Appendix to this chapter.

The first of the two components of the distance effect concerns the distance exponent on visit rate **per 1000 residents**. Figure 5.2 illustrates this variable related to the 'Attractiveness index'. The attractiveness index values have been re-scaled using the 'Mintel equivalent' scale mentioned briefly in Chapter 4 above and developed more fully in Chapter 6 below. This relationship could also be used in estimating the distance exponent for sales forecasting purposes, although for a new centre it would be necessary to estimate the Attractiveness index in advance.

The relationship between individual relative spending and competitor distance following from Equations 5.5 to 5.10 in Table 5.3 concerns the second component – illustrated in Figure 5.3. This relationship, or even better, the non-linear version fitted to the data, could be of use in modelling shopper spending. When using, for example, the Lakshmanan and Hanson (1965) model, the distance exponent could be adjusted arithmetically to correct for the effects of competing centres on individual spending.

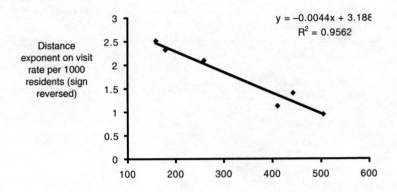

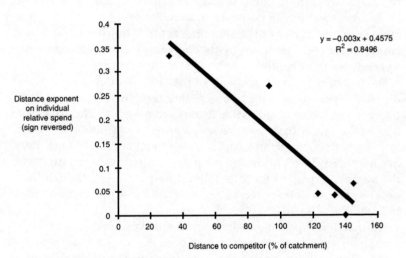

Figure 5.2 Distance exponent on visit rate per 1000 residents *vs.* Brunel measured attractiveness index of shopping centre (corrected for surrounding town where applicable) on the same scale as the 'Mintel' scale.

Figure 5.3 Distance exponent on individual relative spent *vs.* distance from each of the six shopping centres to the nearest 'Substantial competitor' as percentage of the mean catchment distance.

Hypotheses testing

H1   Individual relative spending is significantly related to relative travel distance at some shopping centres but not at others.

For a comparison of the relationships between relative spending and travel distance at each centre, the author has devised a measure of the 'Association' value. This is the square root of the product of the linear regression coefficient and the R^2 value – thus taking account of both the degree of correlation and the 'elasticity'. The significance 'p' values for the 'Association' between individual relative spending and relative travel distance were:

White Water Centre	<0.0001
Blue Rose Centre	0.69
Jubilee Centre	0.62
Metropolitan Centre	0.25
Greenleys	0.99
The Woodlands	0.013.

The association between relative spending and relative travel distance was significant at normal test levels at both the White Water Centre and The Woodlands. Unusually, the value of p = 0.99 at Greenleys indicated that an association between individual relative spending and relative travel distance was very improbable at that centre and implied rejection of H_0.

In order to add to support for H1, it was desirable to confirm that the significant association at the White Water Centre and The Woodlands would be unlikely to arise at random if all respondents were drawn from a single population. To this end, the values for 'Association' with travel distance have been calculated by bootstrapping ten samples of 73 respondents selected at random from all 287. The 'One sample t-test' significance values have been calculated for the 'test values' obtained for the 'Association' at the White Water Centre and The Woodlands. Both were significant at p < 0.05 indicating that it would very unlikely that the 'Association' values between individual relative spending and relative travel distance would have arisen at random if all respondents were drawn from a single population. The results indicated that the null hypothesis could be rejected and therefore **there was support for hypothesis H1**: Individual relative spending was significantly related to relative travel distance at some shopping centres but not at others.

H2   **Variations in the relationships between 'distance' and 'individual relative spending' are associated with the size or 'attractiveness' of shopping centres. Specifically, for the less attractive centres there is more association with distance and *vice versa*.**

H2 and H3 can be postulated as alternatives. Scatter points for the association of relative spending with relative travel distance appeared to be virtually uncorrelated with the 'Attractiveness index' of the shopping centres – but the line of 'best fit' actually had a **positive** slope (the reverse of the H2 postulation) of 0.095. On this basis, the postulation that high values of 'Association' between relative spending and relative distance are associated with low values of shopping centre 'Attractiveness' could be rejected. **Hypothesis H2 was not supported.**

H3   **Variations in the relationship between distance and individual relative spending are associated with whether there are competing shopping centres within the catchment. Specifically, for centres subject to more competitive pressure, there is more association of spending with distance and *vice versa*.**

With a limited sample of shopping centres, H3 cannot be formally tested. Nevertheless, such a relationship is consistent with the data, as illustrated in Figure 5.3. On the basis of these results, H3 cannot be rejected. In view of the rejection of H2, **hypothesis H3 merits further testing.** There is a parallel here with Marjanen's (1993) finding that 'people estimate the more attractive centre to be also more accessible than the smaller one' – wording which implies a comparison between two centres, rather than referring to an absolute attractiveness of a single centre. If a centre is substantially more attractive than its competitors, i.e. less subject to competitive pressure, distance will figure less in shopping decisions.

Implications and conclusions

This chapter set out to investigate the two-component aspects of the distance effect on shopper patronage of shopping centres. A traditional view, that the distance exponent varies according to the size or attractiveness of a shopping centre would appear to be relevant to the first component only – decay in patronage with travel distance measured by visit rate per 1000 residents. The second component, the **individual** desiring, measured by individual relative spending is **not** related to the size or attractiveness of the shopping centre.

So far as can be determined from the investigation of six shopping centres, there is evidence that the second component concerned with individual desiring is related to the presence or absence of competing shopping centres. In this second aspect, 'desiring' (as measured by individual relative spending) varies inversely with the 'value space distance' (the effect of travel distance relative to an alternative centre) from the 'object of desire' (shopping centre). The results suggest that the value space distance is greater (distance exponent numerically greater) when an alternative object of desire (competing shopping centre) is close. If an alternative object of desire is readily available, people are quick to take advantage.

Secondly, and more centrally to the thrust of this current chapter, the modelling of variations in the distance exponent can be put to use in the planning of new shopping centres. It is now possible to estimate shoppers' likely assessment of the attractiveness of alternative proposals and the effect of competing centres. It is thus possible to model, for example, likely catchment area boundaries. This potential will be explored further in the following chapter, Chapter 6 below, which considers how the variable distance exponent can be utilised in determining catchment boundaries.

The significant findings from this chapter are illustrated schematically on the lower left of the diagram, Figure 13.2 in Chapter 13 below, page 243.

Appendix 5.1: Modelling of individual relative spending across all six centres

An overall model has been estimated based on the non-linear curve fitting of the terms of Equations 5.5 to 5.10 inclusive from Table 5.3 above:

$$\text{Relative spending} = a + b \times \text{Relative attractiveness} - c \times \text{Relative distance} \quad (5.11)$$

Where the values of a, b and c are related to the distance to the nearest substantial competitor, d:

Constant $\qquad\qquad a = 17.28 \times \text{Ln}(150 - d) - 25.77 \quad (5.12)$

$$(5.13)$$
Attractiveness coefficient $\quad b = \dfrac{1.9863}{e^{\left(\text{Ln}(150 - d) \times 0.4075\right)}}$

Distance coefficient $c = 0.1296 \times Ln(150 - d) - 0.235$ (5.14)

Although R^2 for this overall model is only 0.18, it is significant at $p < 0.0001$. This degree of fit is at the lower end of what would commonly be accepted as 'modest' (Bryman and Cramer, 1994, page 170). The degree of fit may not appear high, but should be viewed in the light of the finding in Chapter 3 above that the attractiveness attributes **are significantly different** at different centres and any attempt at a universal comparative scale can only be an approximation. The use of local, rather than overall, attractiveness scales would bring R^2 up to over 0.25.

There is no denying that London captures the go-ahead spirit of the age. Property prices have shot up ... as young City types move into flats and studios a short walk from their offices in the Square Mile [financial district]. ... Once nondescript streets boast lively pubs, trendy coffee shops and plenty of good places to eat. ... And the shopping has improved in the past few years, with a good range of outlets selling Paris fashions.

(The Daily Mail, 18 March, 2000, referring to London in 1700, commenting on *1700: Scenes from London Life* by Maureen Waller (2000).

6

Central Place Practice: Shopping Centre Attractiveness Measures, the 'Break Point', Catchment Boundaries and the UK Retail Hierarchy

This chapter is adapted from a paper that first appeared in the *Journal of Retailing and Consumer Services* (Dennis et al, 2002b).[1]

Introduction

The previous chapter, Chapter 5, explored the effects of distance on 'Why people shop where they do?' – not only travel distance/time but also individual perceptions that may equate to social or cultural distance. This chapter uses the author's empirically based measurement system for the attractiveness of shopping centres, in- and out-of-town, developed in Chapter 4 above, with a view to modelling and predicting positions in the retail hierarchy. A greater understanding of the hierarchy can add to an understanding of essential spatial aspects of why people shop where they do, not least, catchment area boundaries. The chapter proceeds as follows. Firstly, a theory of retail hierarchy – Central Place Theory – is briefly outlined. The development of the author's attractiveness model follows and the model is used, in case study examples, to define steps in the retail hierarchy, based on shoppers' choice behaviour. Scales proposed by other researchers are examined and it is demonstrated that such scales can be modified in the light of the empirical research. The unified attractiveness scale used in Chapter 4 above is demonstrated to have utility in predicting catchment boundaries, consistent with the principles of Central Place Theory. Next, 'Break point' theory is re-examined in the light of the attractiveness measurements

---

[1] Dennis C E, Marsland D and Cockett W (2002b) 'Central place practice: shopping centre attractiveness measures, catchment boundaries and the UK retail hierarchy' *Journal of Retailing and Consumer Services*, 9 (4): 185–199.

and variable distance exponents (discussed in the previous chapter, Chapter 5). Finally, the author considers whether, when changes in attractiveness over time are considered, Central Place Theory modelling can become dynamic. In discussing the results, indicators are drawn for possible changes that might be anticipated in the UK retail and population structure.

Central place theory

Central Place Theory is based on classical economic assumptions such as uniformity of consumers and travel, a theory described by Brown (1992, page 40) as an 'elegant and ... much maligned conceptualisation'. Based on the work of the German geographer, Christaller (1933) and economist, Losch (1940), the theory was, according to O'Brien and Harris (1991) 'widely accepted by the planning profession as a model of retail organisation'. O'Brien and Harris considered that Central Place Theory, for example, 'explains why London [UK] contain[ed] the major fashion houses and top stores, and why small places such as Durham [UK] [did] not have department stores.'

The theory has been criticised in recent decades and dismissed as 'more elegant than practical' by O'Brien and Harris, who drew support from Dawson (1979, page 190):

Whilst the theory serves to describe and, in part, explain locational patterns developed prior to the 1960s, it can no longer be used as an ... explanation of present patterns or planning future.

According to Dawson, Central Place modelling was flawed because of the complex nature of retailing and scrambled merchandise mixes. Despite acknowledged drawbacks, in this chapter the author revisits and adapts Central Place ideas in modelling catchment boundaries and positions in the retail hierarchy.

In Christaller's terminology, goods were described in terms of 'threshold' (the population needed to make supply worthwhile) and range (distance from source of supply beyond which demand falls to zero). According to Brown (1992):

Expensive and infrequently purchased ['comparison'] goods ... have higher thresholds and ranges than inexpensive, everyday ['convenience'] purchases ... There will be a large number of purveyors of [convenience] goods and relatively few sellers of [comparison] merchandise.

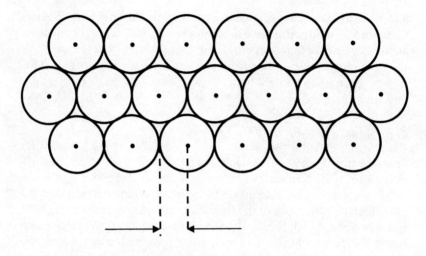

Maximum travel
distance for
convenience goods

Figure 6.1 (a) (i)

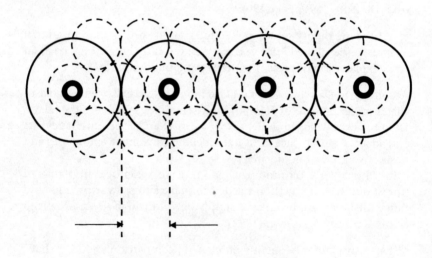

Maximum travel
distance for
comparison goods

Figure 6.1 (a) (ii)

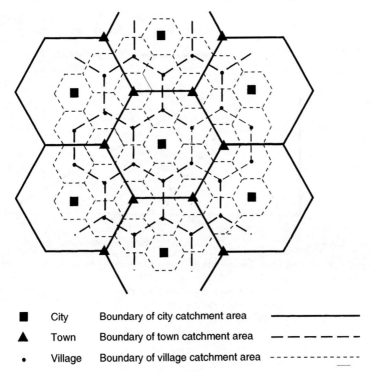

■   City   Boundary of city catchment area   ─────────

▲   Town   Boundary of town catchment area   ─ ─ ─ ─ ─ ─

•   Village   Boundary of village catchment area   - - - - - - - - - - - -

Figure 6.1   Central Place theory – illustration of demand areas
(a) Hypothetical demand cones;
(b) Hierarchy. Notes: (i) Different types and orders of goods supplied from different levels of places will have different ranges and thresholds and thus sizes of market areas. A nested hierarchy will be produced.
(ii) This pattern is known as a K = 3 hierarchy. The k value is determined by the number of lower order centres served by the next higher level of place. The numbers of centres follows a geometrical progression, proportional to 1, 3, 9 and so on according to the number of levels.
Sources: Adapted from (a) Brown (1992); originally sourced from Davies (1976); (b) O'Brien and Harris (1991).

By combining the concepts of threshold and range, catchments are defined in which comparison goods are only supplied from populous 'central' places whilst convenience goods are sold locally. Economic modelling based on these assumptions produces maps of catchments in terms of interlocking and overlapping areas (Figure 6.1).

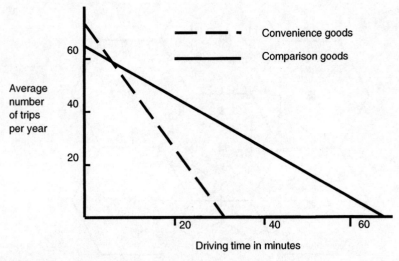

Figure 6.2   Travel time decay curves, comparing convenience and shopping ('comparison') goods. This (US) example indicated shopping frequencies for three regional and three sub-regional shopping centres. Symbols represent the number of trips to those centres for customers at various travel times.
Sources: Jones and Simmons (1990, page 40), based on Young (1975).

Brown pointed out that:

> The spatial arrangement of shopping facilities in the majority of British cities is explicable in terms of central place principles. Typically, this comprises a [comparison] retailing core, a series of [convenience] shopping districts surrounding the core but closer to it than the edge of the city, and a greater number of shopping districts in the inner than the outer parts of the urban area.

Effectively summing up researchers' ambivalent approaches to Central Place Theory, Tang and Ingene (2000) drew attention to essential assumptions that cannot be sustained in reality, for example the homogeneity of households and purchasing demands. Nevertheless, in calibrating their shopping model (using the example of Shanghai), they observed that the retail hierarchy predicted by the theory was actually observed in practice. This chapter explores the use of break point calculations in defining the interlocking and overlapping areas.

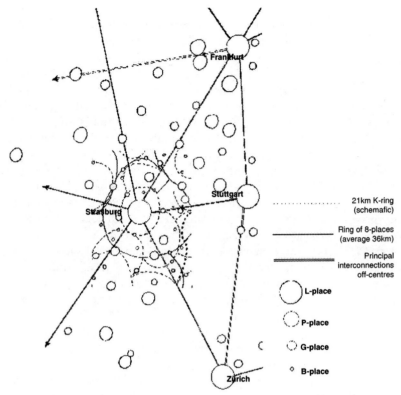

Figure 6.3 The distribution of towns as Central Places in southern Germany
Source: Adapted from Christaller, 1933, page 225.

The retail hierarchy

The distinction between higher order comparison and lower order convenience goods has been observed in empirical data, illustrated for example in Figure 6.2. Christaller (1933, page 58) observed that:

> We always find great numbers of central places of a lower order, i.e. lesser importance and smaller size. Beside them, we find a considerable number of Central Places that have a somewhat greater importance, a still smaller number of places of a higher order, and only very seldom, places of the highest order ... The greater a town is, the smaller is the number ... in its respective category.

Analogous to Reilly's (1929 and 1931) approach to measuring attractiveness, Christaller based his hierarchical system on population
numbers. The (then) standard German classification defined five
categories, from the 'county town' of 2000–5000 to the 'metropolis' of
1 000 000+ population. Despite having apparently utilised these
classifications, Christaller claimed to base his definitions of the hierarchy on the classification of goods on offer. For any particular good, the
outer limit of its range is defined by the distance that shoppers will
travel to obtain that good. Beyond a certain distance they may purchase from another place, or may not purchase at all. The inner limit is
'determined by the minimum sales ... to make the offering pay.'
Christaller claimed to classify towns into categories based on levels of
goods, but the boundaries between the categories seem to have actually
been set according to population numbers. Nevertheless, in southern
Germany, 'especially for the plains ... where there are no natural barriers', the theory 'often determine[d] with astonishing exactness, the
locations of central places' (pages 190–191). An extract from Christaller's mapping is reproduced in Figure 6.3, indicating striking regularity in the distribution of places and hierarchy. Christaller, though,
tested his predictions against the distribution of population (and tele-
phone connections) but did not report doing so against the availability
of the specific goods that are supposed to form the basis of the hierarchy. Other authors have, however, reported confirmatory evidence.
Clark (1982) reported the applicability to market centres in southwest
Iowa (USA); once again, an area where the map can be studied relatively free of the confusing effect of natural barriers. On the other
hand, the author questions whether the (static basis of) Central Place
Theory (i) explains why the biggest shopping centre in the world is
located in a sparsely populated province of a sparsely populated
country (West Edmonton Mall, Alberta, Canada – Finn, 2000); or
(ii) accounts for the shopping centre with the world's highest number
of visitors – over 40 million – being located in a state of only 5 million
inhabitants (Mall of America, MOA, Minnesota, USA – Feinberg et al,
2000). It is the author's contention that the key to an understanding
of the locations of central places is dynamic. For example, if entrepreneurs build shopping centres of sufficient attractiveness (which Finn
and Feinberg have found to underlie the successes of West Edmonton
and MOA respectively), shoppers will come despite travelling long
distances.

Rather than defining hierarchies based on nominal measures such as
population or type of goods, a more rigorous approach is based on

attractiveness. Figure 6.4 illustrates, for example, the retail hierarchy of Cardiff, UK, based on the use of m² selling area as the proxy measure. From the town centre core the hierarchy radiates progressively further out with greater numbers of district centres, neighbourhood centres and finally local centres. An analogous pattern can be demonstrated to surround even a regional shopping centre such as the Harlequin Centre (Watford, UK), where local centres survive and even thrive within a kilometre of the shopping centre. Lakeside (Thurrock, UK) has another shopping centre (in Romford) within the inner band of its catchment area (20 kilometres/15 minutes drive). In order to be viable, those centres lower in the hierarchy need to include a retailer mix appropriate to their position: in Romford, satisfying the shoppers who spend less per visit but come 'three times a week' (the owners, quoted in Retail Week, 6 June 2000).

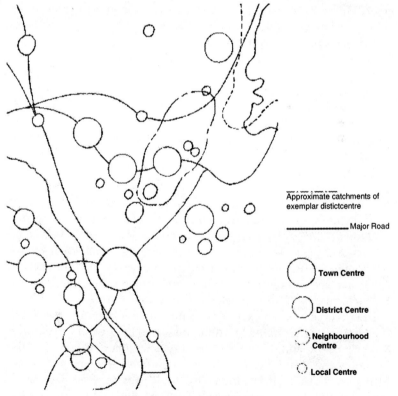

Approximate catchments of exemplar distictcentre

Major Road

Town Centre

District Centre

Neighbourhood Centre

Local Centre

Figure 6.4   The urban retail hierarchy of Cardiff (UK).
Source: Brown (1992); originally sourced from Guy (1984).

Cardiff comprised the basis of a long-term investigation into retail change. Guy (1999, page 458, referring on his 1996 study) observed that 'the development of a few large new food stores coincided with the closure of several smaller ... shops.' Guy described these changes as 'the outcome of a general process of concentration', disproving any static nature of the retail hierarchy. This point was further illustrated in a report of the impact of the Merry Hill regional shopping centre (UK) on the adjacent town of Dudley. On completion of the shopping centre in 1989, a number of major retailers closed their stores and 'in effect moved them to Merry Hill'. Many other shops closed and the premises were reoccupied by low quality and discount stores (Guy, 1999).

In the UK, retail areas have grown in a 'haphazard manner', from origins as markets in the centres of towns and in suburban areas through conversions of other types of property (Guy, 1998). Patterns are not as regular as in, for example, southern Germany or southwest Iowa. Guy criticised Central Place Theory as relying on the notion that consumers would tend to buy the goods required at the nearest available location, an assumption:

> Clearly incorrect for many shopping trips since other determinants of shopping success are also important. ... Consumer choice of shopping destination reflects several qualities, such as variety of goods, price of goods, cleanliness, spaciousness and security of the centre, and quality and quantity of car parking, for example. Central Place Theory, which relies mainly on distance as a choice criterion, becomes inadequate in this situation.

Guy, though, goes on to review dimensions of retail classification systems including goods sold, trip purpose, size of store, store ownership, catchment area, physical form, function, location, development history and type. Guy pointed out that shoppers make their choices of shopping centre destination from an 'evoked set' with respect to a particular combination of location and trip purpose, suggesting a hierarchical classification based on trip purpose and size.

The Goad score is an example of a hierarchical classification system used in the UK. Shopping locations are scored by the numbers of non-food shops. (Reynolds and Schiller, 1992; Schiller and Jarrett, 1985). Reynolds and Schiller examined the cumulative frequency of scores, fitting the divisions in the hierarchy to the gaps between size clusters where possible. The hierarchy classifications illustrate the increases in numbers of centres at the lower levels but cannot be observed to follow the strict geometrical progression of Central Place Theory. The six levels were:

	Multiple branch (Goad) score	*Number of centres*
National	186	1
Metropolitan	93–132	6
Major regional	35–74	99
Minor regional	25–34	60
Major district	6–24	290
Minor district	2–5	370

In this chapter, the author attempts a preliminary exploration of the use of retail attractiveness measures in defining positions in the hierarchies and catchment boundaries for shopping centres and towns. A description of the empirical measurement system for shopping centre attractiveness developed by the author follows. Empirical measurements have been compared with 'retailer count' systems and a unified scale proposed. In a further step, the attractiveness scale has been utilised in defining positions in the retail hierarchy and predicting catchment boundaries, comparing with data not gathered by the author and not used in developing the model.

Propositions

Based on the preceding discussion, two propositions on the development of central places and on consumers' shopping centre choice behaviour can be derived.

P1 Population and retail provision tend to cluster around central places defined on a matrix.
P2 Catchments and the retail hierarchy follow the attractiveness of shopping and town centres.

P1 represents Christaller's 'classical' approach, whereas P2 follows the more recent classification systems of (e.g.) Guy; Reynolds and Schiller. P1 and P2 are not necessarily mutually exclusive, but if P2 is accepted, a trend towards the redistribution of population around attractive shopping destinations might be expected. Accordingly, this study was designed to test, on an exploratory basis, the extent to which P1 and P2 fit available exemplar UK data.

Attractiveness

The methodology for the attractiveness measurements in the context of consumers' choices of shopping centres has been reported in Chapters 2 to 5 inclusive above. Briefly, the survey results took the form of Rating/distinctiveness and Importance measures ascribed by respondents to various attributes at different shopping centres. A regression model was used to model relative spending according to these measures and shoppers' relative travel time or distance to the centres. Both the Rating/distinctiveness and travel terms were relative to competing centres. The attributes were weighted in the model according to their degree of association with relative spending and the results were used to produce an Attractiveness measure for shopping centres on a 0 to 100 scale.

Steps in the retail hierarchy

The positions of steps in the retail hierarchy of shopping centres were investigated by first defining what constituted a 'substantial competitor' in the empirical survey. In this context, a substantial competitor was defined as another shopping centre used by over 25 percent of shoppers at the centre studied. To qualify as substantial, a competitor must be attractive relative to the centre studied. For example, considering centres featuring in this empirical work, the Blue Rose Centre (not its real name) has a competitor of 55 percent of the physical size (m^2 gross selling area) within its catchment. This competitor was used as a main or alternative centre by only 2 percent of the Blue Rose Centre's customers and thus cannot be considered a substantial competitor. Conversely, The White Water Centre's substantial competitor is 95 percent of the size of the White Water Centre and used as a main or alternative centre by 40 percent of the White Water Centre's customers.

Using selling area as a proxy indicator of attractiveness, the defining point for a substantial competitor (used by over 25 percent of a shopping centre's customers) lies somewhere in between above 55 percent and below 95 percent of the size of the centre studied. A mid value of 75 percent has thus been adopted as the defining level of a substantial competitor, based not on selling area but rather on the more precise unified attractiveness scale reported in Chapter 4 above and in the section below. For a competitor to be counted as at the equivalent level in the hierarchy to the centre studied, the competitor must have an attractiveness of at least 75 percent of that of the centre studied. It follows, therefore, that when two shopping centres are compared, if the smaller one has an attractiveness of less than 75 percent of the larger one, the smaller is at a lower level in the hierarchy. Although studies of many more centres are needed to confirm this arbitrary-seeming definition, it is consistent with the results of this study and those of other authors analysed below. That is, a centre at a lower level can lie within the catchment of a larger centre whilst there will be a 'break point' in catchment boundary between two centres at the same level.

Unified attractiveness scale

As used in Chapter 4 above, the Mintel (1997) attractiveness measurement scale for shopping centres and towns is based on numbers of retail outlets, scoring multiples higher than others and certain specific named retailers higher still. In the light of the many considerations that are known to inform shoppers' choices of shopping destinations, measuring shopping centre attractiveness in such a manner initially appears trivial. Nevertheless, evidence in support can be inferred from at least two independent sources. Firstly, Finn and Louviere (1996) investigated all 17 regional and community shopping centres in Edmonton, Canada. The fit of their regression models was 'highly significant, with between 70 percent and 90 percent of image item variance accounted for by the store tenant variables' such as the presence of particular major and discount department stores. Other characteristics had some significant effects, but the additional effect on image was 'generally rather small'. It was concluded that specific anchor stores had a substantial impact on consumers' images of shopping centres, accounting for 'most of the variation in centre patronage'. Secondly, Feinberg and associates (2000) investigated the prediction of (US) mall patronage from attraction scales using stepwise logit regression. In every case, the rating of specific stores that most attracted customers was demonstrated to be the most significant variable. Findings such as these are understandable when it is considered that the most attractive shopping centres will be expected to attract the most successful and popular retailers.

In this study, the 'Mintel' scale correlated well with the empirical measurements from the questionnaire surveys, $R^2 = 0.94$ for Equation 6.1:

$$A = 0.978B \qquad (6.1)$$

Where A is the Mintel score and B the empirical 'Brunel Index' for attractiveness (from the survey-measured weighted attractiveness summations, re-scaled to use an equivalent numerical scale to the Mintel score – Figure 6.5). Corrections must be made, though, for the differences between planned, covered shopping centre attractiveness and the unplanned town centres, and in addition for the effect that the surrounding town area has on shoppers' perceptions of the attractiveness of the centre. The attractiveness measure was significantly associated with shopping centre sales turnover and rental income (R^2 0.99 and 0.98 respectively, reported more fully in Chapter 4).

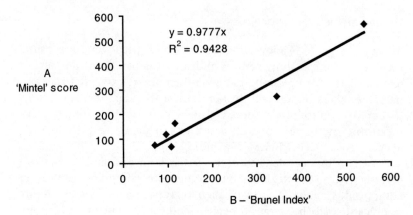

Figure 6.5   'Mintel' scores, A of shopping centres *vs.* the Brunel measured attractiveness index, B of the centres, rescaled on the 'Mintel' scale – corrected for the effect of the surrounding towns where applicable (forced through the origin).

To estimate and plot catchment boundaries maps indicating the locations of towns and shopping centres along with their Mintel scores would be useful. Such maps can be produced to order by data owner(s). The Hillier Parker 'New Guide to shopping centres of Great Britain (Goad Plans/OXIRM, 1991, the 'Goad Plan') is useful in this connection. The Goad Plan is based on the numbers of branches of 113 specific multiple retailers ('Goad scores' – based on one of the examples referred to by Guy and designed to reflect the presence of multiple comparison goods retailers – Reynolds and Schiller, 1992). An extract from the Goad Plan is reproduced in Figure 6.6. The area selected deliberately typifies a part of central England relatively free from natural barriers and having in consequence some regularity in the distribution of towns. Below those towns rated in the Goad hierarchy, there is a level of smaller places, such that, in the Middle Ages (approximately 1100 to 1500 CE), every habitation was within a one-day return walk of a market.

The author has determined the Goad scores to be valid measures of attractiveness for towns, correlating with scales proposed by other research organisations (such as Management Horizons, 1995: for 15 towns also rated on the Goad Plan, $R^2 = 0.88$, significant as $p = 0.01$). The Mintel scores, though, are valid for both towns and shopping centres. To facilitate data handling, the Goad scores have been rescaled to the Mintel equivalents.

Based on the best fit of available data, it has been estimated that, for plotting catchment boundaries, the attractiveness of towns must be scaled down by a fixed percentage compared to shopping centres. Validating the combined scale as linear, estimates of sales values for town and shopping centre combinations together with out-of-town shopping centres correlated well with the combined attractiveness scale (coefficient of determination, $R^2 = 0.92$, significant at $p = 0.01$). It must be stressed that the author's new empirical attractiveness measures should be used whenever practicable. Nevertheless, the scale based on Goad and Mintel values, adjusted for town centres *vs.* shopping centres, can be utilised as an alternative where the empirical measures are not available.

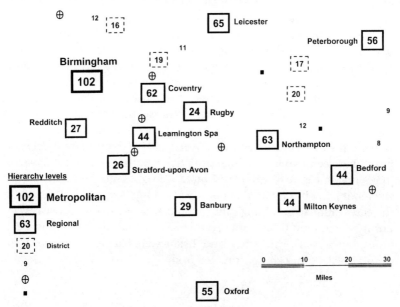

Figure 6.6 Towns and shopping centres in central England.
Source: Extracted and adapted from Goad Plans/OXIRM, 1991.

Break point and distance exponent

There are many theoretical approaches to modelling shopping centre catchment areas but these have 'produced considerable controversy' and models which only work when the fit of the distance component is adjusted by the 'Fiddle Factor' (Rogers, 1984, page 320 drawing on Openshaw, 1973). The complex models tend to be 'unpopular among practitioners' (Breheny, 1988).

This chapter returns to a simpler approach to catchment area boundaries, based on 'gravitational theory' (see Chapter 5 above): calculation of the 'break point' between the catchment areas of two towns or shopping centres. This is often known as 'Reilly's Law' (Reilly, 1929; 1931) although it is usually expressed in a form re-stated by Converse (1949). Although some of the original underlying assumptions of Reilly's Law cannot be supported, in this chapter the method has been updated based on empirical results, overcoming the main disadvantages.

As outlined in Chapter 5 above, the principle of the 'gravitational' theory of retail is that shoppers are more likely to shop in a bigger town, but the attractiveness of a town or shopping centre decreases with distance away. Spend can be considered as being positively related to some measure(s) of 'attractiveness' of the shopping location and negatively related to some measures(s) of unattractiveness or deterrence – such as 'distance'. Reilly (1929; 1931) used an analogy with gravitation as the basis of his 'law' which forms the basis of many approaches to retail location. The frequency with which residents trade with a town is said to be directly proportional to the population and inversely proportional to the square of the distance that they travel. Reilly used 'population' as surrogate measure for attractiveness – but of course, the population measure cannot be applied to today's out-of-town shopping centres.

Reilly's 'Law' was restated by Converse (1949) to estimate the 'break point' between two towns separating the areas of dominance of each, illustrated in Figure 6.7. If, for example, 'A' represents the earth and 'B' the moon, an object placed at point 'x' is more likely to be attracted to the earth. Similarly, although the moon is smaller, an object released at point 'y' will tend to be attracted towards the moon. There must be a point, say 'z', where attraction and distance are balanced. The position of this break point can be estimated from:

$$\text{Break point} \atop \text{(distance from A)} = \frac{\text{Distance A to B}}{1 + \sqrt{\dfrac{\text{Population A}}{\text{Population B}}}} \qquad (6.2)$$

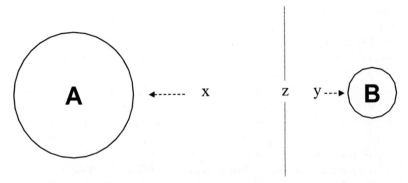

Figure 6.7   Schematic illustration of the 'gravitation' effect and 'break point', z.
Source: The author.

In a shopping application, town A might be Hull (England) with a population of 250 000. B is Beverley, seven miles away with a population of 40 000 (not the true figures but chosen to keep the arithmetic simple). The calculated break point is:

$$\frac{7}{1 + \sqrt{\dfrac{40000}{250000}}} = 5 \text{ miles from Hull}$$

A shopper who lives 5 miles from Hull and 2 miles from Beverley is (predicted by this law to be) equally likely to shop at Hull or Beverley. Someone living say four miles from Hull would be more likely to shop at Hull, whereas a person living less than two miles from Beverley would be more likely to shop there than Hull.

The more general Luce (1959) axiom for human choice behaviour, re-stated by Ghosh and McLafferty (1987) as holding that the probability of a consumer visiting a particular shopping centre is related to the 'utility' of that centre relative to competitors. This approach has proved useful in retail location studies. Firstly, 'attractiveness' (and deterrence) can be considered as a composite of numerous aspects of (for example) a shopping centre: choice of stores, car parking, layout, and toilets among many others. Secondly, the (inverse) effect of distance need not be limited to its 'square'. Re-phrasing, the 'distance exponent' does not necessarily have a value equal to the '–2' of Reilly's analogy with gravity.

More sophisticated and complex methods have been developed for forecasting sales of shopping centres and catchment area boundaries (for example, Huff's 1963; 1964 'spatial interaction'; Lakshmanan and Hansen's 1965 stepwise method; Nakanishi and Cooper's 1974 'multiplicative competitive interaction', and Wilson's 1971 'entropy-maximising'). In such methods, attractiveness can be assessed in a realistic way, and distance exponents other than the –2 of Reilly's simple gravitational model can be incorporated.

In following sections of this chapter, the author addresses the use of varying distance exponent values and more realistic estimates of attractiveness. By substituting 'attractiveness' for 'population', the break point method has been adapted to help predict catchment area for an out-of-town shopping centre as well as for a town. One obstacle is that the simple mathematical solution (Equation 6.2 or variations) does not apply if the distance exponent has more than one value. A methodology will be proposed here for solving the break point in these circumstances. Predictions are tested against data not gathered by the author and not used in developing the models. There is a scarcity of such data published in the public domain, but two surveys mapping customer catchments have been used, a town (Northampton, UK: Martin, 1982) and an out-of-town shopping centre (Meadowhall, UK: Howard, 1993).

Variations in the distance exponent were reported in Chapter 5 above. The distance exponent was demonstrated to be a variable related to attractiveness. The author contends that an estimation of the distance exponent, d, can be predicted from the Brunel Index of attractiveness, B, using a relationship derived from a linear regression (SPSS) in Equation 6.3:

$$d = -0.0044B + 3.19 \qquad\qquad (6.3)$$

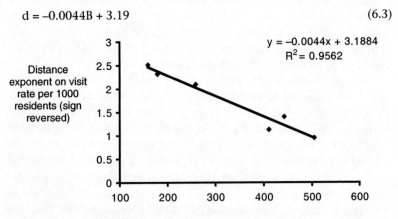

Figure 6.8 Distance exponent on visit rate per 1000 residents *vs.* Brunel measured attractiveness index of shopping centre (corrected for surrounding town where applicable) on the same scale as the 'Mintel' scale.

The empirical data comprising the basis of the relationship are illustrated in Figure 6.8, duplicated for convenience from Figure 5.3 in Chapter 5 above.

The catchment boundary

Martin (1982) demonstrated that Reilly's Law break points could be used to define a notional catchment area boundary, by calculating (and joining) multiple break points with surrounding towns. Martin compared the calculated break points around Northampton (England) and surrounding towns with a survey data contour (from 1350 respondents) enclosing the area from which 90 percent of Northampton's shoppers travelled.

Martin's calculated break points for Northampton produced a catchment boundary in reasonable agreement with survey results – illustrated in Figure 6.9. This provided a quick quantitative method of estimating the catchment area, albeit with two disadvantages. First, there was only a single measure of attractiveness – population. Population must be an inappropriate measure for the attractiveness of the new town shopping centre of Milton Keynes, UK, which acts in effect in a similar way to an out-of-town shopping centre for a large geographical catchment. Second, the distance exponent was treated as a constant although it has been demonstrated to be a variable in Chapter 5 above. The author has re-worked the break point calculations using unified attractiveness scores together with estimated distance exponents (derived from Figure 6.8). An intuitive restatement of the Reilly/Converse break point prediction of the position of the break point between towns a and b would be:

$$\text{distance from a} = \frac{\text{distance from a to b}}{1 + \frac{\sqrt[d]{A_b}}{\sqrt[d]{A_a}}} \tag{6.4}$$

where d^a and d^b are the distance exponents for towns 'a' and 'b' respectively, A_a and A_b their attractiveness scores. Equation 6.4 is, though, only a first approximation of a relationship. No straightforward algebraic solution is readily apparent but the position of the break point can readily be solved graphically. For simplicity, and to avoid the need for solving graphically, the author has devised a stepwise algorithm, outlined below.

Step 1
Calculate a first approximation of the break point from Equation 6.4,

Where d_a and d_b are the distance exponents for towns 'a' and 'b' respectively,

A_a and A_b their attractiveness scores.

Step 2
Calculate the values of the functions:

$$\frac{A_a}{D_a{}^{d_a}} \text{ and } \frac{A_b}{D_b{}^{d_b}}$$

where Da is the distance of the calculated break point from 'a' and D_b the distance from 'b'. At the true theoretical break point the values will be equal. The values of these functions, which are proportional to theoretical trading frequencies for the two centres, are referred to as F_a and F_b respectively. Correct the distance of the break point from town 'a' by multiplying by:

$$\sqrt[d]{1 + \frac{F_a - F_b}{2 \times F}}$$

where d is the higher of the distance exponents and F is the lower the frequency function values.

Step 3
Calculate the F values again for the new break point. The desired F value is the mean of the two new F values. Knowing the F_a value for the distance from 'a' from step 1 and the F_a value for the distance from 'a' in step 2, interpolate (or extrapolate) arithmetically to estimate the required distance from 'a' for the desired F value.

A more rigorous solution is readily obtained solving two simultaneous (nearly) linear equations by similar triangles, but space limitations preclude including the details here. Such a degree of refinement is in any case unnecessary as in the author's experience, the 3-step procedure described has always estimated break point distances within 0.2 km of the theoretically optimum solution.

Martin defined the catchment area in what may seem to be an arbitrary manner – the boundary which enclosed 90 percent of the shoppers, pointing out that 'any attempt to identify more than around 90 percent of catchment area results in absurdities such as claiming that parts of ... America should be included'. The author has investigated the use of values other than 90 percent. No other value was more useful in modelling shopper spend. The value of 90 percent has therefore been retained as a standard (R^2 value in predicting the effect of distance on individual spend 0.85 when using the 90 percent value for defining catchment, compared to 0.62 and 0.57 for 85 percent and 95 percent respectively).

Using the techniques described above, substituting 'attractiveness' for 'population', and using distance exponent values estimated from attractiveness, the author's adapted break point method has been used to test predicted catchment area for an out-of-town shopping centre (Meadowhall, Sheffield, UK) and for a town (Northampton, UK), using Howard's (1993) and Martin's (1982) data respectively. Predicted catchment boundaries have been compared with survey results for these two shopping locations, illustrated in Figures 6.9 to 6.11 inclusive. The

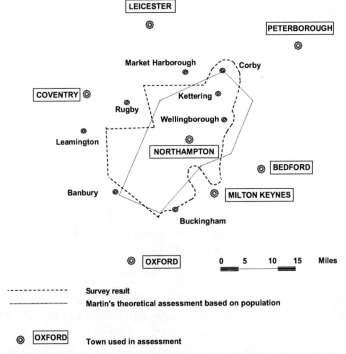

Figure 6.9 Catchment area of Northampton, comparing the theoretical assessment from the Reilly/Converse 'law' with the survey result.
Source: Adapted from Martin (1982, page 71).

author's break point calculations have been based on estimated drive times from Automobile Association data (AA: Routemaster programme, ~1998), plotted *via* the major roads.

For Northampton, illustrated in Figure 6.10, the radii of the predictions in the directions of towns in the vicinity of the catchment boundary fit the survey result well, with a Hoel and Jesson index of fit = 0.82 (equivalent to the R^2 value – Hoel and Jesson, 1982).

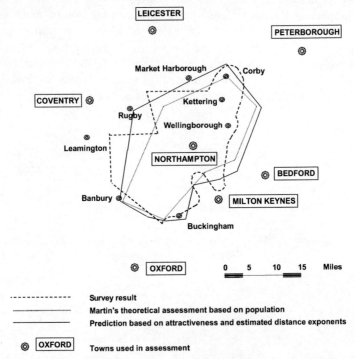

Figure 6.10 Catchment area of Northampton, comparing the theoretical assessment from the Reilly/Converse 'law' *vs.* the survey result, with a plot based on Brunel Index superimposed by the author (based on drive times and predicted distance exponents).

Sources: The author and adapted from Martin (1982, page 71).

For out-of-town regional shopping centres, break point calculations are in the main less applicable than for towns as such centres are usually not surrounded by competitors attractive enough to figure at an equivalent level in the retail hierarchy. Figure 6.11 is an example of catchment data for Meadowhall out-of-town shopping centre, near Sheffield, UK. In directions other than Manchester (a major UK city west of

Figure 6.11 Catchment area of Meadowhall, (Sheffield, UK) comparing the theoretical assessment from predicted 'Brunel attractiveness', distance exponents and population, plus the 'break points' with Manchester (based on drive times) *vs.* the survey result.
Sources: The author, adapted from Howard (1993, page 101) using data from Census of Population (1991) and Routemaster (1998).

Sheffield), the effect of competitors is not relevant and predictions were made using standard calculations based on population, drive time (or distance) and estimated distance exponents only. Populations (residents in households from Census, 1991) in radial segments in the direction of the main population centres have been analysed in conjunction with the (Routemaster, ~1998) drive times together with the estimated distance exponent. Figure 6.11 illustrates the catchment boundary calculated on this basis (for directions other than Manchester) compared with the boundary enclosing 90 percent of respondents (estimated by the author from Howard's respondent 'spots').

The predicted catchment for Meadowhall is less extensive than that observed in the directions of Bradford, Leeds, Nottingham and Derby but at York, Scunthorpe and Lincoln is close to the survey result. In the

direction of Manchester, the catchment area boundary has been calculated using break point calculations – and the fit is considerably closer
to the survey result than is the standard calculation.

Practitioners tend to favour the estimation of catchment area boundaries from drive time isochrones. For example, the author has calculated that the isochrone that enclosed 90 percent of respondents in the
Meadowhall survey was at the 50-minute drive time. This isochrone,
though, extended into the city of Manchester, considerably beyond the
observed catchment. The break point method predicts the catchment
boundary in the direction of Manchester more closely than does either
the standard calculation or the isochrone. The radii of the predictions
using the break point method again fitted the survey result well. When
combined with the standard distance exponent approach for other
radii directions, catchment area was predicted with a Hoel and Jesson
index of fit = 0.77.

Discussion and conclusions

Break point

This chapter has demonstrated an updated break point approach to the
prediction of town and shopping centre catchment areas. Joining the
locus of break points can provide a simple and quick estimate of the
catchment area boundary of a town. Calculations that are more conventional can be used for an out-of-town shopping centre, but even in
this case, if substantial competitors are involved, the break point
method can improve predictions.

In the examples above, the catchment area was defined as enclosing a nominal 90 percent of shoppers. The methodology might
equally be adapted to estimate catchment area boundaries enclosing
other percentages of shoppers. The technique for this extension of
the methodology requires scaling the positions of the other boundaries accordingly. The scaling, though is not directly proportional.
Rather, for example, if the distance exponent happened to have the
'standard' value of '–2', the scaling of the boundaries would then be
on a square root scale. Scaling can readily be performed according to
the actual distance exponent root. By way of example, Figure 6.12
illustrates the contour for Northampton, based on break points,
where the predicted frequency with which residents trade is double
that at the break points locus. From Figure 6.12 it can be estimated
that the residents of Wellingborough, for example, are twice as likely
to shop at Northampton than as the residents of Buckingham. The

method can be used to calculate the contours of any desired value for the probability with which residents shop in a particular shopping location. This technique is important because it allows the break-point calculations to be used in an improved version of (e.g.) the Lakshmanan and Hansen (1965) method for forecasting sales at a centre.

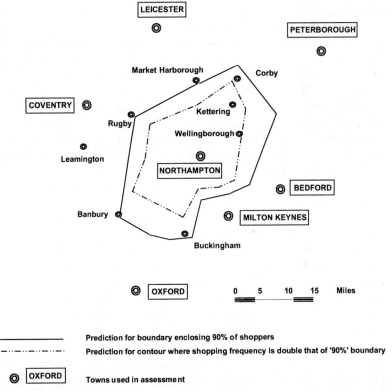

Figure 6.12   Predicted break point boundary for Northampton and the contour where the predicted frequency with which residents trade is double that at the break point locus.
Sources: The author.

The author's modified break point calculations overcome the main disadvantages of the original (Reilly and Converse) procedure: incorrect attractiveness and distance exponent assumptions. As part of a method for predicting shopping centre sales, the author's technique is quicker and simpler in application than the more complex approaches.

Central place practice

In this chapter, the author has eschewed the rigid 'laws of settlement' which, according to Christaller, determined 'the location of central places'. Rather, the dynamic nature of shopper behaviour has been demonstrated with shoppers following the provision of attractive shopping areas. Decisions of developers and planners can lead to the building of large out-of-town shopping centres that re-define the retail hierarchy. As briefly alluded to above, Guy (1996; 1998; 1999) has studied many examples, and concluded that a more flexible interpretation of Central Place Theory is needed for useful application to UK retail. The author shares the view that strict economic assumptions can be relaxed in a more pragmatic approach.

On one hand, the distribution of market towns in central England, illustrated in Martin's study of shopping patterns around Northampton, supported proposition P1. In that approach, population appeared clustered around central places defined on a matrix (classical Central Place Theory), with catchment break points being defined by population (Reilly/Converse). The author, though, has demonstrated an alternative scenario. In line with proposition P2, catchment areas and the retail hierarchy followed the attractiveness of shopping and town centres, which in turn was closely related to the provision of shops that shoppers considered to be attractive. This proposition was demonstrated to hold not only for traditional towns and shopping, but also for new out-of-town shopping centres – thus extrapolating beyond the scope of P1.

The dynamic nature of shopping behaviour following the provision of shops can be further illustrated by comparing the famous, traditional English university cities of Oxford and Cambridge. These are of similar population size (and socio-demographic profile), but Cambridge supports 15 more of the specified multiple comparison goods retailers included in the Goad score (27 percent higher attractiveness score). Reynolds and Schiller (1992) suggested this to be due to Cambridge's expansion in catchment draw resulting from the opening of the Grafton Centre (in-town sub-regional shopping centre) on the edge of the central area. The results from this study indicate a correlation between attractiveness score and sales turnover ($R^2 = 0.99$, as mentioned above and reported in Chapter 4 above). By modelling sales turnover on this basis, it has been deduced that Cambridge's consumer spending is around a quarter more than that of Oxford, directly resulting from the building of the new shopping centre.

In the examples of Northampton and Meadowhall, a fit has been observed between the predicted break points and the boundary containing

90 percent of shoppers. From this, it can be concluded that there is an overlap of catchment area boundaries – close to 10 percent. Shoppers do not necessarily shop at the nearest place that satisfies their requirements for specific goods. Rather, they take into account many aspects of shopping destinations and, when considered on aggregate, distribute their (non-food) shopping expenditure according to their assessments of the attractivenesses of the destinations. Despite the many other considerations in shoppers' decisions of where to shop, there nevertheless appears to be a close association between assessments of attractiveness and the numbers of shops, particularly those shops especially desired by the consumers. This is understandable on the basis that the most attractive shopping centres will attract the most successful retailers. Centres underperforming on attractiveness lack the big name and designer stores.

This chapter has justified one aspect of classical Central Place Theory – the nesting hierarchy of catchments. For example, from Figure 6.10, the town of Market Harborough can be seen to lie within the catchment of Northampton. On the other hand, there is a break point boundary between Milton Keynes and Northampton; although Milton Keynes is closer to Northampton than is Market Harborough. Milton Keynes (and the other towns used in the break point assessments) is on the equivalent hierarchy level to Northampton, based on the rule of at least 75 percent of the attractiveness score of Northampton. Market Harborough, though, in common with a number of smaller towns not used in the break points assessment, is below the 75 percent measure. The author's data (ongoing study, to be reported later) indicates that the typical resident of Market Harborough has some comparison goods expenditure in that market town, but substantially more in Northampton and/or Milton Keynes. In the examples of both Northampton and Meadowhall, the defining level of 75 percent of attractiveness appears to have been effective in defining the level in the hierarchy. Towns below 75 percent attractiveness do not appear to affect the catchment area boundaries of the larger centres.

The author contends that classical Central Place Theory can be modified in the light of proposition P2, taking as a basis the provision of retail offerings, which can be modified by planners and developers. Thus, it can be forecast that movements of population towards the new 'central places' will follow developments of regional shopping centres. This effect has been observed in the USA from as long ago as 1976 (Gosling and Maitland, 1976; Lion, 1976). Young (1985) documented the US trend for residential and office development around 'suburban growth poles' centred on regional, out-of-town shopping centres, sometimes growing to 'minicities' of 300 000 to 500 000 residents (for example Brae, California). In these 'edge cities', 'malls usually function as the village squares' (Garreau, 1991). Des Rosiers and associates (1996, Canada) reported a positive correlation between house prices and proximity to shopping centres. In the UK, it is understood that some of the best-known out-of-town shopping centres (The MetroCentre and Lakeside – Mintel, 1997; Braehead – Lowe, 2000a) have attempted to be reclassified for planning regulation purposes as 'in-town', on the grounds that residential development and other business such as retail parks have been attracted to the area. According to Lowe (2000b), UK shopping centres are becoming 'the new high streets' in a trend even more marked than in the US. All of these indications support an essential tenet of Central Place Theory associating the number of population and provision of services with the availability of shops. Retail has been stated to form 'the heart of virtually all [UK] towns and cities' (Retail Week, 9 June, 2000). That article went on to claim that the first step in urban regeneration is renovating shopping centres and retail, citing the example of the 'transformation of Wood Green Shopping City [that] created a focus for the north London community and improved the surrounding area'. This chapter has demonstrated the link between shoppers and retail attractiveness to be part of a dynamic process in which planners and developers might take the initiative in providing shops, leading to changes in population, expenditure, residence patterns and indeed bringing new life into run-down areas.

If the findings are confirmed by larger studies, there may be a number of implications. Shopping centre developers will be able to more accurately model the likely catchment areas of new or extended centres, and planners predict the impact on existing facilities with more confidence. By progressing to a further stage of modelling, residential developers and institutional lenders can benefit from improvements to the prediction of house price changes. Planners will be able to model the effects of regeneration projects in order to more accurately assess required infrastructure improvements and residential provision associated with retail and shopping centre developments.

The work reported has been exploratory in nature. Confirmatory studies of larger numbers of shopping centres and respondents are recommended. There are limitations to Central Place Theory but the author contends that aspects of Central Place Practice, when suitably modified to place the main focus on the retail provision, are worthy of further consideration by planners, developers and managers. The indications from the results to date, in this chapter and Chapter 5 above, are that, once the strict economic assumptions are relaxed, the principles of Central Place Practice can be applied to both in-town and out-of-town shopping centres, improving the prediction of catchment area boundaries and defining positions of centres in the retail hierarchy. The findings from these two chapters are illustrated schematically in the lower part of Figure 13.1 in Chapter 13 below, page 243.

The following chapter, Chapter 7, drills down into the overall sample of shoppers considered so far, in order to take a marketing segmentation approach to choices of shopping centres. The chapter thus attempts to address questions of why different demographic and other segments of shoppers shop where they do.

Modern Shopping Centre Design and Atmosphere?

Imagine elegant corridors ... [with lighting] reflected in mirrors and marble and by diffused light from glass roofs ... accommodating beautiful shops to satisfy the whims of the passer-by and ... protecting from the vagaries of the weather.

(MacKeith, 1985, describing the Burlington Arcade in London, opened in 1818).

7
Marketing Segmentation for Shopping Centres

This chapter is adapted from a paper that first appeared in the *International Journal of New Product Development and Innovation Management* (Dennis et al, 2001a).[1]

Introduction

The previous chapters of this book have addressed the question of 'Why people shop where they do?' by considering the attributes of shopping centres and aspects of travel time and distance associated with shopper spending behaviour. Despite attention given to why people shop, there has been little previous research into the differences in responses to shopping centre marketing mixes from different segments of shoppers. This is surprising as 'pro-active marketing' has been demonstrated to be central to shopping centre success (e.g. Capital Shopping Centres, 1996; Mintel, 1997, see Chapter 1 above), and marketing segmentation is a well-known component of marketing strategy. This chapter explores the potential to apply market segmentation to shopping centres and draws attention to the superior performance of benefits segmentation based on cluster analysis of the importance that shoppers place on various shopping centre attributes.

The background to market segmentation

Marketing segmentation is not a new tool for retailers. Josiah Wedgwood, the eighteenth century UK pottery entrepreneur referred to in

---

[1] Dennis C E, Marsland D and Cockett W (2001) 'The mystery of consumer behaviour: market segmentation and shoppers' choices of shopping centres', *International Journal of New Product Development and Innovation Management*, 3 (3): 221–237.

Chapter 1 above, targeted an up-market shopper segment, 'the monarchy, the nobility and the art connoisseurs', establishing his own outlet, rejecting Pall Mall as 'too accessible to the common folk' (McKendrick et al, 1982). The objective of market segmentation for retailers is 'to identify reasonably homogeneous groupings, or segments, of shoppers to be the target(s) of retail marketing efforts' (McGoldrick, 2002, page 105).

A priori segmentation

There are many possible bases for segmentation. Retailers have long used *a priori* definitions of their target customers to aim their offering at segments defined by (for example), sex. According to Dholakia (US, 1999), Women report more frequent shopping trips and enjoy shopping more than men, particularly in shopping centres. Most shoppers are female (69 percent of our sample) and shops tend to be designed around the female more leisurely style of shopping. In the UK, though, men are becoming more involved with shopping and shopping centre managers might be advised to segment their offers in order to appeal more to males. Ideas based on our findings are outlined in the 'Why do females and males shop where they do?' section of this chapter below (and see Chapter 10 below for more on the differences between female and male shopping styles).

Other *a priori* segmentation bases include, for example, age or spending power. In the 1980s the (UK) Burton Group had a portfolio of retail brands including (for example), Top Man (target market males, 15–30), Principles for Men (males 25–45), Dorothy Perkins (females 18–30) and Evans (females 25–49). British Shoe Corporation's portfolio of facias included Shoe City (£10–£20, 25–40) and Manfield (£20–£30, 35–45) (McGoldrick, 1990, page 116, citing Euromonitor 1987 and Retail 1989 respectively). Retailers have since tended to rationalise the number of facias in the interests of economies of scale, but the principle of segmentation remains valid.

Post hoc segmentation: lifestyle and psychographics

As Gilbert (1999, page 203) pointed out, following successes in targeting specific groups, retailers such as Habitat and IKEA aimed their marketing mixes at different aspects of lifestyle. 'Lifestyle' refers to consumers' outward characteristics or traits (as opposed to the inner personality) often expressed in terms of the products that people buy. Lifestyle targeting has frequently been based on retailers' subjective descriptions of their target customers – for example, 'Yuppies' (young, upwardly mobile, prosperous people) or 'Dinkies' (dual-income, no kids). The lifestyle approach can, however, be quantified using the 'psychographics' approach. The term usually refers to quantitative research tools used to position consumers on psychological dimensions or to segment them (Boedeker, 1995). Profiles of customer groups can be identified, say from lifestyle questionnaires or loyalty card data, and these profiles can be used as segmentation bases.

It has been argued that 'the benefits customers seek in products are the basic reasons for the heterogeneity in their choice behaviour' (Van den Peol and Leunis, 1999, drawing support from the seminal work of Yankelovich, 1964 and Haley, 1968). Segments based on benefits (referred to as 'importance motivation' clusters in the empirical work for this chapter) tend to be stable and consistent across samples (Calantone and Sawyer, 1978). Van den Poel and Leunis pointed out that benefit segments are identifiable and substantial (Myers, 1976) and better predictors of purchasing behaviour (Wilke, 1970) than, for example, the proprietary geodemographic shopper classifications often used by retailers.

Other segmentation bases include, for example, usership, shopping occasion, attitudes and loyalty – covered more fully in standard texts such as Gilbert (1999); McGoldrick (1990); and Kent and Omar (2003); shopper spending (Suarez et al, 2004); and shopper behaviour (see, e.g. Sinha and Uniyal, forthcoming 2005). In addition, it is recognised that there are many versions of the marketing mix (dating back to Borden, 1941) and its equivalent the 'retail mix' (see for example Dennis et al, 2004; and McGoldrick, 2002). Nevertheless, for simplicity this chapter refers to the marketing mix in terms of McCarthy's (1960) well-known '4Ps'.

Segmentation for shopping centres

Despite the research attention given to market segmentation in general and more specifically, to shopper types, little has been published on segmentation for shopping centres. Still less have UK shopping centre practitioners attempted to differentiate (for example) their marketing communication offerings to attract different customer segments. Some of the main previous research relevant to marketing segmentation for shopping centres is considered below.

Gentry and Burns (1977) examined the attributes most discriminating between those who shop or do not shop in a shopping centre, but their analysis of segments was based on respondents' views of the 'importance' of attributes rather than correlation with patronage. The attributes which overall discriminated most on patronage did not figure in the 'importance' criteria differences between segments. Gautschi (1981) reported the 'elasticities' of patronage frequency of attributes, but the only differences reported between segments were that the elasticities were different for different centres – similar to a finding in Chapter 3 above.

Timmermans et al (1982) recommended segmenting customers with similar images of the retail environment as preferable to relying on socio-economic variables. Oppewal et al (1994) demonstrated that attribute effects are context-sensitive. Oppewal et al (1997) reported important determinants of expenditure, although only two merchandise segments (food and clothing/shoes) were considered. They concluded that 'an attractive mix of merchandise can compensate for larger travel times or smaller centre sizes'.

Roy (1994) correlated shopping centre visit frequency with three motivation segments and three socio-demographic segments. He concluded that the frequent shopper is likely to be '40–60 years old, relatively high income, household size greater than three, not particularly sensitive to deals and who considers shopping to be a recreational experience'. Bloch et al (1994) identified four motivational segments of shoppers. Westbrook and Black (1985) identified six segments that could be differentiated by differences in motivation, but these were not clear-cut. Shim and Eastlick (1998) found that personal, social affiliation and self-actualising values were all predictors of attitudes towards regional shopping centres.

Jarratt (UK, 1996) reported a grouping of attributes reflecting their importance to respondents when shopping. Jarratt grouped the attributes into 'offer', 'service' and 'environment' and used cluster analysis to identify six distinct shopper types. Boedeker and Marjanen (Finland, 1993) used a similar methodology to segment shoppers also into six types. Three clusters that could be described as 'shopping', 'service' and 'apathetic' were common to both of these studies. Boedeker (Finland, 1995) identified two clusters that could be described as 'shopping' and 'service' ('traditional' and 'new type' respectively in Boedeker's terminology). Ruiz and colleagues (Canada, 2005 forthcoming) clustered shoppers by their activities, identifying four segments including what could be described as 'shopping' and 'service' ('Mission' and 'Full experience' respectively in Ruiz's terminology) along with 'Recreational' and 'Browsers'. Investigating grocery shopping rather than shopping centres, Uncles (UK, 1996) found that two groups (broadly fitting the 'service' and 'shopping' descriptions) gave the best fit in describing shopping trip behaviour patterns.

Improvement in model fit was similarly reported by Frasquet and colleagues (Spain, 2001), who used cluster analysis of demographic variables to elicit segments, modelling shoppers' preferences in choices of shopping centres. The modelling gave a better fit by segment than with the whole sample. The shoppers in the very young segment were reported to respond better to changes in (i) retail offer; (ii) atmosphere/leisure; and (iii) accessibility. On the other hand, female homemakers responded better to changes in (i) 'Efficiency' (e.g. one-stop-shopping, time saving) and (ii) travel distance.

Michon and Chebat (Canada, 2002) drew attention to shopping centres' needs for niche marketing (i.e. segmentation). They found that French Canadians were more hedonistic than English Canadians. French Canadians were more orientated towards family, kitchen, brands and fashion but were less interested in fast food then were English Canadians.

As with segmentation in general (Wensley, 1994, page 44) much work on shopping centres has been based on the perceptions and stated preferences of the consumers. Roy's study is one of few to have attempted to correlate attributes of centres with actual shopping behaviour.

Strategic considerations

Little has been written on how shopping centres actually segment their customers in practice. Marketing communications ('promotion' in the marketing mix) usually appear to be based on an undifferentiated approach: 'there's something for everyone at the Blue Rose Centre'. 'Product' is segmented between types of centres – outlet centres *vs.* others, for example. Alternatively 'product' is sometimes segmented into particular areas within centres; for example, one centre might feature the 'New Burlington Arcade' side alley for expensive speciality shops and 'Market Square' outside the main mall for bargains. 'Price' segmentation accordingly follows 'product', with bargain pricing at outlet centres. 'Place' is a differentiator between centres competing to be the most convenient. The Blue Rose Centre, for example, located close to a motorway junction, is convenient for shoppers travelling by car making up 90 percent of their customer base. On the other hand, many shoppers 'pop in' from work on foot to use the Metropolitan Centre.

Marketers aim to satisfy customers better than the competition and thus make a profit. By segmenting markets, benefits can be more closely matched to customer requirements. Providing the costs of segmentation are not too great, satisfying customers better will lead to more profit. The author contends that segmented promotion, product, price and place offers could be targeted to appeal to specific, identifiable shopping centre customer groups. Such a strategy should lead to more satisfied customers, higher sales and profits for retailers and, in the long run, higher rental incomes for the centres.

The design and method for this study

From the brief review above, it is apparent that there is considerable literature on shoppers' choices of shopping centres. Nevertheless, little has been written on the differences in responses to shopping centre marketing mixes from different segments of shoppers. Accordingly, the author has aimed to classify shoppers with reference to their spending behaviour. The results have identified which shopping centre attributes are most associated with higher shopper spending for exemplar shopper segments. Central to the findings is the author's classification based on cluster analysis of benefit 'importance motivation' which has been demonstrated to be a more effective discriminator of shopper behaviour than the more conventional segmentation bases.

Various subset *a priori* segmentation pairs from the sample have been compared: male/female, higher/lower socio-economic groups, higher/lower household income, older/younger and car/public transport. The final and most significant segmentation pair was based on *post hoc* benefit 'importance motivation': those clusters of shoppers considering 'Shops' attributes more important *vs.* those considering 'Service' more important.

The *post hoc* part of this study followed the psychographic approach in grouping customers according to their stated benefit motivations – the importance of attributes of a shopping centre in deciding where to shop. It is contended that this *post hoc* approach to segmentation should be more effective in identifying segments than the more nominal *a priori* segments assigned in advance by the retailer or researcher. Success in segmentation from the retailers' point of view will mean identifying groups whose shopping behaviour is different in order to 'tailor a suitable marketing mix package' to meet customers' needs (Jobber, 1995, pages 5 and 201). The segments used therefore should have a stable response to a particular marketing mix. It is further postulated that the *post hoc* clusters based on stated motivations will be more consistent in response than the more conventional segments.

For each segmentation pair, those attributes significantly associated with individual relative spend have been ranked in order of the degree of association. The results indicate those attributes of the shopping centres that are most critical for each of the segments considered. In many cases, implications for centres' managements have been identified for improving the centres' offer to segments of shoppers and for more appropriate marketing communications targeting.

The work contrasts with other shopping centre studies in two respects. Firstly, the segments considered are examined in terms of which specific shopping centre attributes are most correlated with shopper spending behaviour relative to competing centres. Secondly, ideas for varying the marketing mixes for different segments are suggested. In particular, the marketing mixes most applicable to the two groups of the author's benefit 'importance motivation' shopper classification are considered. Having selected the segments to target, the value and communications offers (marketing mixes) can be designed appropriately.

The empirical work for this chapter consisted of measurements of the attractiveness of shopping centres, together with shoppers' perceived travel distances and times, from shoppers' responses to structured questionnaires, as described in the Methodology section of Chapter 2 above. Briefly, the survey results took the form of Rating/distinctiveness and Importance measures ascribed by respondents to various attributes at different shopping centres. Regression models were used to model relative spending according to these measures and shoppers' relative travel time or distance to the centres. Both the Rating/distinctiveness and travel terms were relative to competing centres. The attributes were weighted in the model according to their degree of association with relative spending and the results were used to produce an Attractiveness measure for shopping centres on a 0 to 100 scale.

In the analysis, the attribute evaluations have been considered as interval rather than ordinal data (Oppewal and Timmermans, 1999). Ordinary least squares regression analysis has then been used to investigate associations between shopping centre attributes and shoppers' spending at the centre studied compared to a competing centre. For example, the attribute most associated with the spending of female shoppers was 'Cleanliness', coefficient of determination, $R^2 = 0.075$.

This means that cleanliness is associated with 7.5 percent of the variation in female shopper spending between centres. All the values reported are statistically significant at 95 percent confidence (p = 0.05). Various types of models based on the combined evaluations of attributes, together with travel distance or time, have R^2 values between 0.16 and 0.40. The derivations of the models can be found in Chapter 3 above.

Results

Table 7.1 lists the attributes that were most significantly associated with individual relative spending for various segments of shoppers ranked in order of association. In the interests of brevity, the table has been shortened to include only the 'top six' attributes for each segment. All those listed were significant at the usual test level of p = 0.05. The number of respondents and the average monthly spending for each segment is indicated in parenthesis. A discussion of the differences between the segments follows below.

Why do females and males shop where they do?

The attributes significant for females were clearly different to those significant for males. Only one of the 'top six' significant attributes for females ('Nice place to spend time') appeared amongst those attributes significant for males. Conversely, three out of the 'top six' attributes for males did not appear on the list for females ('Lighting', 'Sheltered access' and 'No undesirable characters').

It is no surprise that the significant attributes for females were grouped around (i) **experience** and (ii) **shopping**. These two factors were confirmed using maximum likelihood extraction and varimax rotation (point of inflection on the scree plot after two factors) as these procedures were found to produce the highest discrimination between the factors (Kinnear and Gray, 1997 – further details of the factor analysis approach are given in Appendix 7.1 to this chapter below).

The 'top five' attributes in the factors for females were:

	R
Experience:	
Friendly atmosphere	0.71
Light and airy	0.68
Helpfulness of staff	0.64
Cleanliness	0.63
Feeling of spaciousness	0.59

Shopping:

Variety of the stores	0.76
Selection of merchandise	0.73
Choice of major stores	0.72
Quality of the stores	0.60
Big shopping centre	0.43.

The attributes significant for males mainly concerned the **centre** (e.g. 'Lighting' and 'Sheltered access'). Some differences between males and females probably arose because many males were in the centre mainly to accompany females. Therefore, it is natural that for females, who were enjoying the trip, the most significant concerns were 'experience' and 'shopping'. Conversely, males who were simply 'there' were more evaluative of the 'centre'. Nevertheless, separate 'experience' and 'shopping' components were also tentatively identified for males as well as females, albeit with more emphasis on the centre itself ('Lighting' and 'General layout' included in the top five in the respective components – see Appendix 7.1 below for more details).

Upper *vs*. lower socio-economic groups: For managerial, administrative, professional, supervisory and clerical (ABC1s), 'Lighting' and 'Access by road' were significantly more associated. For manual workers, senior citizens and unwaged (groups C2DE), 'Good for children' and 'Quality of the stores' were among the most significant. The differences are to some extent understandable in the light of the observation that upmarket shoppers are more likely to travel by car, whereas those from the lower socio-economic groups are more likely to bring children on shopping trips.

Higher *vs*. lower income groups: 'Lively or exciting' and 'Covered shopping' were significantly more associated for the lower income respondents. The author speculates that lower income (and lower socio-economic group) shoppers might tend to live nearby, patronizing as alternatives small, unexciting local centres. Therefore, they might tend to appreciate the benefits of lively covered shopping centres more than do the more upmarket customers who may take these benefits for granted.

Older *vs*. younger shoppers: 'Eating and drinking' was in the 'top six' for the older shoppers who might be expected shop at a slower pace than younger ones and take more refreshment breaks.

Shoppers travelling by car *vs*. public transport: 'General layout', 'Choice of major stores' and 'Eating and drinking' were in the 'top six' for shoppers travelling by car but not significant for public transport.

Four of the 'top six' were significantly more associated for 'public transport': 'Shoppers nice people', 'Availability of seats', 'Big shopping centre' and 'Value for money'. The author considers that most of these attribute differences are related to differences in spending power. For example, shoppers travelling by public transport are more likely to appreciate (free) seats, compared to the more affluent car travellers who choose to relax in a restaurant, bar or café.

Why do shoppers motivated by the 'importance' of 'shops' and 'service' shop where they do?

An alternative to the *a priori* segmentation approach was the search for clusters of buyers who shared needs or wants for particular benefits – the so-called *post hoc* segmentation. A cluster analysis (using SPSS statistical software) identified distinct segments of shoppers classified by benefits or 'importance motivation'. SPSS cluster analysis attempts to identify relatively homogenous groups or cases (version 11.5 'Help' file). As such, it is of course ideal for marketing segmentation purposes. In this instance, the objective was to identify clusters or segments of shoppers sharing similar motivations for their choices of shopping centres. The variables chosen for the basis of the clusters were, therefore, the 'importance' scores of the shopping centre attributes. The method used in this study was 'k-means', a non-hierarchical clustering method that assigns the cases into groups in such a way as to minimise the squared distances of each value from its cluster centre (Kinnear and Gray, 1997; Pung and Stewart, 1983). On a similar shopping centre study, k-means was found to be 'exceptionally robust and unaffected by data idiosyncrasies' (Sit et al, 2003). K-means also copes well with missing values.

The main attributes which distinguished the clusters (with the average 'importance' scores on the 1 to 5 scale, where 1 is 'no relevance' and 5 is 'extremely important') are listed in Table 7.2. These segments were described as 'Shops importance motivation', Table 7.2(a) and 'Service importance motivation', Table 7.2(b).

The two 'importance motivation' clusters were strikingly different in attributes significantly related to relative spending (Table 7.1). As would be expected, for the 'Shops importance motivation' shoppers 'Quality of the stores' and 'Selection of merchandise' were both in the 'top six'. Perhaps not so expected, a number of 'service' attributes were also significant with 'Nice place to spend time', 'Other shoppers nice people', 'Friendly atmosphere' and 'Lively or exciting' all also in the 'top 6' for the 'Shops' segment.

Table 7.1 The 'top six' significant attributes for each segment, ranked in order of the coefficient of determination, R^2, associated with individual relative spending

R^2		R^2	
FEMALES (199 respondents: £68 per month)		**MALES (88 respondents: £58 per month)**	
Cleanliness *	0.075	General layout	0.104
Nice place to spend time	0.063	Nice place to spend time	0.086
Availability of good toilets	0.056	Lighting *	0.085
Friendly atmosphere	0.053	Sheltered access *	0.081
Selection of merchandise	0.051	Helpfulness of staff	0.069
Eating and drinking	0.048	No undesirable characters *	0.067
ABC1 (168: £73)		_C2DE_ (113: £53)	
Nice place to spend time	0.156	Nice place to spend time	0.049
Lighting *	0.118	Cleanliness	0.044
Access by car *	0.113	Good for children	0.043
Friendly atmosphere	0.101	Quality of stores	0.038
General layout	0.101	General layout	0.037
Cleanliness	0.092	Availability of good toilets	0.036
ANNUAL INCOME £20 000 + (101: £89)		_INCOME UP TO £20 000_ (81: £59)	
Nice place to spend time	0.077	Lively or exciting *	0.077
General layout	0.069	General layout	0.069
Cleanliness	0.062	Covered shopping *	0.062
Availability of good toilets	0.046	Cleanliness	0.046
Selection of merchandise	0.045	Selection of merchandise	0.045
Quality of the stores	0.043	Nice place to spend time	0.043

Table 7.1 The 'top six' significant attributes for each segment, ranked in order of the coefficient of determination, R^2, associated with individual relative spending – *continued*

AGE UP TO 44 YEARS (186: £65)	
General layout	0.070
Availability of good toilets	0.069
Selection of merchandise	0.039
Nice place to spend time	0.038
Lighting	0.035
Value for money	0.034

TRAVEL BY CAR (149: £81)	
Nice place to spend time	0.079
Covered shopping	0.072
General layout	0.069
Selection of merchandise	0.044
Choice of major stores	0.039
Eating and drinking	0.038

SERVICE IMPORTANCE (74: £82)	
General layout	0.104
Relative travel distance	0.099
Cleanliness	0.078
Availability of good toilets	0.069
Nice place to spend time	0.059
Good for children	0.057

AGE 45 YEARS ± (100: £65)	
Nice place to spend time	0.074
Cleanliness	0.058
General layout	0.053
Availability of good toilets	0.046
Friendly atmosphere	0.042
Eating and drinking	0.042

PUBLIC TRANSPORT (57: £60)	
Selection of merchandise	0.155
Quality of the stores	0.131
Shoppers nice people *	0.110
Availability of seats *	0.080
Big shopping centre *	0.080
Value for money *	0.076

SHOPS IMPORTANCE (213: £59)	
Nice place to spend time	0.080
Shoppers nice people *	0.067
Quality of the stores *	0.065
Friendly atmosphere	0.057
Lively or exciting *	0.056
Selection of merchandise	0.052

All listed attributes are significantly associated with individual relative spending at $p = 0.05$.
The number of respondents and the average monthly spending for each subgroup is indicated in parenthesis.
* Segments significantly different at $p = 0.05$ with respect to the association with spending of these attributes (combination of bootstrapping and t-test, procedure as described in Chapter 3 above).

The managers of successful shopping centres have long sought to make shopping an enjoyable experience and to ensure that their shopping centres are lively and exciting places. The findings justify the policy in that such considerations are significant in the choice of shopping centre to those respondents primarily motivated by 'Shopping' as well as 'Service'.

Table 7.2(a)   Shops importance motivation cluster

	Final cluster centre 'Importance' scores
Variety of the stores	3.49
Quality of the stores*	**3.41**
Covered shopping	3.30
Access by public transport**	**3.14**

Table 7.2(b)   Service importance motivation cluster

	Final cluster centre 'Importance' scores
Parking facilities**	4.47
Access by car**	4.29
Cleanliness**	4.22
Availability of good toilets**	4.01
Value for money**	3.99
Helpfulness of the staff**	3.96

Differences between clusters 'Importance' scores significant at: * p = 0.05 ** p = 0.001.
'Importance' scores are on the 1 to 5 scale, where 1 is 'no relevance' and 5 is 'extremely important'. Only attributes above the scale mid-point (3.00) are listed, and each attribute is listed once only, in the cluster where most dominant.

Compared to the 'Shops importance motivation' cluster, the 'Service importance motivation' shoppers are on average slightly higher socio-economic group (63 percent ABC1s *vs.* 59 percent), income (60 percent £20 000 per year + *vs.* 53 percent), and age (42 percent 45 + *vs.* 33 percent) than the 'Shops importance motivation' shoppers. They predominantly travel by car (90 percent *vs.* 52 percent).

Modelling behaviour for shopper segments

Models of relative spending in terms of 'attractiveness' and 'distance' for the various segments are summarised in Table 7.3. These are introduced in the same order as in the reporting of the critical attributes for these groups in the 'Results' section above and in Table 7.1. The models describe the relationships observed between relative spending for the groups *vs.* the attractiveness of the centres and the distance shoppers travel. The first column is the group for which the model applies (the numbers of respondents in each group were indicated in Table 7.1). The second column is the constant from the regression equation, representing the amount of relative spending not associated with the variations in attractiveness and distance. The third and fourth columns are the regression coefficients for attractiveness and distance respectively. The fifth column is the coefficient of determination, R^2 of the regression equation, and the sixth the degree of significance (p-value). These two columns indicate modest correlations. All of the models would normally be described as 'significant'. All except model numbers 7.6 (lower income) and 7.10 (travel by public transport) would actually be considered 'highly significant'. The final column is simply the identification number allocated to each model to facilitate discussion.

For example, for 'Shops motivation' shoppers:

$$\text{Relative spending} = 19.4 + 0.70 \times \text{Relative attractiveness} - 0.21 \times \text{Relative distance} \qquad (7.11)$$

Whereas for 'Service motivation':

$$\text{Relative spending} = 39.6 + 0.54 \times \text{Relative attractiveness} - 0.28 \times \text{Relative distance} \qquad (7.12)$$

These models mean that (with confidence at normal test levels) an increase in the attractiveness of a centre would result in an increase in spending at that centre. For example, for the 'Shops' group (7.11), the increase in spending for a given improvement in attractiveness would be greater than for the 'Service' group (7.12). By going back to the weighting of each attribute carried in the attractiveness model, it is possible to predict by how much spending would be likely to increase for any given improvement in any attribute. The models also mean that spending was inversely related to the distance that shoppers travelled to the centre.

The models are useful in estimating changes in spending that could result from improving aspects of a shopping centre. For the high spending 'Service' shoppers (model 7.12 in Table 7.3), a 25 percent improvement in the ratings for cleanliness and toilets could be associated with an increase in spending for those shoppers of 10 percent,

Table 7.3 Models for shopper segments

	Constant	'Attractiveness' Coefficient	'Distance' Coefficient	Coefficient of determination, R^2	Significance p	Model number
Females	28.3	0.63	-0.24	0.19	<0.0001	7.1
Males	21.1	0.49	0	0.09	<0.01	7.2
ABC1	19.0	0.72	-0.19	0.20	<0.01	7.3
C2DE	34.4	0.50	-0.24	0.13	<0.01	7.4
Income £20 000+	28.6	0.62	-0.24	0.17	<0.01	7.5
Up to £19 000	27.0	0.58	-0.19	0.18	<0.05	7.6
Age up to 44	29.3	0.58	-0.23	0.16	<0.0001	7.7
Age 45 +	18.0	0.61	0	0.14	0.0001	7.8
Car	32.8	0.53	-0.20	0.15	<0.01	7.9
Public transport	31.8	0.58	-0.22	0.19	<0.05	7.10
'Shops motivation'	19.4	0.70	-0.21	0.17	0.0001	7.11
'Service motivation'	39.6	0.54	-0.28	0.22	<0.01	7.12
All respondents	26.0	0.62	-0.20	0.16	0.0001	7.13

equivalent to an increase in the total centre sales turnover of over 3 percent. One measure of the validity of the subgroups is the improvement in 'fit' of the models. 'Service' *vs.* 'Shops' had the best fit, with R^2 increased to an average of 0.195 for the two subgroups. Apart from 'Income' (average R^2 0.175), the models from the other pairs of groups did not improve the fit above the overall level of 0.16. 'Service' *vs.* 'Shops' discriminated well between high and low customer spending, with the 'Service' segment's average stated monthly spending of £82, compared with the overall average of £65.

Discussion and implications

Given the small sample size and number of centres sampled, caution must be exercised in interpreting the results. Nevertheless, some interesting pointers have emerged which, if confirmed by larger studies, could be useful to shopping centre managers. This methodology has identified which attributes were most associated with spending for various customer segments. One of the striking findings to emerge from the conventional *a priori* segmentation concerned the differences between females and males, which will be addressed further in Chapter 10 below. Shopping centres might well benefit from extending their specific appeal to males, who in this survey were responsible for 27 percent of the total stated spending. If the postulation is correct, that many males are predominantly in the centre to accompany females, the idea of the 'men's crèche' may be apt. A waiting and relaxation area could provide entertainments including, for example, computer games and sports videos. These would provide almost ideally targeted media for segmented marketing communications drawing attention to offerings of the centre particularly targeted at the male customer. Some of the largest centres do have such a waiting area – for example, Meadowhall (UK out-of-town regional centre) – often referred to as a 'lounge'. This idea could be further developed by the use of targeted advertising video such as the Captive Audience Network (CAN) project managed by How and Why Ltd. This system is used for example in UK grocery superstores (Tesco) and shopping centres (e.g. The Mall). The effect of such a system on shopping centre image is investigated in Chapter 9 below. Sales of suitable merchandise could even be made directly from the 'waiting' area: 'boys toys', computers, guns (in the US at least) and gifts for females, for example.

There are many other marketing implications of the results. For example, 'Availability of seats' was a significant attribute for shoppers travelling by public transport but not for those travelling by car. On the other hand 'Eating and drinking' was more closely associated with spending for car-borne shoppers. The differences are understandable in that 'Mode of transport' provides a useful indicator of spending power. Thus, it might be expected that when car-borne shoppers wish to relax, they might combine this with expenditure on food and drink. Conversely, when those who travel by public transport want to sit down, they are more likely to look for a (free) public seating area. The finding represents an opportunity for segmentation of the marketing communications. For example, centre marketing managers could place advertisements **on the backs of** buses (to target car drivers and passengers) illustrating customers enjoying **eating and drinking** at the centre. On the other hand, the **insides of** buses could carry pictures of the mall area including the comfortable seating areas.

Marketing communications aimed at public transport users might well hint at the other benefits particularly relevant for this group: 'Other shoppers' who can be seen to be 'Nice people', a 'Big' shopping centre and 'Value for money'.

Consideration should be given to directing a high proportion of the marketing budget towards the higher spending 'Car' shoppers – perhaps helping to achieve a higher proportion of 'nice people' amongst the shoppers? A particular strategy here could be to feature the 'Choice of major stores' in the advertising.

Print media can be selected according to whether readership has a higher proportion of the higher-spending 'ABC1' readers (UK JICTAR scale: managerial, administrative, professional, supervisory or clerical, Adcock et al, 1998, page 95). Advertisements in such publications could emphasise the 'Friendly atmosphere' of the centre. On the other hand, 'C2DE' (manual workers and unwaged) readers could be targeted with messages featuring the children's facilities. This would include the crèche or playgroup but also perhaps mall entertainments such as giant characters from children's television. Such entertainments would also contribute to making a centre 'Lively and exciting', relevant to the 'Up to £19 000' income group.

Advertising can be targeted specifically towards the 'Female' or 'Male' reader. Although media availability is more limited on a local basis, opportunities might exist, for example, in the relevant sections of local newspapers. 'Availability of good toilets' might not be tasteful as a topic for a major advertising campaign, but with some creativity, a theme might be represented around the area of 'Friendly atmosphere' and 'Eating and drinking'.

Despite the undoubted benefits of conventional *a priori* segmentation, the most significant implications of this chapter concern the 'importance motivation' shopper classification. Unfortunately, implementation is not straightforward, in the absence of marketing communications media to target these segments directly. Nevertheless, the higher-spending 'Service importance' segment has a greater proportion of other segments indicating spending power: ABC1s, higher income, older and travel by car. Media (such as the backs of buses again) is available for targeting. One attribute in particular could be selected as relevant to these 'up market' segments: 'Eating and drinking'.

The above ideas have illustrated how two of the '4Ps' of the marketing mix – 'Promotion' (marketing communications) and 'Product' (including 'service' offerings) can be varied in order to appeal to differing customer segments. The results also confirm the potential for tailoring the other two 'Ps', 'Place' (distribution or convenience aspects) and 'Price' – but these are already well known and largely self explanatory. For example, it is no surprise that the results draw attention to the need to provide good parking and easy access by road for up-market, higher spending car-borne customers, whilst not neglecting aspects such as 'Value for money' and 'Availability of [free] seats' for those with less spending power. Managers cannot afford to ignore the interests of the less-affluent customers or those using public transport: shoppers travelling other than by car represented 30 percent of stated expenditure at the sample shopping centres. Tenant mixes should be chosen to offer not just high quality and major stores, but also to include at least some discount outlets and/or access to local shops.

Differentiated marketing can be applied to shopping centres, with at least some potential for adjusting each of the '4Ps' of the marketing mix to appeal to different customer segments, even within the same centre. The essential implication for shopping centres is the potential for segmenting shoppers by the benefits that they seek, using the author's 'importance motivation' classification. There is a strong case for utilising customer registration or loyalty scheme records to target the higher spending 'service importance motivation' customers directly using (for example) direct mail.

Conclusions

Consumer behaviour is diverse and not always easy to explain. In drawing attention to differences in behaviour between identifiable market segments, this chapter has illustrated patterns which underlie (if not explain) some of the diversity in 'why people shop where they do'. Chapter 10 below attempts a preliminary investigation of the 'why' for one of the segment pairs: males *vs.* females. New ideas have been presented for ways in which shopping centres might use varied marketing mixes to attract and satisfy specific customer segments. Standard *a priori* segmentation bases can be usefully used to better satisfy customers differentiated (in these examples) by sex, socioeconomic group, income, age and type of transport.

On the other hand, it was postulated earlier in this chapter that *post hoc* 'importance motivation' segmentation would be more effective than the simpler, more conventional approaches. This has been demonstrated to be the case, as motivation clusters discriminated the groups on spending behaviour more effectively than did other bases studied. Models of spending behaviour based on these motivation clusters fitted better than the other segmentation groups, so responses to marketing mixes within the motivation clusters should be correspondingly more consistent.

Based on the survey results from the shopping centres studied, shoppers' 'motivations' can be divided into two classifications:

- 'Service' or 'Experience' and:
- 'Shops' or 'Shopping', also containing a range of 'Service' or 'Experience' elements.

These categories reflect two of the shopper types reported by Boedeker (1995), Jarratt (1996), Boedeker and Marjanen (1993), Ruiz et al (2005 forthcoming) and (for grocery shopping) Uncles (1996). In extending beyond these two clusters there is little consistency with the findings of other authors. It is therefore concluded that a two-cluster motivation classification is likely to prove one of the most useful and robust segmentation bases for shopping centres.

There are fewer customers motivated primarily by 'Service' or 'Experience' but they tend to be the higher-spending ones. An important message for shopping centre managers is that even for those customers particularly interested in 'Shops' or 'Shopping', 'Service' and 'Experience' attributes are significantly associated with spending behaviour. In planning the offer to customers and the marketing communications, managements should keep in mind that the 'Experience' factor is more associated overall with shopper spending than is the 'Shopping' factor (see Appendix 7.1 to this chapter below and Equation 7.14).

Information from a customer database can be used to identify needs of different groups of customers. This knowledge can help shopping centres to improve marketing communications and customer satisfaction. Cluster analysis has identified a group of customers that shopping centres and retailers will want to target: high-spending 'Service' shoppers. How can they be identified, given the high costs of a data warehouse? Firstly, this experimental study has demonstrated that a full data-warehouse system is not essential. Analysis, identification of target segments and assessment of cost-effectiveness can be carried out on a small sample, with only simple processing needed on a complete database. As in this experiment, the SPSS program can be used – saving the costs of custom software. For future, larger-scale projects, though, the author recommends the use of a multi-agent system. Such systems can handle text alongside quantitative data and furnish individual shoppers with a 'personal agent'. This represents customized marketing segmentation – a software 'personal shopper' for every participating consumer. It could be argued that such a system might not work in the UK cultural context. For the customers, though, this would be a small step from the well-established loyalty card. The customer might only be aware of the difference when presenting a 'smart card' to obtain benefits or information. Customers having a personal agent could receive communications specifically targeted to their needs and wants. There are a number of ways that this could be achieved, but one of the simplest would be for customers to present their card for reading at an information kiosk in order to receive personalized vouchers and information sheets.

Customer data could be based on data sourced from loyalty schemes. LeHew and Fairhurst (USA, 2000) found that 'Frequent shopper clubs' were more prevalent in more successful shopping centres than in less successful ones (although the difference was not statistically significant). Similarly, LeHew and colleagues (USA, 2002) concluded that attributes such as the tenant mix influenced loyalty attitudes more than did loyalty schemes. Nevertheless, in that study, actual purchasing loyalty was not as high as attitudinal loyalty. Therefore, this author recommends the frequent shopper reward scheme as a way of encouraging purchasing behaviour loyalty from the attitudinally loyal (i.e. receptive) customers.

Worthington (1999) reviewed the typology of local loyalty cards in the UK. Integrated chips (e.g. Nottingham), and magnetic stripe payment (Hereford; Lakeside) or non-payment (Chester; Meadowhall) are applicable and cost-effective for cities and regional shopping centres. The main distinguishing feature of the higher-spending

'Service' shopper cluster was the preponderance of the car as the means of travel – 90 percent of the group. Therefore, for smaller centres, a scheme could be based on parking. For in-town centres that charge for parking, a solution could be the 'car park membership scheme'. Shoppers would buy a 'carnet' of tickets at a discount and fill in a detailed 'lifestyle' questionnaire including the information needed for the database. Car park schemes are already in use in Australia (Worthington and Hallsworth, 1999). For centres that offer free parking, the suggestion is to recruit shoppers at a kiosk in the car park, offering incentives such as a prize draw.

Some shopping centres (e.g. Lakeside UK out-of-town regional centre) have discontinued loyalty schemes, partly because, with heavy data handling, they were not cost-effective. Another problem is major retailer tenants objecting to shopping centres sharing their proprietary data. With improvements in technology and increased awareness of the benefits of *post hoc* marketing segmentation, the barriers may be overcome in the future. For example, Meadowhall (UK out-of-town regional centre) has a 'Go Shop' smart card with which shoppers can view offers and information from kiosks (and from home *via* the Internet). The system captures extensive information on consumer profiles and preferences, which is already shared with some retailers. Bar codes are read from vouchers. With increasing acceptance by retailers of the benefits of data sharing, there is also the potential to add in transaction data. At Meadowhall and also at the newer Centre West (UK in-town sub-regional), an intranet has been installed connecting each retail outlet with the management office, specifically for sharing information. Retailers can view market reports comparing and contrasting local figures against national statistics. Of particular interest is the facility to share information on customer profiles. Retailers are learning the benefits of information sharing – not least through the requirement to provide it as part of newer tenancy agreements. It is possible that the approach might be developed further into tracking customer transaction data *via* the use of the smart card. Data such as this, combined with psychometric information from the registration form, can by used for segmentation purposes, for example as illustrated in the k-means cluster analysis.

The results can be used to illustrate the potential cost effectiveness of such an approach. As already noted, an improvement of 25 percent in the ratings for 'cleanliness' and 'toilets' could be associated with an increase in spending by the 'Service' shoppers of 10 percent. The 10 percent increase for this group would add 3 percent to the total centre sales turnover. A regional shopping centre would gain tens of millions of pounds in sales, with retailers seeing a seven-figure increase in gross profits. In the medium term, rental incomes follow sales: shopping centre owners could expect £1 million plus in increased rents.

Finally, the author accepts that there have been many limitations in this small exploratory study. The benefits predicted are purely speculative at this stage. Therefore, a more extensive pilot and research program is recommended. This could take the form of (1) a further questionnaire survey with more respondents and shopping centres; (2) A pilot scheme based on exchange of customer information for parking discount benefits (at a paid-for car park); and (3) A pilot 'personal agent' trial based on a smart card. This trial could run on shopper data at a single shopping centre gathered by, for example, a car park membership scheme as outlined above. If this pilot were to achieve no more success than confirming the effects of cleanliness and toilets found in this exploratory survey (which was carried out at nominal cost), the centre could expect a medium-term increase of £1 million in rental income alone. There is a clear case for the cost-effectiveness of further research in this area.

This part of the book has explored why people shop where they do in terms of the attributes of shopping centres that are associated with shopping behaviour. Part III considers shoppers' decision making processes in choices of shopping centres, starting with Motivation theory in Chapter 8.

Appendix 7.1: Factor analysis models

The main modelling procedure used in Part I of this book has been of the **external** item analysis type, correlating attributes with the dependent variable 'relative spending'. In contrast, the factor analysis procedure reported in the 'Why do females and males shop where they do?' section of this chapter above was an **internal** item analysis, grouping attributes that correlate with each other. Factor analyses internal item analysis models for relative spending have been calculated for comparison with the external item analyses models. The degree of fit was very close to the results for the external item analysis models reported in this chapter and Chapter 3 above, although the overall significance 'p' values were not as high on account of having the extra term. In the interests of simplicity, only one model is reported here – the female shoppers example. The 'male', 'public transport' and 'service' segments were too small for this type of factor analysis, but the factor analysis models for all the other segments followed the same form. Non-linear models were explored, but the linear versions fitted better. The exemplar factor analysis model for the female shoppers was:

$$\text{Relative spending} = 68 + 7.86 \times \text{Experience} + 7.00 \times \text{Shopping} - 0.30 \times \text{Relative distance} \qquad (7.14)$$

Coefficient of determination, $R^2 = 0.19$, significant at $p = 0.001$ (for comparison, the equivalent external item analysis model R^2 was also 0.19, but at $p = 0.0001$).

The separate 'Experience' and 'Shopping' factors were distinct for the 'All respondents' group and for the following segments:

- Female
- C2DE socio-economic group
- Age 45 + and
- Car transport to the shopping centre.

In order to explore whether the components for males might be separated, a Principal Components Analysis was carried out for the Female and Male segments as an alternative to the Maximum Likelihood factor analysis (a type of analysis needing fewer cases). As an additional simplification necessary because of the small number of cases, the attributes entered were restricted to those significant for males in Table 7.1, plus those in both factors for females. The point of inflection of the scree plot was at the two-components solution for both segments. The components were separated (as with the previous factor analyses) using varimax rotation. The components for the female segment contained the identical elements to those in the factors reported in the 'Why do females and males shop where they do?' section of this chapter above. The components for males could also be interpreted as having 'experience' and 'shopping' components, although not these were not as clearly defined as for females, with attributes more general to the centre itself included in both components. The 'top five' attributes in the components for males were:

	$\underline{R}$
Experience:	
No undesirable characters	0.81
Cleanliness	0.75

Light and airy	0.70
Friendly atmosphere	0.67
Lighting	0.63

Shopping:

Quality of the stores	0.75
Selection of merchandise	0.71
Variety of the stores	0.70
Big shopping centre	0.60
General layout	0.47

Bearing in mind the very small number of males (88) for this type of analysis, these components must be viewed with caution. Nevertheless, the findings are consistent with the wider importance of 'experience', even for males; albeit with an increased relevance for attributes concerning the centre itself.

The first true shopping centre is said to have been a 50-shop, three-level enclosed arcade opened in 1829 in Providence, Rhode Island, USA (Dawson, 1983).

Part III

Consumer Decision Processes in Shopping Choices

8

Shoppers' Motivations in Choices of Shopping Centres

This chapter is adapted from two papers delivered at the *International Conference on Recent Advances in Retailing and Services Science* (Dennis and Hilton, 2001; Dennis et al, 2002c)[1,2]

Introduction

Part II of this book mainly concerned questions of 'Why people shop where they do?' (choices of shopping centres) by considering the attributes of centres associated with shopper spending. Part III explores shoppers' decision processes, starting with motivations in this chapter. The following chapter, Chapter 9, considers the mechanism of the influence of shopping centre environment and atmosphere, whereas Chapter 10 speculates on how shopping styles may have evolved.

A number of authors have investigated shoppers' motivations with a view to understanding choices of shopping centres (e.g. Bloch et al, 1994; Dawson et al, 1990; Dellaert et al, 1998; Roy, 1994; Wakefield and Baker, 1998). In Part I above, a positive image of a shopping centre was demonstrated to be associated with greater patronage behaviour at that centre (see also e.g. Finn and Louviere, 1996; Frasquet et al, 2001; and Severin et al, 2001). Nevertheless, prediction of shopping behaviour is an inexact science. This chapter reports a preliminary attempt

---

[1] Dennis C E and Hilton J (2001) 'Shoppers' motivations in choices of shopping centres', *8th International Conference on Recent Advances in Retailing and Services Science*, Vancouver, EIRASS.
[2] Dennis C E, Patel T and Hilton J (2002) 'Shoppers' motivations in choices of shopping centres, a qualitative study', *9th International Conference on Recent Advances in Retailing and Services Science*, Heidelberg, EIRASS.

to understand the formation of shoppers' images of shopping centres in terms of motivation – 'the driving force for ... behaviour' (Sheth et al, 1999).

Many theories of motivation are based on needs – according to Sheth, there are perhaps a thousand or more needs. Examples include Maslow's seminal (but much criticised) hierarchy (1943) and McClelland's Primary Social Motives (1961) – developed into shopping motivations by, for example, Tauber (1972) and Westbrook and Black (1985).

Maslow's theory was based on a study of neurotic people and he was unconvinced of its applicability to other fields. It is unclear why there are five basic needs and why they should be ranked in that particular hierarchy. Nevertheless, his analysis has remained popular, possibly because as materialistic consumers, we find the idea of developing interests in 'higher things' intuitively attractive (Gilbert, 1999). According to Evans and colleagues (1996), drawing support from Wahba and Bridwell (1976), there is more empirical support for Alderfer's (1972) 3-level ERG model than for the Maslow hierarchy:

> Once the basic physiological needs such as thirst and hunger have been reasonably satisfied, we start being aware of the need to be safe and secure. These are the existence needs. Then it becomes important to feel accepted and loved by others, the relatedness or social needs.

The study of needs related specifically to customers' behaviour is well established. Early examples included Murray's (1938) 'psychogenic needs' and Dichter's (1964) 'consumption motives'. A number of researchers have investigated shoppers' motivations in choices of shopping locations (e.g. Bloch et al, 1994; Boedeker and Marjanen, 1993; Dawson et al, 1990; Marjanen, 1997; Roy, 1994; Shim and Eastlick, 1998; Tauber, 1972; Westbrook and Black, 1985). Shim and Eastlick (1998) found evidence for a hierarchical relationship with values influencing attitudes that in turn affected behaviour at regional shopping malls. Specifically, social affiliation and self-actualisation values were significantly associated with shopping behaviour. Roy (1994) correlated shopping centre visit frequency with three motivation segments, 'functional', 'deal proneness' and 'recreational'. He concluded that the frequent shopper was likely to consider shopping a 'recreational experience'. Bloch and associates (1994) identified four motivational segments of shoppers: 'mall enthusiasts', 'traditionalists', 'grazers' and 'minimalists'. The experience-motivated grazers had the highest activity on the 'passing time' and 'consumption of products' factors, visited most stores per visit and visited the mall most often. In a marketplace environment, Dawson and colleagues (1990) found that consumers with strong 'experiential' motives reported higher pleasure and satisfaction than those with strong 'product' motives.

Westbrook and Black (1985) reported modest success in confirming the existence of seven theoretically rooted dimensions of (department store) shopping motivation. These were: (1) Anticipated utility of prospective purchases; (2) Enactment of an economic shopping role; (3) Negotiation to obtain price concessions from the seller; (4) Optimisation of merchandise choice in terms of matching shoppers' needs and desires; (5) Affiliation with reference groups; (6) Exercise of power and authority in marketplace exchanges; and (7) Sensory stimulation from the marketplace itself.

A number of studies of shoppers' choices of shopping centres have concentrated on extrinsic motivation – the need to fulfil a specific objective or avoid a negative outcome. On the other hand, Vallerand (1997, page 281, referring to psychology globally rather than shopping in particular), hypothesised that intrinsic motivation – pleasure or satisfaction from undertaking the activity – would have 'the highest level of self-determination'. To some extent, this view is supported in the retail literature, with the various studies pointing to the importance of motivations such as social affiliation, self-actualisation and experience. This chapter has therefore set out to investigate whether there is evidence for dimensions of exemplar motivation theories figuring in shoppers' opinions of shopping centres, alongside more well known attributes such as the variety of stores and the specific stores wanted by individuals, and also whether shoppers are mainly motivated by higher or lower level motivations. A complicating factor, though, is that shoppers' motivations apparently vary from one shopping centre to another. In Chapter 3 above, for example, it was demonstrated that the attributes most associated with shoppers spending behaviour were significantly different at different centres. This chapter also investigates whether shoppers' motivations are different at different shopping centres. Two studies have been performed in order to investigate these questions:

Study 1: Quantitative. This section reports a structured questionnaire survey of shoppers at two UK shopping centres (n = 100).

Study 2: Qualitative. This section draws on the results of the six focus groups and 20 semi-structured interviews reported in Chapter 4 above, plus a final focus group specifically aimed at eliciting meanings for the motivation dimensions in greater depth.

Study 1

Method for Study 1

Study 1 concerned a structured questionnaire survey of shoppers at two UK shopping centres, The Woodlands and The Metropolitan centres (not their real names). The total number of respondents was 100, equally divided between the two. A structured questionnaire was designed to assess shoppers' motivations for shopping at each centre and the extent to which the centre satisfied these motivations. From the many possible needs, those selected as representative of motivation theories included firstly, at least one from each step of Maslow's hierarchy and McClelland's primary social motives and secondly Vallerand's intrinsic motivation. Extrinsic motivations such as the stores, products and brands liked by respondents were also included, as were the functional economic motives (Roy, 1994) of value-for-money and bargains.

For example, the question representing the strength of Maslow's 'Safety; security' motivation dimension was:

I shop at [the Woodlands] because I feel it is a safe environment to shop in (covered centre, no traffic, security guards).

The responses were coded on a 1 to 5 Likert scale, where 1 represented 'strongly disagree' and 5 'strongly agree'. Each 'motive strength' question was followed up by an equivalent 'evaluation' question:

To what extent does [The Woodlands] satisfy this objective?

Responses to the evaluation questions were also coded on a 1 to 5 scale, where 1 represented 'very dissatisfied' and 5 'very satisfied'. Put in the framework firstly of the ERG model (adapted from Evans et al, 1996), followed by Vallerand's intrinsic motivation, these questions are listed in Table 8.1. In this framework, the dimensions are given Maslow's names and are listed in his hierarchy descending order. The McClelland 'Primary Social Motive' dimensions are named in parenthesis.

Table 8.1 Motivation questions illustrated in the framework of the ERG model followed by intrinsic

Motivation group	Motivation dimension	Question
		I shop at the centre ...
Growth	Self-actualisation	As it provides a means of escapism from my daily routine.
	Self esteem	Because I like to shop at a centre which promotes an up-market image.
		When I buy products for myself I feel happier and more attractive.
Relatedness	Love	Because you can find luxury items and gifts.
	Social	With friends as a social occasion.
	Belongingness, (Affiliation: McClelland)	Because my friends and colleagues shop here.
	(Power: McClelland)	Because I enjoy sales assistants educating me in the choice of products available.
Existence	Safety, security	Because I feel it is a safe environment to shop in (covered centre, no traffic, security guards).
	Physiological	Because in addition to store choice it provides important facilities (e.g. toilets, cafes, seats, lifts, wheelchair access).
Intrinsic	Knowledge	I like to research about products I am interested in buying.
	Accomplishments (Achievement: McClelland)	I know when I have finished shopping I will feel a sense of accomplishment.
	Stimulation	I enjoy shopping in a physically stimulating environment (e.g. space, layout, window displays).

With the exception of 'negotiation' (not a common activity for UK shoppers), the questionnaire covered all of Westbrook's and Black's 'major dimensions of shopping motivation'. Other questions concerned details such as income, age, sex, occupation, frequency of visit, travel time and distance. The main dependent variable was the 'overall opinion of the centre', coded on a five point scale from 1 = very bad to 5 = very good.

Results

The initial stage in processing the results was, for each motivation question, to multiply the 'strength' of the dimension by the 'evaluation' of the extent to which the centre satisfied that objective – the standard 'expectancy – value ' approach, justified in more detail in Chapter 2 above. These values were correlated with respondents' overall opinions of the centres (for convenience, rescaled on to a 1 to 100 scale). The 'top 10' are listed in Table 8.2, ranked in order of Pearson's correlation coefficient.

All of the motivations were assessed for correlation with shoppers' overall 'image' or opinion of the shopping centre. In the event, many of the motivation dimensions were **not** significantly associated with overall opinion of the centres. Interestingly though, of those that were, half were higher-level motivation dimensions ('Love' and 'Self-actualisation'), alongside more conventional attributes such as 'Variety of Stores' and 'Compare brands and prices'.

Table 8.2 Top 10 motivation dimensions ranked in order of correlation with overall opinions of the centres

Rank	R	Question	Motivation dimension	
1	0.18	Luxury items and gifts	Relatedness: love?	***
2	0.12	Variety of stores	Extrinsic	***
3	0.08	Stores I like to frequent	Extrinsic	***
4	0.07	Up-market image	Growth: self-actualisation	***
5	0.05	Escapism	Growth: self-actualisation	*
6	0.04	Compare brands and prices	Extrinsic	*
7	0.033	Happier and attractive	Growth: self esteem	
8	0.031	Safe environment	Existence: safety, security	
9	0.027	Facilities	Existence: physiological	
10	0.024	Stimulating	Intrinsic: stimulation	

*** Significant at $p = 0.001$
* Significant at $p = 0.05$.

There were clear differences between the centres, and it would have been preferable to have sufficient results to study each centre separately. At the more up-market Woodlands, the ones at the top of the association scale were higher-level motivations ('Love', 'Self-esteem' and 'Accomplishment'), ahead of more conventional attributes such as 'Variety of Stores' and 'Compare brands and prices'. At the more down-market Metropolitan Centre, where shoppers usually visit with a specific store objective, 'Variety of stores' came out top, but the two higher-level dimensions of 'Self-actualisation' and also 'Love' followed, ahead of facilities, brands and all other attributes.

Factor analysis and models

The motivation items most associated with image were entered into a factor analysis (SPSS). Those selected were the 'top 10', plus 'Accomplishment' (significant at The Woodlands). Maximum Likelihood extraction was used with Varimax rotation – found in a previous study to give good discrimination between the factors (see Chapter 7 above). Items of factor loading below 0.25 were excluded. Five clearly distinct factors were obtained (down to Eigenvalue 1.0) with no significant inter-correlation between the factors – illustrated in Table 8.3.

Table 8.3   Motivation factors and loadings

Question		Loading R				
Factor:	1	2	3	4	5
Variety of stores	0.92	0.34			
Luxury items and gifts	0.43				
Stores I like to frequent		0.93			
Accomplishment			0.89		
Escapism				0.73	
Happier and attractive	0.26		0.25	0.45	
Facilities			–0.31		0.56
Up-market image		0.29			0.39
Compare brands and prices					0.33

These could be interpreted as three 'stores and facilities' factors (1, 2 and 5) plus two 'satisfaction' factors (3 and 5). The five factors (with the dimensions on which they loaded positively in ranked order) were named as in Table 8.4.

Table 8.4   Motivation factors with ranked dimensions

Factor number	Factor name	Ranked dimensions loading in factor
1	Variety	Variety of stores Luxury items and gifts Happier and attractive
2	Stores	Stores I like to frequent Variety of stores Upmarket image
3	Accomplishment	Accomplishment Happier and attractive
4	Self-actualisation	Escapism Happier and attractive
5	Physiological	Facilities Up-market image Compare brands and prices

Multiple regression (SPSS) was then performed to investigate the association between the factors and the respondents overall opinion of the centre. The following model was obtained:

$$\text{Overall opinion} = 69 + 0.23 \times \text{Variety} + 0.18 \times \text{Stores} +$$
$$0.19 \times \text{Self-actualisation} + 0.25 \times$$
$$\text{Physiological} \tag{8.1}$$

$R^2 = 0.22$. The 'Accomplishment' factor was omitted as not significantly associated with overall opinion. In Equation 8.1 above, the remaining four factors were all significant at $p = 0.05$.

Attributes such as the variety of stores and the specific stores wanted by shoppers are well known as determinants of shopping preference and investigated in more detail in Chapter 3 above. In line with the aims of this chapter, in order to clarify other motivation dimensions, a second factor analysis was performed, omitting the store variables. Four factors were extracted using a similar procedure, illustrated in Table 8.5.

The four factors were named respectively, 'Self-actualisation', 'Love', 'Accomplishment' and 'Self-esteem'. The so-called 'Love' factor 2 is hardly a true factor, consisting of only a single item. Nevertheless, in the interests of simplicity, the nomenclature of 'factor' has been

Table 8.5 Motivation factors – omitting stores variables

Question		Loading R			
Factor:	1	2	3	4
Escapism	.99			
Luxury items and gifts		.98		
Accomplishment			.70	0.31
Facilities			–0.51	0.38
Happier and attractive	.31		0.33	
Upmarket image				0.46
Compare brands and prices				0.45

retained. Again the factors were regressed against respondents' overall opinions of the centres, to produce the model:

$$\text{Overall opinion} = 68.5 + 0.35 \times \text{Love} + 0.29 \times \text{Self-esteem} \qquad (8.2)$$

$R^2 = 0.23$. The 'Self-actualisation' and 'Accomplishment' factors were omitted as not significantly associated with overall image. The remaining two factors were both significant in Equation 8.2 at $p = 0.01$. It is noteworthy that the model **without** the usual stores dimensions performed slightly better than did the original model.

The same two factors were regressed against individual shopper visit frequency per year, producing the model:

$$\text{Visits per year} = 3.3 + 0.24 \times \text{Love} + 0.23 \times \text{Self-esteem} \qquad (8.3)$$

The R^2 in this case was only 0.12, but each of the factors in Equation 8.3 was significant at $p = 0.05$. By including travel distance the performance of the model improved to $R^2 = 0.17$, i.e. the lower end of 'modest'.

Study 2

Postulations

The literature suggests that needs can be classified and ordered into those that are 'higher order' and those that are 'lower order'. Whilst it is difficult to test directly the preconditions of steps in any hierarchy, related postulations are possible. For example, higher order *vs.* lower order needs and the extent to which they are satisfied affect shopping attitudes in choices of shopping centres. Specifically, in this study we have attempted exploratory qualitative testing of:

P1 Shoppers' evaluations of 'good' dimensions will be of higher order at a more attractive centre than they are at a less attractive centre

P2 Shoppers' evaluations of 'bad' dimensions will be of higher order at a less attractive centre than they are at a more attractive centre.

Although not part of the empirical work reported here, a practical value of testing these postulations will arise if it can be demonstrated that a more attractive centre (as measured for the purposes of testing the postulations) is more successful in terms of sales turnover and rental income than is a less attractive centre. Other exploratory work (for example as reported in Chapter 4 above) has demonstrated that this is indeed the case. Therefore, there is a corollary that a shopping centre that is more successful in satisfying shoppers' higher-order motivation dimensions will also be more successful in commercial terms.

Method for Study 2

This study included focus groups, personal constructs and semi-structured questionnaires. The first stage in the qualitative study took the form of six focus groups, previously reported in Chapter 4 above. The participants were shoppers familiar with the two shopping centres. The initial six groups comprised six to eight participants each, many of whom (for convenience) were university students in the West London (UK) area. Students' views may not be representative of all UK shoppers. Therefore the sixth focus group was carried out with 10 participants including both sexes with a range of ages and socio-economic classifications. The participants in this final focus group were not previously known to the facilitator or to each other. These six focus groups were aimed at eliciting what participants considered 'good' and 'bad' about the centres, and what the participants' views were about the centres' 'personalities'.

The constructs arising from the focus groups were coded manually and assigned into motivation categories. The categories were based on those that had been used in the quantitative study (classified for convenience around those of Maslow, Alderfer and Vallerand). These three bases were each amenable to arranging into ranked order – Maslow's being written as a hierarchy, Alderfer's having three levels, and Vallerand's 'intrinsic' having 'the highest level'. A further category that we have termed 'behavioural control' was needed to encompass constructs such as 'Access' (drawn from the Theory of Planned Behaviour, Ajzen, 1985; 1991). As an enforced control rather than a positive motivation, this category was classified at the lowest rank of the hierarchy. The categories were simplified to the minimum number that retained clear distinction between the levels:

Rank	Construct category
1	Self-actualisation; stimulation; self-esteem; knowledge; accomplishment
2	Relatedness; love; social; belongingness; power
3	Safety/security
4	Extrinsic
5	Physiological; Behavioural control.

For further processing, the rankings were converted into a 'virtual' interval scale. Chignell and Patty (1987) reviewed various methods for accomplishing this task. The more complex techniques are suitable for analysing large numbers of items. For the relatively small number of constructs in this study, the simplest was most relevant (applying the principle of Occam's razor in avoiding needless complexity – Breakwell et al, 2000). Accordingly, the ranks have been converted to values that are the reverse order of the ranks (Guildford, 1954). With this simple scale, the highest level constructs, stimulation, self-esteem, knowledge and accomplishment, scored the maximum 5 on the 1 to 5 scale. At the other end of the scale the most basic physiological and behavioural control motivations were scored at the lowest level of 1. The rating scores assigned to the other levels were linearly distributed along the intervening integers. This rating scale was then applied to the 'good' and 'bad' constructs elicited from the focus groups in order to assess at which centres both the good and the bad constructs were at a higher level.

A final focus group was designed specifically to add depth to the motivation constructs, as a follow-up to the quantitative motivation studies. The participants in this case consisted of doctoral students and research assistants – 'shoppers of tomorrow', but more mature as shoppers than the undergraduates of the first five groups. The topic for this final group concerned shopping motivation in general rather than being specifically a comparison of the two centres. Rather than attempting to reach a consensus, the participants in this group were known in advance to differ in their views on shopping. The facilitator accordingly attempted to draw out the **differences** in motivations. As applicable to this specifically targeted type of focus group, the number of participants was smaller – four. Following an unprompted discussion of shopping motivations, the participants were prompted with statements similar to those used in the structured questionnaire of the quantitative study. For example, for 'self-actualisation', the group was asked to discuss the statement 'I go shopping as it provides a means of escapism from my daily routine'.

As a follow-up to the exploratory qualitative studies, a semi-structured questionnaire was carried out with a further 40 respondents (reported in Chapter 4 above). The respondents were selected on a convenience basis from shoppers known to shop at the centres. The semi-structured questionnaire was based on constructs derived from the first six focus groups.

Results of Study 2

The constructs that emerged from the first six focus groups were summarised in Table 4.1 in Chapter 4 above, repeated in Table 8.6 in Appendix 8.1 of this chapter below, this time with the constructs classified according to motivation dimensions. These indicated consistent themes. The descriptions from the final (more representative) group included that if the Metropolitan Centre were an animal, it would be a 'cat or a dog – not exciting, just OK'. On the other hand, The Woodlands would be a 'tiger, lion or peacock: strong, vibrant, big and colourful'. If the Metropolitan Centre were a person, it would be 'dull, boring and old-fashioned – lower working class or elderly'. The Woodlands would be a 'trendy, prestigious, very smart person of good taste who enjoyed leisure'. The ten focus group participants from the final group considered the Metropolitan Centre to be inferior to The Woodlands across a wide range of attributes, including choice of shops, eating places, crèche facilities and attractiveness in general.

Exemplar results from 40 semi-structured questionnaire interviews comparing the two centres were reported in Table 4.2 in Chapter 4 above. For example, typical comments imagining the centres as cars included:

- Metropolitan: Working class, low profile image
- Woodlands: Class, status, style.

The results of the quantitative Study 1, the first six focus groups, and the semi-structured interviews reported in Chapter 4 provide triangulation giving reasonable confidence in a finding that:

- The Metropolitan Centre is not liked by participants and tends to be used to satisfy lower order needs

– The Woodlands is liked by participants and tends to be used to satisfy higher order needs.

Using the method outlined above, it has been possible to assess the levels of the good and bad motivation constructs at each centre. For example, 'Access by all types of transport' was identified as a 'good' construct at the Metropolitan Centre by two of the focus groups. The level score for this construct was 2 × 1 = 2 (2 focus groups mentioned a level 1 construct). Multiplying the level by the number of focus groups that mentioned the construct and then adding gave a total value of 12 for good constructs at the Metropolitan Centre. This value was distributed over 8 constructs (6 separate constructs elicited, but 2 of these were each mentioned by two different focus groups). The mean value for the level of the 'good' constructs at the Metropolitan Centre was therefore 1.5 on the 1 to 5 scale (12/8). Converted to a 0–100 scale, this is 13 percent. Continuing the procedure to the good and bad constructs at each centre gave the following, all scored on the 0–100 scale:

	Good constructs	*Bad constructs*
Metropolitan Centre:	13	39
The Woodlands:	35	6

These figures are a measure of the levels of the good and bad constructs at each centre, such that the lowest level constructs would score 0 and the highest 100. This means that constructs that the focus group participants considered good about the Metropolitan Centre were considerably lower level than those on which the centre was considered bad. On the other hand, the constructs that the focus group participants considered good about The Woodlands were considerably higher level than those on which that centre was thought to be bad. These results support postulations P1 and P2.

Extracts from the final focus group aimed at adding depth to understanding of the motivation dimensions are included in Appendix 8.2 of this chapter, along with the prompts. A discussion of the main dimensions follows.

Self-actualisation

In the quantitative study, this was significantly associated with respondents' overall opinions of the centres. Nevertheless, it did not arise in the first six focus groups, nor unprompted in this one. Prompted, there was minimal agreement, which could be interpreted more in terms of enjoyment than self-actualisation:

'I go round the garden centre and fantasise ... it's a pleasant day out'.

A more typical response was:

'No, shopping is only routine'.

Despite this, the participants explained many non-routine shopping motivations at length, as summarised below.

Stimulation

In the quantitative study, this was not significantly associated with overall opinions of the centres, but was (just) included in the Top 10. Aspects such as decor and atmosphere were mentioned unprompted in three of the earlier focus groups. In this group most of the participants considered enjoyment to be an important motivation for shopping, with unprompted comments including:

'I need recreational ... When I get bored, [I] go shopping – I'm easily tempted; I like nice shopping centres, a relaxed atmosphere'.

To an extent, this extract seems contradictory. Shoppers may shop to relieve boredom, i.e. for stimulation or enjoyment, but this does not mean the search for a high state of arousal: enjoyment is greater when shopping in a relaxed atmosphere. There is a preference for the stimulation of markets and small shops:

'*[In] Paris there is a market on every street*'.
'Paris has more small bars, it's one reason why we travel'.

Again, the variety aspect of shopping in Paris (France) is stimulating, but one of the reasons for enjoying it is the bars – which perhaps help make shopping a more relaxing experience.

Self esteem

In the quantitative study, this was not significantly associated with overall opinions of the centres, but was included in the Top 10. A related dimension (lack of class shops) was mentioned unprompted by one of the earlier focus groups. The prompted 'personality' sections of the earlier focus groups came up with clear descriptions that could easily be interpreted in self-esteem terms. For example, the Metropolitan Centre 'crumpled suit', 'untidy' *vs*. The Woodlands 'designer suit', 'trendy'. The comparisons were clearly confirmed in the qualitative part semi-structured questionnaire responses, reported above, with for example, the Metropolitan 'low profile image' *vs*. The Woodlands 'class, status, style'. In this focus group, when prompted, most participants denied being directly influenced by self-esteem considerations. Typical comments included:

'Try to resist exploitation'.
'Pleasure in buying for some people, not me'.
'I like somewhere friendly that looks nice and meets a bare minimum standard'.

One participant gave weak acknowledgement to self-esteem as a motivation:

'Difficult, yes, but it doesn't compare with other things that make me happy'.

Knowledge

This was not significantly associated in the quantitative study and did not emerge from the first six focus groups. In this group it was mentioned only when prompted, when the male participants referred to a purposeful shopping style:

'Definitely re Internet – find out for myself'
'I over-research'.

Accomplishment

In the quantitative study, 'Accomplishment' was significant only at the more attractive centre, The Woodlands. The construct did not emerge from the unprompted discussion but following the prompts, there was agreement about the feeling arising from completing something difficult, rather than as a motivation in itself:

'Yes, when I have finished shopping for clothes because its so hard'
'Sometimes it's a relief'.

Love

In the quantitative survey, the dimension that we have described as 'love' was top-ranked, highly significantly associated with shoppers' overall opinions of the centres. Nevertheless, it did not emerge unprompted from any of the focus groups. Prompted, the participants were not in agreement, but two made comments along the lines of:

'When I buy for someone else, I don't feel guilt'.

Social

Social aspects were not included in the Top 10 from the quantitative study, and did not emerge from the first six focus groups. In this final group, though, the social dimension came through strongly both prompted and unprompted, with typical comments including:

'Shopping has become going out, meeting friends, coffee, Starbucks, Pret a Manger'.

Belongingness

Again, this was not included in the Top 10 from the quantitative study, and did not emerge from the first six focus groups. Even prompted, though, in this group, 'belongingness' did not come through as a motivation distinct from 'social'.

Power

Similarly, 'power' was not included in the Top 10 from the quantitative study, and did not emerge from the first six focus groups or even from this group when prompted.

Safety, security

This was not included in the Top 10 from the quantitative study. It was mentioned unprompted by one of the first six focus groups but not unprompted by this one. When prompted, participants implied that security was not actually a motivation, but would be a de-motivator if it were bad:

'Never occurred to me, never had trouble or it might be important'.

Physiological

This dimension was included in the Top 10 from the quantitative study, but with the relatively small number of respondents, was not significantly associated with overall image. Physiological aspects were mentioned unprompted by two of the first six focus groups. In this group, when prompted, there was acknowledgement of aspects such as cafés and seats, but this was not strongly emphasised. There was an implication of higher-level motivation in one comment:

'Only cafes – Starbucks'.

The reference to the fashionable Starbucks brand might be more related to 'self-esteem', 'social' or 'belongingness' than to 'physiological'.

Discussion and conclusions

Firstly, in Study 1, the significant motivations varied between the two centres studied. Specifically, at the more attractive centre, the main motivators were the higher order 'Love', 'Self-esteem' and 'Accomplishment'. At the less attractive centre, the main motivator was 'Variety of stores' (although 'Self-actualisation' and 'Love' followed, ahead of facilities, brands and all other attributes). These differences in shoppers' motivations between shopping centres provide a parallel with the differences in attributes significantly associated with spending reported in Chapter 3 above. This provides triangulation and support for the finding in answer to Research Question (iii) in Part II: the variables affecting shoppers' spending are different at different shopping centres.

The quantitative work in Study 1 drew attention to the importance of higher order needs in shoppers' evaluations of shopping centres. Those significantly associated with overall opinions of the centre were the ones that we have named 'Love', 'Self-esteem' and 'Self-actualisation'. The qualitative work in Study 2 has explored some of the complexities of the higher order constructs.

Love. Buying gifts for others is a strong shopping motivation for some shoppers, even though seldom acknowledged as a direct motivation. Many people enjoy shopping as an activity for its own sake; when buying for someone else the activity can be guilt free.

Self-esteem. Shoppers want to be thought of as the type of people who shop at a centre with associations of high class and style. This applies even to shoppers who shop at a centre with the opposite associations (and this is despite a reluctance of shoppers to acknowledge such aspects as a motivation).

Self-actualisation and **Stimulation**. Shoppers were reluctant to acknowledge escape from the daily routine as a motivation but typically preferred to claim that shopping is only a routine activity. Despite this, the unprompted discussions almost exclusively concerned the non-routine and enjoyment aspects of shopping. Rather than using Maslow's highest-order self-actualisation terms, though, shoppers are more down-to-earth in describing shopping as, for example, a pleasant day out. Therefore, we have concatenated these into a single motivation construct that we have called 'Stimulation'. This includes the relief of boredom – often referred to as 'retail therapy' and was well illustrated by the enthusiastic, positive discussion of the markets and bars of Paris.

The quantitative Study 1 did not investigate whether or not a hierarchy of motivation needs existed. This qualitative work has indicated the existence of a hierarchy, although perhaps not in Maslow's sense (of higher needs being dependent on lower needs being satisfied). Needs have been demonstrated to be higher or lower order. A shopping centre's ability to satisfy higher order needs plays an essential part in the centre's attractiveness to shoppers and in its commercial success.

The qualitative Study 2 has supported the postulations. Firstly, shoppers' evaluations of 'good' dimensions were of higher order at the more attractive centre than they were at the less attractive centre. Secondly, shoppers' evaluations of 'bad' dimensions were of higher order at the less attractive centre than they were at the more attractive centre.

The higher-order needs, confirmed and triangulated from the quantitative and qualitative studies, confirmed the prominence of enjoyment in shopping motivation. Enjoyment is important to the shoppers in obtaining satisfaction and this benefits shopping centres by improving sales turnover and rental income. The main higher order needs are those that we have named **love**, **self-esteem** and **stimulation**.

The qualitative Study 2 has also drawn attention to the importance of the **social** dimension. In the quantitative study the social aspects were not significantly associated with respondents overall opinions of the centres, and we have only limited evidence of this motivation. Shoppers possibly consider socialising to be a function of the people that they shop with rather than the centre itself, and therefore not related directly to opinions of the centres. Whatever the reason, further investigation is needed on the social issues.

Finally, this work has been exploratory and the findings cannot be generalised. Further work is in recommended: extending the quantitative study to more shopping centres; and more focus groups specifically targeted to shopping motivations.

The significant findings from this chapter are illustrated schematically on Figure 13.1 in Chapter 13 below, page 243, in the centre part of the diagram, with the chapter number (8) annotated on the paths. The following chapter, Chapter 9 considers shoppers' choices of shopping location from an Environmental Psychology perspective, including how the overall image of a centre (the dependent variable from this chapter) is associated with shopping behaviour.

Appendix 8.1: Constructs from the first six focus groups

The focus group records were coded and interpreted by the author. The constructs in Table 8.6 below are considered to summarise the essence of what participants of the first six groups considered good or bad about the centres or illustrative of their 'personalities', as reported in Table 4.1 in Chapter 4 above, page 59. In the version below, the constructs have been classified according to motivation dimension.

Table 8.6 Constructs from the first six focus groups

Metropolitan Centre: 'Good' constructs		
Access by all types of transport	B, D¹	Behavioural control
Car park	D, K²	Behavioural control
Functional shopping, convenience, good for quick shop	C	Extrinsic
Good for specific item	F	Extrinsic
Value for money	K²	Extrinsic
Shops like computer games and music attractive to teenagers	S	Extrinsic

Metropolitan Centre: 'Bad' constructs		
Security	B, S	Safety, security
Teenagers	B, S	Safety, security
Lack of class shops	D	Self esteem
Centre too small	K²	Extrinsic
Limited breadth of offering	C	Extrinsic
Crowded	K²	Behavioural control
Limited opening hours	K²	Behavioural control
Not enough toilets	K²	Physiological

Table 8.6   Constructs from the first six focus groups – *continued*

Metropolitan Centre: 'Bad' constructs		
Dark	F	Stimulation
Poor ambience, atmosphere	C	Stimulation
Poor surrounding facilities	C	Extrinsic
No attractions or personality. Used to be good for families, now 'Poundsaver'	S	Stimulation

The Woodlands: 'Good' constructs		
Wide range of good quality shops for all the family	B	Extrinsic
More variety, better quality bigger shops	F	Extrinsic
Good security	B	Safety, security
Good décor and layout	F	Stimulation
Crèche	F	Physiological

The Woodlands: 'Bad' constructs		
Not enough car parking	B	Behavioural control
Expensive parking	K^2	Behavioural control
Town centre layout confusing	B	Behavioural control
High prices	K^2	Extrinsic

[1] The initial letters are code identifiers for the focus groups
[2] Focus group K was the final, more representative, one.

Appendix 8.2: Extracts from the final motivation focus group

The extracts have been collected below under the motivation category headings, with the prompts where used included in square brackets. Names have been changed. Unprompted comments that have been categorised under these headings follow the prompted ones where applicable. The + sign is used as a convention to record that the second and possibly subsequently named participants expressed agreement with a statement made by the first named. For example, 'JOHN + GRAHAM: Part of shopping as experience' means that John said 'part of shopping as experience' and Graham agreed.

Self-actualisation

[AS IT PROVIDES A MEANS OF ESCAPISM FROM MY DAILY ROUTINE] JOHN: No, I enjoy shopping but I don't get lost in a world of whatever. GRAHAM: Yes, I don't have a garden, so I go round the garden centre and fantasise; I like fantasy; it's a pleasant day out. SUZANNE: No, shopping is only routine.

Stimulation

[I ENJOY SHOPPING IN A PHYSICALLY STIMULATING ENVIRON-MENT.] JOHN + GRAHAM: Part of shopping as experience. SUZANNE: Likes little shops. [UNPROMPTED] MADELINE: There are not enough farmers' markets in cities, not like Paris where there is a market in every street. GRAHAM: Paris has more small bars, it's one reason why we travel; foreign supermarkets have better fresh food – they are better linked to the locality. GRAHAM: + MADELINE: The UK is too centralised. MADELINE: I like to FEEL, so I'm not an on-line shopper; I need price and quality; recreational; my husband says, when Madeline gets bored, she goes shopping – I'm easily tempted; I like nice shopping centres, a relaxed atmosphere; location is important, the [White Water Centre] is 10 minutes, I have been to the Chimes. JOHN: The shops in the Pavilions are closing down, but I still go there in case anything catches the eye – I park in the Chimes to go to Starbucks. GRAHAM: I shop at Whitelys because of the ambience of the old department store.

Self esteem

[WHEN I BUY PRODUCTS FOR MYSELF, I FEEL HAPPIER AND MORE ATTRACTIVE] GRAHAM: + JOHN: More in control or accomplished is more to the point; I tend to resist those feelings, i.e. try to resist exploitation; self regard, yes – largely related to 'good choice'. JOHN: Always pleasure in buying for some people, not me. SUZANNE: Difficult, yes, but it doesn't compare with other things that make me happy. [BECAUSE I LIKE TO SHOP AT A CENTRE WHICH PROMOTES AN UP-MARKET IMAGE]. JOHN: + SUZANNE: No; it depends how up-market – designer suit shops are intimidating; I like somewhere friendly that looks nice and meets a bare minimum standard. SUZANNE: + GRAHAM: I associate up-market with high prices, e.g. Liberty's. GRAHAM: I never go to Debenhams because of the down-market atmosphere; Barker's in Kensington High Street (House of Fraser) sells the same things as House of Fraser Oxford Street, but nicer.

Knowledge

[I LIKE TO RESEARCH ABOUT PRODUCTS I AM INTERESTED IN BUYING.] SUZANNE: Yes, if it means I talk to friends. JOHN: Definitely re Internet – find out for myself, especially for bigger items – less for day-to-day. GRAHAM: I over-research, over-deliberate, over-rationalise.

Accomplishment

[I FEEL A SENSE OF ACCOMPLISHMENT.] SUZANNE: Yes, when I have finished shopping for clothes because it is so hard. JOHN: Yes, from the process. GRAHAM: Sometimes it's a relief, e.g. got the bed. [FROM 'SELF-ESTEEM'] GRAHAM: + JOHN: More in control or accomplished is more to the point; I tend to resist those feelings, i.e. try to resist exploitation; self regard, yes – largely related to 'good choice'.

Love

[BECAUSE YOU CAN FIND GIFTS]. SUZANNE: I like to buy for other people rather than myself, the pleasure of buying for godchildren, friends and family. JOHN: I buy gifts for myself; when I buy for someone else, I don't feel guilt: 'I shouldn't buy this, but it's OK if it's for someone else'; I like to buy little gifts – unexpected ones. GRAHAM: No. GRAHAM: + JOHN: Anxious when Christmas shopping. SUZANNE: + JOHN: + GRAHAM: It's different when I HAVE to buy the gift. [LUXURY ITEMS FOR MYSELF] SUZANNE: No, not things that I can't afford. JOHN: No, not expensive things, I get more pleasure from bargains. GRAHAM: No, I'm brand-averse.

Social

[WITH FRIENDS AS A SOCIAL OCCASION]. JOHN: not the shopping, the before, during and after coffee; we often go together [with a group of friends], when shopping, mainly do our own thing, but go to some places together. GRAHAM: Yes, for lifestyle shopping [see under 'Belongingness']; even ordinary shopping can be quite enjoyable; in a village, meeting a significant other, older people – can be important. JOHN: Sainsbury's is quite social when a bunch of students do it together. [RE EXPERIENCE BENEFITS AND INTERNET SHOPPING] JOHN: Shopping on the Internet takes away the social benefits, but I can still shop on-line then go to Starbucks; but I still enjoy it [Internet shopping] for the pleasure of buying; I like the actual BUYING, on-line takes away the waste of time; but if I did all my shopping on-line, it wouldn't ruin my social life – I could still go for coffees – but I never do go to Starbucks unless I'm shopping. [UNPROMPTED] JOHN: Starbucks has taken over – I might visit a shop or two as well; my friends go to work there – you see people with laptops, the prices are high, but even students go because of the atmosphere; Costa coffee is the same or better, but not the same atmosphere; I shop on-line a lot, but Starbucks etc. has become quite a ritual – with friends. GRAHAM: I like the restaurants on the top floor of Whitelys it's an ideal shopping centre; I go by bus to IKEA for an outing, the café and chocolate mocha; at IKEA the café is the key – people socialising; the café at the V&A is very nice, but I object to the prices; even a small bookstore has a good, very busy café. MADELINE: Shopping has become going out, meeting friends, coffee, Starbucks, Prèt a Manger.

Belongingness

[BECAUSE MY FRIENDS AND COLLEAGUES SHOP HERE]. JOHN: + SUZANNE: No, except for recommendations. SUZANNE: I like to go if a friend asks, but not as a social thing. JOHN: I wouldn't go on my own; I enjoy going with someone else. GRAHAM: I always go clothes shopping on my own; I go with someone to lifestyle shops; some, like Heals and Habitat are very social – either with friend or [significant other]. GRAHAM: I enjoy the lifestyle [television] programmes – e.g. Grand Designs – very similar to going round the shops, a very social thing.

Power

[BECAUSE I ENJOY SALES ASSISTANTS EDUCATING ME IN THE CHOICE OF PRODUCTS AVAILABLE.] SUZANNE + JOHN + GRAHAM: I would rather do my own thing, otherwise I feel obliged. I would rather go with a friend. JOHN: Sales staff should be there if needed – I don't mind a quick approach, but not a hard sell. GRAHAM: If approached by a shop assistant, I hope that they'll go away, EXCEPT e.g. when doing DIY and I want specialist advice, e.g. Dixons, I want to talk about computers – can't rely on them knowing, I'd rather talk to friends.

Safety, security

[BECAUSE I FEEL IT IS A SAFE ENVIRONMENT TO SHOP IN (COVERED CENTRE, NO TRAFFIC, SECURITY GUARDS).] GRAHAM: + JOHN: + SUZANNE: I'm never aware of being threatened in London; I wouldn't not go to a centre because of that. JOHN: prefers shopping centres – no, never occurred to me, never had trouble or it might be important. [Hygiene].

Physiological

[BECAUSE IN ADDITION TO STORE CHOICE, IT PROVIDES IMPORTANT FACILITIES (E.G. TOILETS, CAFÉS, SEATS, LIFTS, WHEELCHAIR ACCESS).] JOHN: Only cafés – Starbucks. GRAHAM: I try to avoid a day spent recreational shopping – prefer the high street – take what's available. SUZANNE: I would rather have seats, but I can't do anything about it.

The first purpose-built out-of-town shopping centre is reported to have been the Country Club Plaza, Kansas City, USA, opened in 1923 (McGoldrick and Thompson, 1992b, citing Sternlieb and Hughes, 1981).

9
An Environmental Psychology Approach to Consumers' Choices of Shopping Centres*

This chapter is adapted and summarised from a paper originally presented at the *British Academy of Management Conference* (Dennis et al, 2004)[1] and summarises essential findings from a paper still in the course of preparation for publication in an academic journal elsewhere at the time of writing.

Introduction

The previous chapters have investigated shoppers' choices of shopping centres by considering the attributes of shopping centres and motivations of shoppers. In this chapter we explore how managers can manipulate atmospheric stimuli (using an exemplar stimulus) with the objective of increasing shoppers' approach behaviours such as spending. Despite substantial research (see summary in Turley and Milliman, 2000), the processes of perception of stimuli and conversion into actions are still not fully understood. This chapter addresses the mechanism by which perceptions of a stimulus act to change consumers' images of a shopping centre and/or its retail stores and products and thus increase pleasure and/or arousal emotions. If these effects can be further understood, management might be able to design atmospheric stimuli to increase: (i) **arousal** (e.g. using fast tempo music), (ii) **pleasure** (e.g. by pleasant video images) or (iii) the **image** of a shopping centre or stores (e.g. by providing relevant

---

* This chapter by Charles Dennis and Andrew Newman.
[1] Dennis C, Newman A, Zaman S, Nicholas R and Grundy A (2004) 'Manipulation of stimuli in a retail setting: a study into the effects of Captive Audience Network screens on shopping centre customers', *British Academy of Management Conference*, Fife, Scotland, University of St Andrews.

audio-visual information). In this chapter we explore whether the effects of stimuli can be linked to approach variables such as shoppers' spending. The exemplar stimulus for this chapter was a trial of Captive Audience Network (CAN) screens at the Delphi Centre, an in-town, sub-regional shopping centre in the South East of England (not its real name).

Captive Audience Networks

A CAN (sometimes called a 'private TV channel') might consist, for example, of a plasma screen in a retail or public place showing video material. Clarke (2003) drew attention to figures on retail media effectiveness showing that in-store media is 'four times as effective as the TV advertising people see at home'. CANs have been used in a number of retail settings as advertising media but also have uses in improving customer satisfaction. For example, an experiment in a retail bank reported a 5.9 percent improvement in customer satisfaction as a result of installing a CAN (Thomke, 2003). CANs are used in some shopping centres with two objectives:

(i) To charge advertisers for advertisements and thus produce revenue directly. This is an important function of a CAN, but outside the scope of the current chapter.
(ii) By the use of interesting, entertaining and/or informative content, to increase shoppers' pleasure, positive mood and image of the shopping centre and stores. Thus, it is hoped that approach behaviours such as spending will also increase. This aspect of CANs is the focus of the current chapter.

Conceptual framework

Pleasure and atmosphere – To date, there has been little research on the effect of CANs on shoppers' moods, pleasure and shopping behaviour. This is an important omission, as it has been demonstrated that even a small improvement of a single component of the image of a shopping centre can potentially improve financial results significantly (see Chapter 7 above). It is difficult to prove that environment influences spending, but work in Chapter 4 above has succeeded in demonstrating that the image of shopping centres is significantly related to sales and rental income. Similarly, Turley and Chebat (2002) drew attention to a number of studies of store image indicating an association between image and consumer purchasing behaviours (e.g. share of household spending, Hildebrandt, 1988; store loyalty, Sirgy and Cocksun, 1989).

Shopping environments are a substantial component of image, and therefore it is reasonable to infer that the environment of a shopping centre does influence shopper spending. Turley and Milliman (2000) reviewed experimental atmospheric and servicescape (first coined by Bitner, 1992) studies and noted that the link between atmosphere and sales is 'very strong and robust'. Out of 28 studies that used sales as a dependent variable, 25 found some statistical relationship between changes in the retail environment and sales. A study by Spies and co-workers (1997) compared two stores differing in atmosphere, but otherwise very similar. Shoppers' moods were measured before, during and after shopping. It was concluded that better store image and information rate were associated with pleasant atmosphere, enhanced mood, goal attainment and higher spending on unplanned purchases. The most important store characteristics were those that helped shoppers to achieve their shopping goals.

For decades retailers and researchers have been aware that shopping is not just a matter of buying products but also about experience and enjoyment (see Martineau, 1958). For example, in Chapter 3 above, it was found that service and experience attributes were more associated with shoppers' choices of shopping centres than were shops and merchandise. This was confirmed for specific retailers by Newman and Patel (2004), and linked explicably to the profitability of the business. In other contexts, the legibility of the setting, and therefore the perceived clarity of company image, has been linked to the reputation of the retailer (See Newman, 2002). The latter research took place in a busy shopping mall inside an international airport terminal. Enjoyment and entertainment have been demonstrated to be important benefits of shopping (e.g. Babin et al, 1994; Sit et al, 2003; Yoo et al, 1998), valued by consumers, and reflected in their spending (e.g. Donovan et al, 1994; Jones, 1999; Machleit and Mantel, 2001; Sherman and Smith, 1987; Smith and Sherman, 1993).

Customers' pleasure emotional responses and impulse purchasing can increase in a store with a pleasant atmosphere compared to an unpleasant one (Ang and Leong, 1997; Spies et al, 1997, referred to above). Management-manipulated cues such as aroma or music can increase pleasure, arousal and spending (e.g. Mattila and Wirtz, 2001). The effects of emotional aspects such as pleasure have been found to be additional to cognitive image variables such as price, variety and quality of the merchandise (Donovan et al, 1994) Shoppers' moods can influence behaviour **after** the decision to shop has been made, and therefore extra spending may depend on marketer-driven stimuli (Sherman and

Smith, 1987). Visual merchandising has been demonstrated to be a cause of additional spending and there is some evidence that spending is also influenced by information rate (Spies et al, 1997). In summary, there is considerable evidence to support the fact that pleasure and atmosphere influence shopper spending, albeit mainly gained at the store rather than the shopping centre level.

Shopping centre image attributes – We postulate that a CAN may be considered as a sophisticated method of visual merchandising, contributing to pleasure, atmosphere and therefore associated with increased spending. It can be postulated that a CAN will provide shoppers with useful information, increase pleasure and therefore also increase spending. Atmosphere is notoriously difficult to measure, but the basis of this research mainly took the form of more concrete measurements of 'image'. In our context for this chapter as in Chapter 3 above, image is a concept used to mean an overall evaluation or rating of something used in such a way as to guide actions (Boulding, 1956). Image includes both functional qualities and the 'aura of psychological attributes' (Martineau, 1958, p. 47). For example, shoppers are more likely to buy from a store that is considered to have a positive image on considerations such as price, customer service or atmosphere. This is an approach that has been demonstrated to work in store image research over many years (e.g. Berry, 1969; Lindquist, 1974).

Shopping centres with strong images have been demonstrated to have higher sales turnover, catchment area and rental income than those with weaker images – see Chapter 4 above. The study reported in Chapter 4 triangulated the image findings using structured (plus semi-structured) questionnaires and focus groups, testing the image models against sales turnover estimates and also against data not used in generating the models, i.e. published catchment and rental income figures.

Image measurements have demonstrated that a positive image of a shopping centre or a retail store is associated with greater patronage behaviour at that centre (see Chapter 4 above and e.g. Newman and Patel, 2004; Finn and Louviere, 1996; Severin et al, 2001). Although it may be a circular argument, the image measure(s) used should predominantly include aspects that can be postulated as being related to spending. For example, 'general layout' should be included because in Chapter 3 above, this was found to be the image attribute most correlated with spending at shopping centres. Even more critical measures of layout that offer greater and more precise indicators of image components show significant impact on approach behaviour, and therefore propensity to spend more money (Newman, 2002).

The direct measurement of actual spending behaviour is often impractical. An example of such an approach might be the use of EPoS data as an input into an econometric model. Unfortunately, there are likely to be so many other variables (weather, interest rates, competitor advertising and many others) affecting sales that any attempt at modelling is likely to be confounded. Therefore, the indirect measurement of image is preferable in this application. As stated in this section above, the measurements of image should be those that are as closely related as possible to shopper spending. The starting point in developing a measure of shopping centre image was therefore the selection of elements of image that are likely to relate directly to shopper spending.

Firstly, we consider the 'top ten' attributes from the study in Chapter 3 above that was specifically aimed at eliciting the image attributes associated with shoppers' spending relative to competing centres. The attributes are listed in Table 9.1 (Table 3.3 from Chapter 3 above, page 44, reproduced here for convenience), ranked in order of association with reported spending. These were the attributes most associated with relative spending at six shopping centres (all were significantly so at $p = 0.05$). They are not necessarily the attributes that the respondents considered most 'important' as the 'weight' also takes into account the degree and strength of the association of the respondents' rating of the attribute with relative spending. Hence 'weight' was intended to model the weight that the attribute carried in shopper spending decisions. In Table 9.1, less significant attributes have been omitted, but the numerical values were scaled such that when all attributes were included, the weights totalled 100. These are the attributes that the author found to

Table 9.1   Attributes ranked by association with shopper spend at shopping centres

Rank		Attribute weight
1	General layout	11.4
2	Access by car (roads)	7.8
3	Nice place to spend time	6.7
4	Cleanliness	6.0
5	Covered shopping	4.5
6	Quality of stores	3.9
7	Shoppers nice people	3.9
8	Availability of toilets	3.9
9	Friendly atmosphere	3.8
10	Helpfulness of staff	3.1.

Source: The study reported in Chapter 3 above.

carry most weight in the regression model of shoppers' relative spending in choices between competing shopping centres.

A number of other authors have developed or used shopping centre attribute image lists (most summarised in Sit et al, 2003 but McGoldrick and Thompson, 1992a; b; and Severin et al, 2001 could be added). Most of these studies did not seek to link image attributes to shopper spending. However, the Newman and Patel (2004) work linked such attribution to retailer profitability. McGoldrick and Thompson (1992a; b) did model reported relative spending between two shopping centres. Their image attributes were categorised using factor analysis rather than individual attributes. The factors significantly associated with spending (p = 0.05) were named: (i) user friendliness and (ii) recreational experience. The attributes that loaded highest (R > 0.5) included four of those already listed in Table 9.1, however Recreational Experience ('In-place' to go when the weather is bad) and User Friendliness (Security) are added.

Two further studies are also relevant. Finn and Louviere (1996) found that stores are central to image and patronage. 'Quality of stores' is incorporated in Table 9.1, but two further attributes (Wide selection and Low prices) were found to be critical, together accounting for 86 percent of the variance in the share of shopping centre choice. Finally, Severin and colleagues (2001) confirmed many of these attributes to be associated with relative spending, stable across time and between countries. It was therefore considered that attributes such as these can confidently be used as the bases for shopping environment, stores and products image dimensions.

Emotion – As mentioned, controllable cues such as music and aroma have been found to influence emotion and spending (e.g. Chebat and Michon, 2003; Newman 2003; Mattila and Wirtz, 2001). Most research has been based on a stimulus-organism-response (S-O-R) framework, based on the model by Mehrabian and Russell (1974 – the 'MR' model). The components were:

(i)   **Stimuli – environmental**: e.g. store image and atmosphere components such as layout, design, colours, music and odours
(ii) **Organism – emotions**: (i) pleasure/displeasure; (ii) arousal/no arousal; (iii) dominance/submissiveness – the Pleasure/Arousal/Dominance (PAD) model
(iii) **Responses – shopping behaviour**: approach/avoidance behaviours, e.g. (i) time spent in store; (ii) money spent; (iii) number of items bought and prices; and (iv) intention to revisit the store.

In most studies, pleasure has clearly predicted response-shopping outcomes, but the influence of arousal is not as clear (e.g. Chebat and Michon, 2003; Donovan et al, 1974). In one of few studies to consider the effect of atmosphere in a shopping centre (as opposed to a store), Wakefield and Baker (1998) found that 'Excitement' strongly influenced repatronage intentions. Parsons (2003) found that entertainment (which, like excitement, may be linked to arousal) increased visits to a shopping centre but did not increase the value of sales. Sit and colleagues (2003) found that shopping centre shoppers could be clustered into 'pro-entertainment' and 'anti-entertainment' segments, with only the 'pro-entertainment' ones seeking stimulation and excitement. Work by Newman (2003) in an airport retail setting found that the arousal dimension suggested feelings of calm or even sleepiness, which stem from low 'load' environments. Pleasant atmospheres generate greater levels of arousal leading to greater approach behaviour. In our research this would equate to the likelihood of spending more money. Hence, arousal was retained in our models on the grounds that a conditional interaction can be demonstrated between pleasure and arousal (e.g. Chebat and Mechon 2003; Russell and Pratt, 1980).

The dominance/submissiveness emotion scale has usually been deleted from studies using the MR framework on the grounds of lack of empirical support (Donovan et al, 1994) and we therefore postulate that there is **no** significant link between dominance/submissiveness and spending.

Chebat and Michon (2003) compared the MR model with an alternative theoretical framework, Lazarus's (1991) cognitive theory of emotions (the 'CE' model). If applied to our application, the effect of environment and emotion would be reversed, such that the environment image variables would be intervening between the mood variables and the shopping behaviour responses. The more relevant finding for this study was that to improve their model, Chebat and Michon included direct paths from their atmospheric stimulus (aroma) to mood variables **and** image variables.

Travel time and distance – In Chapter 3 above it was demonstrated that the influence of travel time and distance on relative spending varied for different shopping centres. Chapter 5 above presented empirical evidence supporting the hypothesis that this was due to competitive differences. Specifically, for a centre subject to little competitive pressure, there was little association of spending with travel time and distance. The Delphi Centre does not have any competitor at the same (or higher) level in the retail hierarchy (see Chapter 6 above) within its catchment. Therefore, it was postulated that travel time and distance would **not** be significantly associated with approach variables at the Delphi Centre.

Models

The main objective of this chapter was to explore the mechanism by which a stimulus acts to increase spending by increasing emotion and perceptions of image. The main postulation is based on the widely used MR model. A CAN is postulated to positively influence shopping centre environment image, thus increasing shoppers pleasure, positive mood and hence spending.

P1 A controllable atmospheric stimulus can improve the image of a shopping centre and (through intervening emotions) increase approach behaviour such as spending.

As mentioned in the section above, Chebat and Michon, 2003 found support for the CE model, in which shoppers' moods are considered to influence perception. As most researchers have favoured the MR model, the MR model was postulated in preference the CE model here. Nevertheless, as this study specifically concerned the mechanism of an atmospheric stimulus (CAN), the relevant findings from Chebat and Michon (2003) were taken as the basis of Postulation 2.

P2 A controllable atmospheric stimulus can act directly to increase emotional responses and thus indirectly increase approach behaviour such as spending.

The essential points here (apart from reversing the interaction of image and emotion) were the direct paths from the stimulus (CAN) to the emotion variables in addition to the image variables.

The dependent approach variables include spending and related behaviours and defined by Donovan et al (1994) were:

- Likelihood of spending more money than intended
- Time spent shopping
- Number of items bought and
- Frequency of visits.

Method

The authors tested the postulated paths in a study described more fully elsewhere (Dennis et al, 2004). The fieldwork took place at the Delphi

Centre, a sub-regional shopping centre in the southern part of the UK. The method consisted of quantitative survey research. The survey interview instrument was an assisted self-completion questionnaire, requiring respondents to rate the screens and their content, plus the shopping centre and various emotions. In keeping with this type of survey design we utilised 5-point bi-polar scales (e.g. very poor to very good). The questions were based on a developed list of elements and the dependent approach variables from the section above. In order to provide a control and comparative data for the modelling, respondents were required to similarly rate their alternative shopping location and provide comparative information on shopping-related activity. The quantitative survey sample consisted of a total of 315 completed questionnaires. The sample demographic profile was reasonably representative of shoppers at the centre in terms of their spending.

Findings

As the detail of the results will be published elsewhere, only the overall summary of the confirmation and modification of the postulated paths is reported here. Firstly, compound variables were elicited, representing the main variables. A small number of items were dropped as not consistent with the other items in the dimension (Cronbach Alpha). The final compound variables (all relative to the respondents' main alternative shopping location, in the same manner as described in Chapter 2 above) were:

Approach:
- Spending
- How long spend shopping
- Number of items bought
- Likelihood of spending more than intended.

Pleasure:
- Happy
- Pleased
- Content.

Arousal:
- Excited
- Wide awake
- Stimulated.

Image of stores and products:

- Quality of the stores
- Wide selection of products.

Image of shopping centre environment:

- General Layout
- Nice place to spend time
- Cleanliness
- Covered shopping
- Other shoppers nice people
- Availability of good toilets
- Helpfulness of staff
- 'In-place' to go
- Security.

The results were analysed using the SPSS Amos structural equations programme with Maximum Likelihood estimation. Firstly, Model 1 testing P1 had a very good fit, although the paths 'CAN screens – Image of shops and products' and 'Image of shopping centre environment – Arousal' were not significant.

The model testing P2 also fitted well, although not as high a fit as Model 1. Three paths were not significant: 'CAN screens – Image of shops and products', 'CAN screens – Image of shops and products' and 'CAN screens – Arousal'.

Model 1 was found to be preferable to Model 2, but from P2 there was evidence that the CAN stimulus acted to increase 'Pleasure' both directly and through the Image of the shopping centre environment. Through 'Pleasure', both routes acted to increase 'Approach'. The effect of the CAN screens was small, but significant, and acted only through 'Image of the shopping centre environment' and 'Pleasure', not directly. The significant paths have been incorporated into the illustration of the overall findings of the work reported in this book in Figure 13.1 in Chapter 13 below.

The simple image model

It is useful to explore whether the effects of controllable atmospheric variables such as a CAN on approach variables such as spending can be quantified. The principles developed in Chapter 3 and validated in Chapter 4 above were therefore applied to the CAN.

The simple image model was based on the so-called expectancy × value compensatory approach of multiplying 'rating' by 'importance', as used (e.g.) by James and colleagues (1976); and for shopping centres (e.g.) by Gentry and Burns (1977) and for Part II of this book, described in Chapter 2 above. This was the basis of the model used in Chapter 4, demonstrated by triangulation to measure the image of shopping centres in a manner relevant to their business success.

The 'CAN' variable was significantly associated with the 'Approach' variable (although the structural equation modelling reported above has demonstrated that association to be through the 'Image of the shopping centre' and 'Pleasure' variables rather than directly). The individual image items were all very highly significantly associated with the perceived 'Overall image', supporting their use in the disaggregated model. The main dependent compound variable 'Approach' was demonstrated to result in more robust models than the single approach variables individually.

Apart from the CAN, all the variables used in the image model have been demonstrated to be related to approach variables in previous work (see Chapter 4 and also, e.g. Finn and Louviere, 1996; McGoldrick and Thompson, 1992; Severin et al, 2001). The CAN variable has not been studied previously, but can provisionally be included with the other image variables on the grounds of significant association with Approach and significant paths in the structural equation model.

A statistically significant simple image model (linear regression, SPSS) was derived using the procedure described in Chapter 3 above, following the form:

$$\text{Approach} = \text{Constant} + \text{Regression coefficient} \times \text{Image variables} \tag{9.1}$$

The components of the Approach variable all represent items likely to be related to sales, therefore any uplift in Approach can be estimated to be equivalent to an uplift in like-for-like sales. As a component of Image, CAN therefore represents a quantifiable proportion of image. The potential uplift in sales arising from the CAN was therefore be estimated.

Rental income

In the long run, an increase in sales turnover for retailers can be expected to result an increase in rental income for the shopping centre.

Some shopping centres receive part of their rental income from turnover-related rents, but even for those using fixed rents, there are periodic opportunities for rent reviews and attracting new tenants. The modelling in Chapter 4 above has demonstrated a close relationship between the attractiveness of shopping centres and their rental incomes. The relationship between Sales and Image was close to, but not exactly, linear, the relationship of best fit (from Figure 4.1 in Chapter 4 above) being:

$$\text{Sales (notional units)} = 0.0014 \times \text{Image}^2 + 1.11 \times \text{Image} \qquad (9.2)$$

Using this equation and the linear relationship between Rental income and Image (see Figure 4.2 in Chapter 4 above), the hypothetical increase in rental income was also calculated.

This figure necessarily must be viewed with caution as long term forecasting is fraught with difficulties, and the actual mechanism of rent increases varies from centre to centre. Nevertheless, a more attractive centre with a higher sales turnover has more pull in attracting higher-status retailers and can expect to receive appropriately higher rents. The best estimate of the size of the effect is that **the Approach variables (our most robust measure of like-for-like retail sales) were uplifted by *1.5 percent* by the CAN Screens**. In the long term, this might perhaps be associated with an increase in rental income of around *1.3 percent*.

The size of the effect the CAN screens on Image (and hence the Approach variables) was small but statistically significant. This was exploratory research at a single location, but if applied to a shopping centre the size of, say, Lakeside in Thurrock, UK, the owners would typically have to invest around £12 million on refurbishment or extension (e.g. an extra 1500 square metres of gross lettable area, GLA) to obtain a 1.5 percent increase in sales turnover. The associated return on investment in terms of rent increases would be expected to be around £0.6 million per year. This helps put into context the part that an atmospheric stimulus such as a CAN could play in improving the shopping environment.

Discussion

The findings of the study summarised here demonstrated that a controllable atmospheric stimulus such as CAN screens can act to increase both pleasure and shopping centre image, and through both routes, increase approach behaviours such as spending.

Atmospheric stimuli such as a CAN should therefore be designed predominantly to increase shopper pleasure (for example including pleasant scenes), but also to take into account the image of the centre (for example with information about the benefits of the centre). There is no need for high arousal approaches such as high volume, fast tempo music.

The CAN in this chapter was estimated to have contributed to the image or atmosphere variables of the shopping centre, uplifting approach variables such as shopper spending by an estimated 1.5 percent. With simple adjustments to the CAN, such as the size of the screens, style of music, information content etc., it is known that the CAN could be adjusted so as to meet shoppers' requirements more closely. Therefore, the 1.5 percent figure might be regarded as a minimum starting point that might easily be exceeded in an updated system.

Conclusions and implications for management

The shopping complex described in this chapter is well known in the region comprising a typical single storey format with a blend of retail provision and supporting amenities. In all, 60 retailer brands including Marks & Spencer, Waitrose and WH Smiths attract a broad cross section of the population indicative of the region. In operators terms, the degree to which shoppers are prepared to, and actually do spend time within the retail space is a function of the attractiveness of the centre. In terms of attribution, centre attractiveness may be reduced to a range of factors such as branded retail concessions, convenient location, parking and more specific facilities such as restaurants, toilets and changing rooms. The perceived attractiveness of such retail centres has been linked empirically (see, for example, Chapter 4 above) to a range of image related attributes or pull factors.

Given the competitive nature of shopping centres, and the considerable economic pressure expected in the future, market-oriented operators will be forced to make differential changes to the total proposition to survive. As well as changes to the retail mix; a successful retail strategy necessitates continuous realignments to a range of tangible and intangible factors (such as atmosphere) in line with customer expectations. In our research a number of postulations were presented that tested the notion that Captive Audience Networks (CAN) could positively influence consumers' perceptions and that such technology could, conceivably, increase like-for-like retail sales.

It is useful at this point to reconsider the components that constitute image within the context of a retail centre, and the implications of these for the operator. How the centre's shoppers perceive retail space relies fundamentally on the operator's manipulation of numerous factors or cues that stimulate feelings and customer expectations. Such cues act as symbols facilitating judgements, and may be used to reinforce customers' expectations. As with retail store interiors, shopping centre concourses need to be fine-tuned and *constantly* re-evaluated and altered to follow the pattern of customer expectations, and (quality) marketing orientation (Newman and Foxall, 2003).

Although centre management take on the responsibility for attracting suitable consumer groups they are not on the other hand liable for the conversion rates of individual retailers. When management's marketing efforts succeed in improving conversion, and particularly where a measurable uplift in like-for-like retail sales (as in our study) is achieved, this is likely to have a positive influence on tenant occupation. As a promotional tool, the CAN network technology offers the means to reach all age groups with messages that raise the image of the centre and its offering.

As the CAN network technology has been shown to be an important component of layout and atmosphere, the precise tuning of this centre attribute will vary with the shopping centre and target market. Identification of the target market is critical if management wishes to align the informational content to specific needs. Centre image is hard won and delicately balanced. In a broad sense, the information carried by the system should be related strategically to the population of the centre. In essence, images should offer a 'slice of life' in keeping with the population profiles and surroundings. For example, topics such as opening hours, local events, and community information regarding the local farmer's market would personalise the message for spectators. An element of seasonality would help to transfer the entire centre during festive occasions such as Christmas and Easter. We can see from this that plasma screen technology can greatly impact on the image of the shopping centre *per se*.

This chapter has established a strong link between mood inducing technology / image attributes and shopping centre / retailer performance. Moreover, the work clearly contributes to the sphere of retail and shopping centre strategies. We have demonstrated that a strategic emphasis on functional attributes like parking and toilet facilities alone is insufficient in a modern society. Only the integration of a full range of marketing communication activities, or market-orientated approach is likely to inspire contemporary consumers. The study provides the basis for much more precise targeting and leads to quality marketing orientation and retailer image development. However, more research is needed to evaluate the degree to which individual on-screen images contribute to overall image, and how perceived images vary within and between consumer groups. The relative size and *shape* of screens is also of importance if the retail setting is to retain the relevance it has enjoyed to date.

As referred to earlier, the significant paths confirmed by the work reported in this chapter are illustrated schematically in the top left of the diagram in Figure 13.1 in Chapter 13 below, page 243. The following chapter, Chapter 10, continues the exploration of shopper psychology with a preliminary attempt at a deeper understanding of the 'why' from an Evolutionary Psychology perspective.

When a sewer burst in a Norwich, UK, street in 1965, it was closed for repairs. The expected drop in sales never happened and Norwich became the first city in the UK to eliminate traffic permanently from a central commercial street (Brambilla and Longo, 1977).

10
An Evolutionary Psychology Approach to Understanding the 'Why' of Shopping Behaviour: the Savannah Hypothesis of Shopping

This chapter is adapted from a paper on work-in-progress originally presented at the *11th International Conference on Recent Advances in Retailing and Services Science* (Dennis 2004).[1]

Introduction

'Life is just a rather complicated form of chemistry'
(Gribbin, 2002: xvii)

So far this book has attempted to answer the question of 'Why people shop where they do' (choices of shopping centres) by considering the attributes of shopping centres affecting shopper behaviour and, in the previous chapter, the possible processes by which the environment of a shopping centre affects shopping behaviour. This chapter reports a tentative preliminary attempt to search for a deeper 'why'. Are shopping styles culturally determined? Or have humans evolved to shop the way that they do? Up to the time of writing, the quantity of data gathered for this study has been very limited. Nevertheless, the results are included here to illustrate the current state-of-play and the potential of this new approach.

Explaining and predicting human behaviour is an extraordinarily complex process, dependent on many considerations including instinctive, physiological, rational and emotional ones. One argument, though, is that all these emanate from chemical changes in the brain – exemplified by the well known 'fight or flight' reflex associated with the

---

[1] Dennis C E (2004) 'The savannah hypothesis of shopping', *11th International Conference on Recent Advances in Retailing and Services Science*, Prague, EIRASS.

'adrenaline rush' of the hormone cortisol affecting emotion (fear), physiology (heart rate) and action (fight or flight). If the argument is true, it
begs the question, why should brain chemistry perform in this way? The
answer, according to evolutionary psychologists, is that such processes
have evolved by the 'survival of the fittest' – a proposition that may have
intuitive logic in the case of 'fight or flight'. Our ancestors were those
that were successful in either their fight or flight, and we can take it that
those less successful were less likely to survive and reproduce! The argument does not demand the absence of free will, although many of us
would accept that free will is guided as much by emotion as it is by logic.
The basic premise is that we like (positive emotion) the things that make
us more likely to survive or reproduce, for example: food; drink; sex;
safety and security; socialising; power; and, central to the basic postulation of the paper, this author suggests: **shopping**.

The evolution of life goes back to a primeval soup some billions of
years ago, but we take up the story from the time of a major ice age
four million years ago. The forest covering most of Africa retreated and
many tree-dwelling apes died. Some found ways of living in the open
savannah. The more resourceful ones were the ones that were more
likely to survive and reproduce (Winston, 2002). The Savannah
Hypothesis holds that human psychology has been shaped by the need
to evolve and adapt to the savannah environment: 'selection has
favoured preferences, motivations and cognitions to explore and settle
in environments abundant with the resources needed to sustain life'
(Buss, 1999: p. 83). Evolutionary psychologists have cited as evidence
human preferences for natural (rather than human-made) environments (Orians, 1980; 1986). Applying this to shopping, we can
observe, for example, preferences for natural daylight, water features
and greenery in shopping centres.

For a window on what life might have been like as the human race
evolved in the African savannah, we can look at today's hunter-
gatherer societies such as the Kung San of the Kalahari. Females tend to
carry babies, are based around the camp and do the gathering of foods
such as mongongo nuts. Males on the other hand are more likely to
protect the group and do the hunting. Humans may have evolved in
such a way that those best at their respective roles have been more
likely to find a mate and to survive. For males, it entailed being good
hunters: fast, strong, powerful and decisive. For females, this meant
excelling in gathering: finding the best food and other materials for
the family. Both sexes would look for those respective qualities in a
potential mate, resulting in persistent traits. These differences in mate

seeking behaviour have survived into a wide cross section of modern cultures (Buss, 1999).

In western consumer societies, gathering may have translated into comparison shopping, hunting into earning money to support the family. According to Dr Geoffrey Miller (then) of University College, London (UK – reported in the Daily Mail, 10 May 2001): 'It started with body painting, ornaments and fur' According to Miller, for females, shopping for fashion items is a form of sexual signalling. Women must keep giving off these signals to prevent their mates from straying. A man, on the other hand, may purchase expensive symbols to demonstrate his fitness as a provider, but tends to lose interest once the chase is over (Miller, 2001).

Even in the US, where gender equality in the workplace is greater than most countries, differences in shopping styles can be clearly observed. The female style involves searching, comparing, weighing the advantages and disadvantages of alternatives, finding the best value and taking a pride in the shopping activity (Underhill, 1999). This pride is justified as on average women make a 10 percent better cost saving than men do, making women the 'better shoppers' (Denison, 2003). Women have a more positive attitude to shopping and see the activity as a satisfying experience in itself. For women, shopping is a leisure and social activity in which they are more involved (Bakewell and Mitchell, 2004) and can express love for families and their social network (Miller 1998; Miller et al, 1998). Women shopping together spend nearly twice as long in store as do men shopping with women or other men (Underhill, 1999). Married women tend to take primary responsibility for shopping for the household (Dholakia et al, 1995). For adolescent girls, entertainment was as important a part of their shopping centre trips as was shopping for goods and services (Haytko and Baker, 2004). On the other hand, men see shopping as a mission and tend to go straight for what they want in a purposeful way (Underhill, 1999). For men, the focus is on the speed of the shopping process, achieved by sticking to familiar brands (also used by men as symbols of economic power) and by either visiting a familiar store and buying quickly or by being indifferent to which store is selected (Bakewell and Mitchell, 2004). Male emotional response to shopping comes at 'the kill' – the actual moment of purchase when their heart rate quickens. The stereotypes are not 100 percent accurate but in the UK have been found to apply to 80 percent of women and 70 percent of men (Denison, 2003). The styles have been found to be equally valid for e-shopping (Lindquist and Kaufman-Scarborough, 2000) see Boxes 10.1 and 10.2.

As with bricks shopping, the stereotype reverses when the product purchased is technical and expensive (Dholakia and Chiang, 2003).

Female shopping style – the gatherer
* Ritual of seeking and comparing
* Imagining and envisioning the merchandise in use
* Tally up the pros and cons
* Take (justified) pride in ability as shoppers
* The total shopping process (not just buying) is a leisure activity
* Women like to spend longer shopping than men do
* Women visit more shops than men do
* Women shop more often than men do
* Social interaction is an important part of shopping
* Women shop to express love for families and social networks

Male shopping styles – the hunter
* Men are incisive, decisive and determined shoppers
* Men's excitement with shopping is at the moment of 'kill' (purchase)
* Men try to complete the shopping activity in the shortest possible time
* Men prefer top brands, both as symbols of economic power and to save time
* Men's lack of patience means they often miss the best buy
* The men who do enjoy shopping shop for **power**: control over household products; and **achievement**: shop to win.

* But the stereotype reverses when the product is technical and expensive. Men do take a pride in shopping for (e.g.) cars and computers (and women are purposeful for those products).

Box 10.1   Are they from Venus or Mars?
Sources: Allegra (2002); Bakewell and Mitchell (2004); Denison (2003); Dholakia (1999); Dholakia and Chiang (2003); Lindquist and Kaufman-Scarborough (2000); Miller (1998); Miller et al (1998); Otnes and McGrath (2001); Underhill (1999).

The basis of evolutionary psychology has been founded on research demonstrating consistency of mating behaviour across widely different cultures. That is, if mating behaviour were culturally determined, it would tend to be significantly different between cultures. If mating behaviour is not culturally determined, it is therefore argued to be genetically based – i.e. people evolved to behave in those ways. The evolutionary approach can thus be challenged if female and male social cultures can be shown to converge in response to cultural changes of gender equality:

To the extent that traditional sexual division between wage labor and domestic labor disappears and women and men become similarly distributed into paid occupations, men and women should converge in their psychological attributes.

(Eagly and Wood, 2002)

Is this cultural stereotyping? Or is there any truth in this research? BBC News (2003) ran a story on the Denison (2003) research asking readers to post their own answers to these questions. Of 64 replies posted, 19 asked further questions or made different points ('Louise [who hates shopping] – will you marry me?' *Debt-ridden husband*). Of the remainder:

* 22 percent disagreed with the stereotypes
* 78 percent agreed.

Box 10.2   Male and female shopping stereotypes?

The Savannah hypothesis of shopping

The Savannah hypothesis of shopping can be stated as:

H1 Female and male shopping styles are evolutionarily determined, reflecting the gatherer and hunter roles respectively.

Using a parallel with Eagly's and Wood's (2002) challenge to Evolutionary Psychology in general, H1 can be tested as below:

H1a The differences between female and male shopping styles, reflecting the gatherer and hunter roles, are reasonably homogenous across various national cultures.

Testing the Savannah hypothesis of shopping

The objective of this chapter is to attempt to challenge the Savannah Hypothesis of Shopping in a similar way to that in which Eagly and Wood (2002) are seeking to challenge evolutionary psychology in general. If it can be demonstrated that male and female styles of shopping are converging, the hypothesis that these are evolutionarily determined could be rejected. Of course, 'it is difficult to predict anything, especially the future' (Dan Quayle, former US Vice President). Nevertheless, the chosen method here has been to attempt to forecast, using innovator/early adopter opinion leaders as judges, writing miniscenarios of male and female shopping styles across a range of national cultures in order to attempt to predict the degree of convergence. The participant judges to date have comprised Masters and MBA students of Marketing and Retail at three southern UK universities.

Such students were chosen as being young marketers who within a few years are likely to be earning and spending significantly more than the general population. They have the typical characteristics of opinion leaders (involvement and familiarity with the topic – Foxall et al, 1998), and also innovators and early adopters (younger, higher income and socio-economic status – Rogers, 1995). Thus, they are likely to be not only familiar with the latest marketing trends but also to be involved in forming the future of marketing, retail and shopping.

Fourteen 'mini focus groups' wrote shopping scenarios about the national culture(s) that they were most familiar with. Fourteen cultural nationalities were represented: nine judge participants represented the UK national culture, eight continental European, 25 Asian and two African, i.e. 44 judge participants in total.

Results

Analysis of the results of the scenarios indicated (percent of participant judges):

Hypothesis H1a

The differences between female and male shopping styles, reflecting the gatherer and hunter roles, are reasonably homogenous across various national cultures.

Support Hypothesis H1a	100 %
Reject Hypothesis H1a	0 %

Forecasts for the future

If shopping styles converge in the future, this will challenge the Savannah Hypothesis of Shopping. Although the forecasts from the participant judges are purely speculative, they do come from early adopters/opinion leaders. Therefore, they might provide some challenge to the hypothesis if female and male shopping styles can be demonstrated to be likely to converge, reflecting increasing gender equality in the workplace in some national cultures. The results based on the forecasts were (percentages of participant judges):

No future convergence is forecast	50 %
Some future convergence is forecast	50 %

In support of the Savannah Hypothesis, for example, the Greek national shopping culture was described as:

> *'Females motivated by emotion, spend a great amount of money [and] time, fashion sensitive.*
> *Males practical-orientated, lack of time, target orientated.'*

As an example of current support with partial future convergence forecast, a group representing the Indian national culture agreed that the sex and shopping stereotypes currently apply, but predicted for the future:

> *'Clothing – [these sex stereotypes will] not converge.*
> *Entertainment – converge.'*

The highest degree of forecast convergence concerned Turkey, where the female and male shopping styles:

> *'Seem to be closing in, but the mid point may never be reached.'*

In general, there were differences in shopping styles between the national cultures, but the differences between males and females seem to have been reasonably consistent across them. One of the biggest differences was between two countries that are actually close geographically and in cultural background: France and England. According to the participant judges, in France both sexes:

> *'Like shopping in markets and independent shops [much more than in the] UK – less out-of-town, love the stimulation of the market.'*

This was consistent with comments made in a focus group reported in Chapter 8 above, where UK shoppers found the markets and bars in Paris to be stimulating, and indeed, to be a reason for travelling to France.

Conversely, two of the most closely matched national cultures in terms of shopping style are furthest away geographically and in cultural background: the USA (based on the Underhill, 1999 description) and Japan, with the Japanese shoppers:

> *'Females fussy about product, price, quality, brand. Seek bargains, shop for satisfaction. Take time, brand, image and fashion conscious.*
> *'Males emphasise function.'*

Hypothesis H1a has received total support in terms of the current differences in shopping styles. For the forecasts to challenge the Savannah Hypothesis of Shopping, it would be necessary to link the forecast convergence of shopping styles to increasing gender equality in the workplace. This has not yet been indicated in the results: convergence has **not** so far been forecast for countries such as France and UK. Limited convergence has been forecast for countries such as India and Turkey – i.e. countries **not** noted for workplace gender equality.

Discussion and conclusion

In Chapter 7 above, attention was drawn to differences in shopping behaviour between female and male UK shoppers. Specifically, females tended to be more concerned with both the experience and the shops/products aspects than males were. This chapter has investigated male and female shopping styles across a range of national cultures. On the basis of the results of this small, preliminary study, the Savannah Hypothesis of Shopping cannot yet be rejected. Shopping styles were reasonably consistently different between males and females across a range of national cultures, mirroring the hunter and gather roles. On the basis of the limited evidence gathered so far, it is not possible to predict with confidence any significant changes in these differences.

The implication for shopping centres and retailers is that appropriate retail mixes may be reasonably stable across national cultures. Segmentation of offers may be more important for groups such as males *vs.* females rather than adapting to individual national cultures.

Part IV considers the potential impact of e-shopping on shopping centres. The next chapter, Chapter 11 concerns shoppers' motivations for e-shopping.

The growth of shopping centres in the UK actually began in 1964 with the Bull Ring in Birmingham (rebuilt in 2004) followed by other town centre schemes such as the Arndale Centre in Doncaster in 1968 (Davies and Bennison, 1979).

Part IV
Futurescapes

11
Shoppers' Motivations for E-shopping

This chapter is adapted from a paper delivered at the *International Conference on Recent Advances in Retailing and Services Science* (Dennis and Papamatthaiou 2003)[1]

Introduction

The previous parts of this book have mainly concerned 'Why people shop where they do?' in terms of choices of (bricks) shopping centres. For the future, shopping centres are facing increasing competition from e-retailers. This part of the book addresses e-shopping. Firstly, this chapter explores shopper's motivations for e-shopping rather than bricks (physical store) shopping.

Although several authors have commented on shoppers' motivations (See Chapter 8 above and e.g. Bloch et al, 1994; Dawson et al, 1998; Roy, 1994; Wakefield and Baker, 1998; Westbrook and Black, 1985), to date there has been little research into motivations for e-shopping and little comparison with shopping centres. A number of the studies of 'bricks' shopping have drawn attention to the importance of higher level shopping motivations as compared to utilitarian ones such as products and prices. For example, the quantitative Study 1 in Chapter 8 above indicated that 'Love', 'Self-esteem', 'Self-actualisation' and 'Accomplishment' were more prevalent than conventional attributes such as 'Variety of stores' and 'Compare brands and prices'. The qualitative Study 2 using six focus groups, found that the 'good' constructs

---

[1]Dennis C E and Papamatthaiou E (2003) 'Shoppers' motivations for e-shopping', 10th *International Conference on Recent Advances in Retailing and Services Science*, Portland, OR, EIRASS.

were higher order at a more attractive centre than at a less attractive one and *vice versa*. For 'bricks' shopping, entertainment has been demonstrated to be a component of image and a motivator for some shoppers (Sit et al, 2003). Many classifications of shopping motivations have been proposed, but commonly a distinction is drawn between lower level or utilitarian motivations as compared with higher level or hedonic ones (see Chapter 8 above and e.g. Babin et al, 1994).

According to 'Wheel of retailing' theory new formats such as e-retail enter the market on the basis of utilitarian offers and low prices (Dholakia and Uusitalo, 2002). Few studies have attempted to test this proposition by examining the extent to which e-shopping is motivated by price, although Foucault and Scheufele (2002), in a study of student textbook purchasing, found that price was **not** significantly associated with online buying. On the other hand, that study did indicate a strong link between talking about e-shopping with friends and intention to e-shop in the future.

Kolesar and Galbraith (2000) reviewed the importance of higher level needs such as personal interaction and control, pointing out that e-retailers have difficulty in satisfying customers needs for these. On the other hand, they pointed out that loyalty and affinity programmes can be successful in satisfying self-esteem and belonging needs. Their study, though, did not gather primary data. Rohm and Swaminathan (2004), in a study comparing a sample of e-shoppers with non-e-shoppers found that social interaction, variety seeking and convenience were all significant motivators for e-shopping. Recreation, although a motivator for bricks shopping, was not significant for e-shopping. Those authors concluded that e-shopping appealed more to functional shoppers than to recreational shoppers. This was consistent with the results of Lee's and Tan's (2003) experiment with 179 undergraduate participants. The study found that shoppers were more likely to shop in store for products/services high in purchase risks. The results, though, were statistically significant for services only as opposed to tangible products.

On the other hand, we consider that the variety seeking motivator is consistent with the substantial use of e-shopping for 'hedonic' goods and services such as books, music and travel. Childers and colleagues (2001) found enjoyment to be a strong predictor of attitude towards e-shopping. In that study, 'usefulness' and 'enjoyment' were equally predictive of attitude overall. Usefulness was the better predictor for grocery, enjoyment more so for the examples that the authors described as 'hedonic': Amazon, Hot Hot Hot (sauces), Wal-mart, K Mart and Bookstore.

The aim of the current chapter is to add to understanding of e-shopping motivations and examine potential implications for e-retailers.

Research framework

The study of e-shopping motivations entailed investigating the hedonic aspects of e-shopping in comparison with the more utilitarian, goal-orientated ones. Childers et al (2001) used the term **'enjoyment'** to embody the hedonic aspects, while **usefulness** and **ease of use** denoted the utilitarian ones. Usefulness refers to the value of the outcomes, whereas ease of use concerns the process of e-shopping without any great difficulty or effort. In studying these constructs, Childers and colleagues invoked the 'Technology Acceptance Model' (TAM), developed by Davis (1989) to model users' adoption of information technology at work. Childers and colleagues built on the TAM model by adding three more constructs, **convenience**, **navigation**, and **substitutability**. Convenience concerns, for example, saving time or shopping 24/7. Navigation concerns flexibility in tracking down products and information and the ability to move fluidly through the shopping environment (Novak et al, 2000). Layout alternatives have been addressed in detail by Vrechopoulos (2001; Vrechopoulos et al, 2002; 2004) – considered further in the 'Discussion' section of this chapter below. Substitutability means the ability of e-shopping to substitute for the lack of sensory inputs.

In the Childers study, usefulness, ease of use, convenience, navigation and substitutability were all found to contribute significantly to **attitude** to e-shopping. E-retailers will be more interested in modelling e-shopping **behaviour** rather than just attitude. Attitude/behaviour modelling has been improved in recent years by the addition of two further variables to the basic model. These are, firstly, the **subjective norm** (SN), i.e. an individual's perception of the social pressures to perform or not the (e-shopping) behaviour (Ajzen's and Fishbein's 1980 'Theory of Reasoned Action'). Secondly, **perceived behavioural control** (PBC) refers to people's perceptions of their capability (ease/difficulty and availability of resources) of performing a behaviour such as e-shopping. Modelling behaviour from the three constructs, attitude, SN and PBC constitutes Ajzen's (1991) 'Theory of Planned Behaviour' (TPB). TPB has been little used to date in retail studies, but by way of example King and Dennis (2002; 2003) triangulated using quantitative and qualitative techniques to demonstrate improvements to the basic attitude/behaviour model that arose from including the SN and PBC variables. Shim and colleagues (2001) demonstrated that attitude towards e-shopping and PBC were a predictors of intention to e-shop (along with information search and previous e-shopping experience), but in that study, SN was marginally significant only at $p = 0.10$. Although not specifically using TPB, Foucault's and Scheufele's (2002) study effectively confirmed one of the aspects of SN in e-shopping, demonstrating the significance of discussing with friends. In both TAM and TPB, the variables are supposed to be conceptually independent of one another (Davis, 1989; East, 1997).

This current chapter aims to investigate e-shopping behaviour by testing the broad postulation that the dependent variables reported frequency and value can be modelled using the extended TAM model and TPB as a framework. The independent variables were attitude (components: enjoyment, usefulness, ease of use, convenience, navigation, and substitutability), SN and PBC. The matrix of specific hypotheses is in Table 11.1. For example:

H1v Reported e-shopping value is significantly associated with enjoyment

H7f Reported e-shopping frequency is significantly associated with subjective norm (SN).

Table 11.1 Hypotheses matrix

Reported e-shopping is significantly associated with:	E-shopping value	E-shopping frequency
Enjoyment	H1v	H1f
Usefulness	H2v	H2f
Ease of use	H3v	H3f
Convenience	H4v	H4f
Navigation	H5v	H5f
Substitutability	H6v	H6f
Subjective norm (SN)	H7v	H7f
Perceived behavioural control (PBC)	H8v	H8f

Procedure

The main research instrument consisted of a self-completion questionnaire. The dependent variables were elicited from the questions 'How often do you use the Internet for product purchases' and 'How much do you spend approximately on online purchases'. For the independent 'attitude' variables, each component (i.e. for H1 to H6 inclusive) consisted of three questions. Two questions were included for SN (H7), representing the two dimensions of SN: the support of friends and family and the online buying behaviour of people important to the respondent. For PBC (H8) a single question was included, concerning the knowledge and ability to make a purchase on the Internet. The questions for the independent variables were recorded on 5-point Likert-type scales, 'strongly disagree' to 'strongly agree' or 'very unlikely' to 'very likely' as appropriate. For analysis, these answers were coded '1' to '5' and used as if they were continuous scales.

Respondents consisted of a convenience sample of undergraduate students at a west London (UK) university. One hundred and sixty self-completion questionnaires were distributed and 150 usable, completed responses received back. This sample cannot be considered representative of all UK e-shoppers. Nevertheless, there are a number of reasons why a sample of university students is particularly suitable for exploratory work. Firstly, university students tend to be more active e-shoppers than the general population and the sample included a high proportion of e-shoppers. Sixty percent reported having e-shopped at some time (7 percent described themselves as 'regular Internet shoppers'). Secondly, graduates have historically been found to have higher discretionary income than non-graduates. The students in the sample can be considered as the 'comparison shoppers of tomorrow'. Thirdly, the sample was younger and better educated than the national average shopper, i.e. having the typical characteristics of 'opinion leaders'. Shoppers such as these are likely to be early adopters and their questionnaire answers are therefore possibly indicative of future shopping patterns.

Results and analysis

The first stage in processing the results was to construct compound variables for those having more than one item. The variables are listed in Table 11.2, along with the Cronbach alpha. To test the hypotheses, each variable was investigated for association with the dependent variables using ordinary least squares (OLS) linear regression. The regression beta coefficient and the R^2 values are included in Table 11.2 as indicators of the strength of the association of the variables. The p-values are also included as a measure of the significance of the association of the variables. The independent variables are ranked in order of degree of association with reported e-shopping spending.

Table 11.2 Compound variables and their association with reported e-shopping

Variable	Alpha	Beta	R^2	p	Beta	R^2	p
PBC	N/A	0.50	0.25	0.000	0.46	0.21	0.000
Convenience	0.67	0.44	0.19	0.000	0.39	0.15	0.000
Usefulness	0.70	0.34	0.12	0.000	0.36	0.13	0.000
SN	0.26	0.30	0.09	0.000	0.25	0.06	0.002
Navigation	0.37	0.29	0.08	0.000	0.34	0.12	0.000
Ease of use	0.61	0.29	0.08	0.000	0.31	0.10	0.000
Enjoyment	0.69	0.28	0.08	0.001	0.36	0.13	0.000
Substitutability	0.56	-0.01	0.00	0.94	-0.01	0.00	0.91

The substitutability variable was not associated with the e-shopping measures and the p values of >0.9 can reasonably justify rejection of hypotheses H6v and H6f. Substitutability was therefore omitted from further processing. All other hypotheses were highly significantly supported, i.e. H1, H2, H3, H4, H5, H7 and H8, v and f variants of each.

Using either the beta coefficients or the R^2 as parameters, the first three variables in the ranking are the same for association with both e-shopping spending and frequency: 'PBC', 'convenience' and 'usefulness'. It is interesting to note, though, that in terms of frequency, 'enjoyment' was equally ranked with 'usefulness'. It is intuitively natural that the main variables associated with e-shopping concern the ability to do so and the convenience relative to 'bricks' shopping. Once these lower level motivations are accounted for, the higher level motivation of 'enjoyment' is just as strong a determinant of e-shopping frequency as is 'usefulness'. 'Usefulness' concerns the outcomes of the shopping processes and it is therefore logical that this variable has a higher ranking for spending than for frequency – i.e. when the motivation is to buy, the successful outcome is to have spent.

The alpha value is an indicator of the degree of association of the individual components of the compound variables. In each case, the association was significant ('usefulness' at $p = 0.05$, all others $p = 0.001$). Nevertheless, for the components of compound variables to be considered as measuring identical constructs, higher alpha values would normally be expected, particularly for SN and Navigation. Therefore these compound variables were not suitable in their present form for modelling e-shopping behaviour. In order to progress to such a model, the variables were first disaggregated into component items (see Appendix 11.1 to this chapter, Table 11.7). This disaggregation allowed the hypotheses to be re-tested against the individual components. In this re-test, each individual component of 'substitutability' remained **not** significantly associated with the dependent variables; H6v and H6f were confirmed **not** supported. All three components of 'usefulness' were significantly associated with both dependent variables; H2v and H2f were confirmed supported. PBC consisted of only one item and remained supported. For each of the other attitude variables and also SN, one of the individual items was not significantly associated with one or both of the dependent variables. The effect can be summarised as below:

- Hypotheses confirmed supported – H1f, H4v, H5f
- Hypotheses receiving qualified support – H1v, H3f, H3v, H4f, H5v, H7v, H7f.

Table 11.3   Principal components analysis

Component	Item	Loading R
TAM component	Clear and understandable	0.75
	Convenient for me	0.70
	Useful for buying whatever I want	0.66
	Enhances my effectiveness in shopping	0.65
	Not boring	0.38
TPB component	Friends and family would support my buying through Internet	0.81
	I have the knowledge and ability to make a purchase on the Internet	0.61
Navigation	Allows flexibility in tracking down information	0.89
	Allows me to move more fluidly through the shopping environment	0.61
Involvement (enjoyment)	Involves me in the shopping process	0.88

From the above, it can be seen that the hypothesised extended TAM plus TPB relationship is not an ideal model, despite most of the hypothesised relationships receiving at least qualified support. Because of inconsistency in the items of the hypothesised dimensions, examination of the disaggregated items was necessary to confirm the hypothesis testing. Unfortunately, these disaggregated items cannot readily be combined directly into a superior model due to multi co-linearity and duplication. In the next stage, those items not significantly associated with the dependent variables were discarded. Secondly, a simplified model was derived based on Principal Components Analysis with Varimax rotation. Limiting extraction to Eigenvalues over 1.0, and suppressing component scores below 0.35, the four components reported in Table 11.3 were obtained. Each item has been included once only, in the component in which it loads highest. The first component included only items hypothesised from TAM, i.e. 'clear and understandable' (ease of use); 'convenient for me' (convenience); 'useful in buying whatever I want' and 'enhances my effectiveness in shopping' (usefulness); and 'not boring' (enjoyment). This component has therefore been named 'TAM component'.

Table 11.4 Stepwise linear regression of reported e-shopping spending vs. components

Component	Beta	R^2 change	R^2 cumulative	p value
Constant (scaled equivalent to beta)	0.46			0.000
TPB component	0.47	0.22	0.22	0.000
TAM component	0.27	0.07	0.29	0.000
Involvement (enjoyment)	0.23	0.05	0.34	0.001
Navigation	0.16	0.03	0.37	0.016

Similarly, the second component included only items hypothesised from TPB: 'Friends and family would support my buying through Internet' (SN) and 'I have the knowledge and ability to make a purchase on the Internet' (PBC). This component has therefore been named 'TPB component'. Again, conveniently from the broad postulation, the second component included only navigation items: 'Allows flexibility in tracking down information' and 'Allows me to move more fluidly through the shopping environment'. Accordingly, this component has been named 'Navigation'. Finally, the fourth 'component' contained only one item loading above 0.35: 'Involves me in the shopping process', originally hypothesised as 'enjoyment'. This component has therefore been named 'involvement (enjoyment)'.

Table 11.5 Stepwise linear regression of reported e-shopping frequency vs. components

Component	Beta	R^2 change	R^2 cumulative	p value
Constant (scaled equivalent to beta)	0.35			0.000
TPB component	0.40	0.22	0.16	0.000
TAM component	0.34	0.11	0.27	0.000
Involvement (enjoyment)	0.23	0.05	0.32	0.001
Navigation				N.s.

This exploratory components analysis has actually produced models superior to those originally hypothesised as the extended TAM plus TPB model. The OLS multiple regressions of the components *vs.* reported e-shopping spending and frequency are reported in Tables 11.4 and 11.5 respectively.

Discussion and implications

This chapter set out to test the general postulation that e-shopping behaviour can be modelled using the extended TAM and the TPB. With the exception of the 'substitutability' aspect of TAM, This general postulation has been supported. A number of the specific hypotheses following from the general postulation have also been supported. On the other hand, the most satisfactory way to model the data has been demonstrated **not** to be based on the assumption that the variables of these theories were independent of one another. The more flexible approach using principal components analysis still supported the postulated theories in general but resulted in the omission of some of the measurement items from the final models and the qualification of some of the specific hypotheses. The final summary of the specific hypotheses tests is reported in Table 11.6. The dimensions have been ranked in overall order of significance based on the consistency of support on both dependent variables (Table 11.6), the order of entry of components into the multiple regressions (Tables 11.4 and 11.5), the item loadings in the components (Table 11.3) and the ranking in the first stage hypotheses tests (Table 11.2).

Table 11.6   Hypotheses results in ranked order of significance of the dimensions

Reported e-shopping is significantly associated with:	E-shopping value	E-shopping frequency
Perceived behavioural control (PBC)	H8v: Supported	H8f: Supported
Usefulness	H2v: Supported	H2f: Supported
Convenience	H4v: Supported	H4f: Qualified support
Enjoyment	H1v: Qualified support	H1f: Supported
Subjective norm (SN)	H7v: Qualified support	H7f: Qualified support
Navigation	H5v: Qualified support	H5f: Qualified support
Ease of use	H3v: Qualified support	H3f: Qualified support
Substitutability	H6v: Rejected	H6f: Rejected

Perceived behavioural control, PBC

Overall, this was the most significant dimension. It consisted of the single item: 'I have the knowledge and ability to make a purchase on the Internet'. It is understandable that someone without the knowledge or ability is unlikely to e-shop. The general population is likely to include a higher proportion than in this sample of people lacking such skills and this may well be one of the main factors inhibiting the growth of e-shopping. E-retailers would be well advised to keep the process as simple as possible. Mailshots or mail order deliveries could include simple education literature and perhaps a demonstration CD or DVD. In this sample, 96 percent knew how to use the Internet and 100% had access at the university (87 percent had access at home). The knowledge and ability lacked must therefore have referred mainly to the making of purchases, rather than the use of the Internet. E-retailers might therefore be well advised to implement market education programmes on how to e-shop.

Usefulness

This was the second-ranked dimension. The original compound variable contained three items relating to enhancing effectiveness in shopping, usefulness in buying desired products and improvement in shopping ability. Each of these was individually significantly associated with both dependent variables. With an alpha value of 0.7, the compound variable was a more consistent measure than were the other compound variables (except for substitutability). Only 'useful in buying whatever I want' appeared in the final component analysis model, but the compound variable could arguably be substituted with reasonable confidence. Turning this finding around, it is as expected that a lack of usefulness in buying desired products would be associated with less use of the Internet for shopping. E-retailers are recommended to ensure that they include the widest and/or deepest ranges of products, taking advantage of e-commerce's strength in facilitating distribution chain efficiency and product sourcing. For a retailer selling a huge range of products, flexibility and fluidity of navigation must be central to shoppers maximising the usefulness – addressed under the 'navigation' section below.

Convenience

This was the third-ranked dimension. Each of the three items was significantly associated with e-shopping spending although one, 'less time consuming' was not significantly associated with e-shopping frequency. Shoppers who are concerned about saving time may well buy more per session rather than at frequent, lower value sessions, as a time-saving strategy. Only one item, 'convenient for me' appeared in the final component analysis model. E-retailers should ensure maximum convenience for shoppers. Simplifying and speeding-up the process and providing simple, 24/7 help facilities can improve the convenience of many sites.

Enjoyment

Enjoyment has often been reported as a motivator for 'bricks' shopping (see Chapter 9). This chapter, as with the Childers et al (2001) study also demonstrated enjoyment to be an important dimension for e-shopping. The Childers work found enjoyment to be more important for e-shopping that they described as hedonic as opposed to utilitarian. Most of the e-shopping carried out by this sample would appear to fall into the hedonic category, with Amazon most popular; CD Wow; eBay (auctions); Ticketmaster (show tickets); Ryannair, EasyJet, and Opodo (air tickets) also used frequently. Tesco and Sainsbury (grocery supermarkets) were also mentioned, but as only two percent of the sample bought groceries by e-shopping (possibly low because some e-grocers refuse to deliver to university halls of residence), it was not possible to analyse separately those who shopped for utilitarian products.

All three of the enjoyment items were significantly associated with e-shopping frequency, although one, 'fun for its own sake', was not significantly associated with spending. This is understandable as shoppers who e-shop for fun rather than to purchase products are presumably likely to buy less products. Similarly, in Table 11.2, enjoyment ranked only seventh in association with spending, but third equal in association with e-shopping frequency. There is an exact parallel here with bricks shopping, where entertainment promotions were found to increase visit frequency by more than the increase in sales (Parsons, 2003). Parsons pointed out that customers could be drawn in by appealing to hedonic motivations, and then switched to buying through the use of utilitarian (e.g. price-based) ones. The other two items appeared in the final component analysis model: 'not boring' as an item in the TAM component and 'involvement' as a component on its own. Childers and colleagues pointed out that navigation and convenience were also 'immersive, involving characteristics of the interactive experience'. They recommended including 'images, video, colour, humor, sound, music, games, animation and all the other aspects of interactive, networked multimedia that make it enjoyable' – i.e. web atmospherics. We would add a specific recommendation that e-retailers should address 'involvement' directly. Ideas include chat rooms; bulletin boards; customer written stories and product reviews; suggestion boxes; personalisation of the web site offers; and even customisation of the products. Many of these techniques are used enthusiastically by eBay (auction site) and Amazon, first and second ranked UK e-retailers respectively. eBay are particularly strong on involvement, with visitors spending on average one hour and 11 minutes on the site, one of the longest of UK e-retailers. Visitors return to the site frequently to check on items they are buying or selling. eBay is one of few UK e-retailers to achieve over one billion page views per month (www.nielsen-netratings.com). With users finding enough interest to return again and again, it can be postulated that a highly involving site would also be expected to be 'not boring' – and maybe also 'fun for its own sake'. Some ideas on customisation and personalisation follow, largely drawn from Chicksand and Knowles (2002).

Customisation

Customisation refers to self-designed products. Shopper involvement in the design of the products adds considerably to the personal feel of the shopping experience. Shopper satisfaction can be enhanced by more closely matching to exact needs. For example clothing could be customised using a body scan. Shoppers can visit selected Levi stores for the scan, which is then held on a database. In theory, this could then be used for e-shopping, incorporating a 3D virtual closet. Shoppers could be confident that the clothes would fit (but Levi themselves do not actually sell *via* e-retail). In the case of Nike, shoppers can customise shoes, not just colours and styles but also for example with a name or message. A potential drawback of this system, though, is concern over what happens if the customer wants to return the product for any reason? Fanbuzz e-retail clothes, allowing shoppers to decide their own styles, colours, graphics and sizes. These custom items are 10–20 percent more expensive than non-custom ones, but many customers are prepared to pay more for customised products (Evans, 2001).

Personalisation

Again taking the example of clothing, the Eddie Bauer 'virtual closet' allows shoppers to match up items with a 'Style Builder'. Some clothing e-retailers such as Land's End keep a database of sizes and items bought that is available on your next visit, personalising the experience and saving purchase time. The technology allows shoppers to create virtual models of themselves online to try on clothes – claimed to increase the likelihood of a sale by 19 percent (Lorek, 2001). In the case of cosmetics, EZFace provide a preview of beauty products demonstrated on a photo of the shopper – and a chat line so that shoppers can discuss the photo with friends, also improving the involvement (enjoyment) component.

Subjective norm (SN)

The originally hypothesised SN compound variable contained two items, but only 'friends and family would strongly support my decision to e-shop' was significantly associated with the dependent variables. This is in line with the Foucault's and Scheufele's (2002) finding that there was a strong link between talking about e-shopping with friends and intention to e-shop in the future. 'Buy online because people who are important to me do it' was not significantly associated. The qualified support for the hypothesised SN relationship reflects the finding of Shim et al (2001) that SN was only partially associated with intention to e-shop (p = 0.1). The finding of this chapter is more precise, though, with the **direct** input of friends and family significant, but e-shopping because others do so was not significant. Some of the recommendations for enjoyment are also relevant to SN, as the most involving web sites (such as eBay) facilitate the building of e-friendships – and presumably such e-friends are likely to be supportive of e-shopping.

Navigation

All three of the items in the compound navigation variable were significantly associated with e-shopping frequency; although the 'finding products' item was not significantly associated with spending. This is counter-intuitive, as finding products would be expected to be pre-requisite to buying them. Further research is needed to investigate this apparent anomaly. The other two items, 'flexibility' and 'fluidity' conveniently loaded together in the same component in the final model. The navigation component, though, only appeared in the 'spending' model and not the 'frequency' model. Childers et al (2002) suggested that the main elements of navigation are: (i) Clear layout and easy navigation, e.g. a navigation bar on the top of each page; (ii) One-click (or at least minimum click) purchase; and (iii) The provision of useful links, e.g. to more product or subject information. The e-store layout is central to navigation. In the 'bricks' store, layout contributes to image and manipulates shopper traffic flow. Layout of the 'clicks' store can be seen as performing similar functions for online shoppers. There are a variety of different patterns of layout used instore, some of which can be thought of as having equivalents online. The main types of 'bricks' layouts are: grid; guided flow; free-flow and

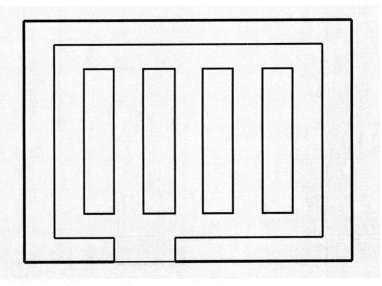

Figure 11.1 Simplified representation of a grid layout instore
Source: The author.

boutique. Vrechopoulos (2001) has proposed a combination layout for
e-retailing, which he has dubbed 'free-grid'.

Grid The grid layout, illustrated schematically in Figure 11.1, is
commonly applied instore for bricks grocery supermarkets. It is charac-
terised by long rows with limited passage between the aisles. High-
demand and high margin items are typically positioned near the
entrance where they will be seen by most shoppers. An advantage of
this layout is the possibility of designing shopper flow so that most
shoppers see most of the store. Guided flow, illustrated schematically
in Figure 11.2, is a variant of grid. It consists of one long path giving
massive exposure of the product range. In the clicks store the 'grid'
layout, illustrated schematically in Figure 11.3, has a similar effect to
grid and guided flow. For e-retail websites, the linear navigation layout
usually does not lead through all pages, but rather section-by-section
through a hierarchy. Customers have to navigate through the main
product categories and sub-categories to find an end product. In this
form of layout, shoppers cannot access an end product from the home
page or the main category level. Once shoppers are at the end product
level, they cannot directly reach an end product from a different
category. As with the bricks store, a disadvantage of this layout is that

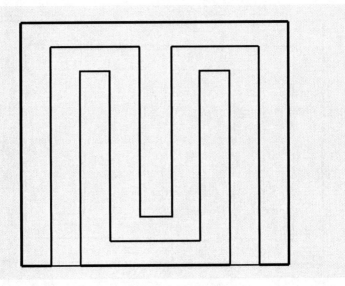

Figure 11.2   Simplified representation of a guided flow layout instore
Source: The author.

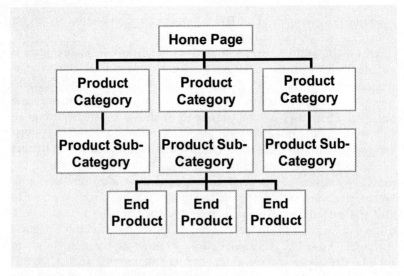

Figure 11.3   Simplified representation of a grid layout e-retail store
Source: The author, based on Vrechopolis, 2001; 2004.

it can exhaust the patience of shoppers, detracting from enjoyment and ease of use.

Free-flow   This layout, illustrated schematically in Figure 11.4, is frequently used by bricks department and fashion stores. It is better for 'lifestyle' displays, with products displayed by usage pattern rather than product category. A major disadvantage compared to the guided flow in particular is that shoppers often miss many products. In the e-store version, illustrated schematically in Figure 11.5, shoppers entering an e-retail website free flow layout can go immediately to an end product by using a catalogue or a search system. The layout allows customers to directly access any page in the e-store from any other page. Some types of e-retail website restrict navigation in a similar way to the boutique variant, such that shoppers can access only those end products that are placed in 'department' in which they are navigating at the time. To obtain wider free flow access they have to move to another department.

Free-grid   Vrechopoulos (2001) carried out experimental research into e-shoppers' preferences for site layout. As a result, He proposed a hybrid layout combining a grid hierarchical tree structure with free-flow's navigation capability illustrated schematically in Figure 11.6. Shoppers can either move through the e-store in a logical progression through departments or obtain direct access to end products using a

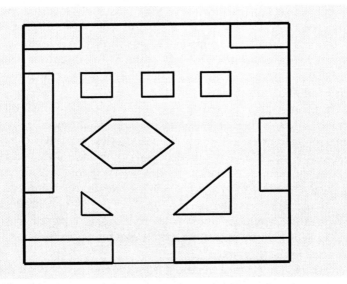

Figure 11.4   Simplified representation of a free-flow layout instore
Source: The author.

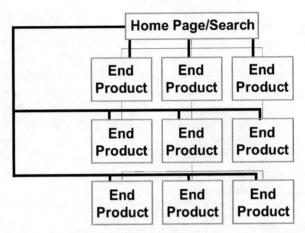

Figure 11.5   Simplified representation of a free-flow layout e-retail store
Source: The author, based on Vrechopolis, 2001; 2004.

search engine or catalogue. Product categories, sub-categories and end products are displayed through-out the shopper's visit to the store. The catalogue displays the lists corresponding to the level in which the shoppers are at the time, i.e. main categories, sub-categories or end products. Participants in the Vrechopoulos study reported that they preferred the catalogue to be 'left-framed'. A screen display divided into two frames is recommended; although this does mot necessarily imply the use of 'Frames' software. Rather, the intention is to show navigation information in a reasonably consistent format down the left hand edge of each page.

The main choices of the shopper entering the so-called free-grid layout are: 'Press to see the main categories' or 'Search'. At any time during the visit, shoppers can return to the main categories and navigate in a linear fashion. Search can be by: product categories and sub-categories; end products; or keyword/free-text. At each level, the contents are displayed in the main section of the screen, with the relevant catalogue level in the left frame. For example, having searched for an end product, that product with description, information and price is displayed in the main screen, whilst at the same time the other products in the sub-category are listed in the left frame.

Vrechopoulos claimed the benefits for the shopper of the free-grid to be the combination of **entertainment** (as with free-flow surfing – the enjoyment dimension) with **content** (simple to find with the hierar-

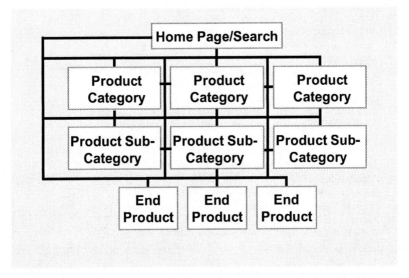

Figure 11.6 Simplified representation of a free grid layout e-retail store
Source: The author, based on Vrechopolis, 2001.

chical grid – the navigation dimension). Vrechopoulos found that the entertainment aspect improved image and web atmosphere, by not rushing shoppers to leave the store as soon as they have made their intended purchase. The benefit for the e-retailer is better shopper satisfaction than the hierarchical grid (not having to wade through irrelevant pages) combined with a longer shopper dwell time and hopefully a higher spending than usual with more conventional layout designs. The free-grid layout and the recommendations in Box 11.1 should considerably assist the flexibility and fluidity aspects of navigation.

Ease of use

Two of the ease of use items were significantly associated with both of the dependent variables, but 'requires mental effort' was not. Perhaps this is because the main alternative to e-shopping, 'bricks', also requires mental effort? One of the items, 'clear and understandable' loaded in the 'TAM' component in the final model. Ease of use is important because switching costs are lower on the web – customers are more promiscuous than in store and more likely to switch from a poor website. The average user is impatient and many are not computer literate. Therefore, usability is a key criterion. According to Childers et al (2001), in addition to navigation issues, a major element

- Provide a simple and concise hierarchical tree structure with information on the layout of categories and sub-categories
- Provide alternative search and navigation facilities
- Keep product assortment and layout constant during navigation
- Continuously display the catalogue and search facilities in the left frame
- Display in the catalogue only the level that shoppers are in (product category, sub-category or end product)
- Where possible, avoid forcing shoppers to scroll up, down or sideways
- Provide a simplified store map with links continuously in the left frame
- Provide a continuous shopping basket management display with running total and easy increase/decrease quantities and select/unselect products
- Design the layout to present relevant personalised, entertaining and dynamic features to the shopper (e.g. personalised product recommendation, frequently updated content and information)
- Include illustrations and product information for each end product
- Include an 'add to basket' button within each product description
- Display product in the main (right frame) screen, one product at a time.

Box 11.1   E-store layout tips
Source: Adapted from Vrechopoulos (2001).

of ease of use is simplicity – complicated graphics and sophisticated design get in the way of buying. A McKinsey study found that the average web user is impatient, and the quicker they can find their way around sites, the more likely they are to purchase (McGovern, 2002). The 'layout' recommendations under 'navigation' above are aimed at improving ease of use and in particular making the use of an e-retail site clear and understandable.

Haubl and Trifts (2000) investigated how e-retailers could enhance ease of use by providing interactive decision aids. Their experiment indicated that both a 'Recommendation Agent' (RA) and a 'Comparison Matrix' (CM) improved ease of use and encouraged e-shopping. The RA allowed shoppers to more effectively screen a potentially large set of alternatives, using their own attribute importance weights and minimum acceptable attribute levels. The CM allows shoppers to organise information about multiple products and to rank alternatives according to any attribute. At one time, the Lycos search site was developing the PersonaLogic system for products such as cars. Shoppers would answer a few questions on how much they wanted to spend, what features were important to them and so on. They could also specify whether particular attributes (say, number of seats, air bags, power or fuel economy) were 'nice to have' or mandatory. They would also make trade offs between (e.g.) lower price/higher reliability, better safety/higher performance and so on. The result would be an ordered list of models that best fitted the requirements. Such systems are still rare but there is considerable potential for developing future use. Some 'Shopbots' (e-shopping aids that compare offerings from different e-retailers) use simplified versions to aid shopper decision-making (e.g., see the US-based www.activebuyersguide.com for cameras, computers, electronics and pets).

Substitutability

This is the one aspect of the hypothesised models that was rejected. This means that with reasonable confidence we can **reject** an association between the belief that e-shopping can substitute for 'bricks' shopping and e-shopping behaviour. The finding indicates that shoppers do not expect e-shopping to substitute for 'bricks' shopping in terms of knowledge of product and its quality. This is in contrast to the Childers et al (2001) study where substitutability was found to be associated with attitude to e-shopping. The reasons for the discrepancy between the two studies (Childers USA shoppers compared with this chapter UK) merits further investigation.

Conclusions

With the exception of the 'substitutability' dimension, which was not associated with e-shopping, the postulated extended Technology Acceptance Model (TAM) and Theory of Planned Behaviour (TPB) were supported in general terms. On the basis of these results though, these models are best applied with a degree of flexibility. In particular, for successfully modelling e-shopping behaviour, the assumption of independence of the variables should be relaxed. In this instance, exploratory component analysis provided the most satisfactory model. The main hypothesised dimensions (except for substitutability) were still represented in the final model. These were, in order of significance: Perceived behavioural control (PBC); Usefulness; Convenience; Enjoyment; Subjective norm (SN); Navigation; and Ease of use. This research has been exploratory in nature, and further investigation is recommended, in particular to confirm the components and develop more concrete recommendations for e-retailers.

The following chapter, Chapter 12, continues the e-shopping theme with a comparison of e-shopping with shopping centres.

Note

Other variables not included in the theoretical analysis may affect attitude and e-shopping behaviour. One major, oft reported concern is security (see, e.g. Fenech, 2000). Although not hypothesised as part of the theory treatment, three 'security' items were included in the questionnaire. One, 'the e-retailers are trustworthy' was significantly associated with both dependent variables. Including this variable did not however improve the final models.

Appendix 11.1

Table 11.7 Disaggregated items, ranked by degree of association with e-shopping value

Item	Construct	Value R^2	Sig.	Frequency R^2	Sig.
I have the knowledge and the ability to make a purchase on the Internet	PBC	0.246	***	0.21	***
The e-retailers are trustworthy	Security	0.22	***	0.15	***
Internet allows me to shop whenever I want	Convenience	0.20	***	0.19	***
Using the Internet for transactions is convenient for me	Convenience	0.14	***	0.17	***
Internet enhances my effectiveness in shopping	Usefulness	0.13	***	0.15	***
My friends/family would strongly support my decision to buy a product/ service through the Internet	SN	0.09	***	0.06	**
Online shopping involves me in the shopping process	Enjoyment	0.07	**	0.06	**
Internet allows me flexibility in tracking down information	Navigation	0.07	**	0.06	**
Online shopping is boring (scale reversed)	Enjoyment	0.06	**	0.10	***
Internet is useful in buying whatever I want	Usefulness	0.06	**	0.07	***
Internet allows me to move fluidly through the shopping environment	Navigation	0.06	**	0.04	*
Internet for shopping purposes is clear and understandable	Ease of use	0.05	**	0.09	***
Online shopping is easy	Ease of use	0.04	*	0.05	**
Internet improves my shopping ability	Usefulness	0.04	*	0.04	*
Online shopping is less time consuming	Convenience	0.04	*	0.004	
Online shopping is fun for its own sake	Enjoyment	0.02		0.06	**

Table 11.7 Disaggregated items, ranked by degree of association with e-shopping value – *continued*

Item	Construct	Value R^2	Sig.	Frequency R^2	Sig.
Online shopping does not require a lot of mental effort	Ease of use	0.02		0.02	
It is better for me to purchase a service than a product, concerning the ability to examine a product's quality, size etc.	Substitutability	0.02		0.005	
Internet allows me to judge a product's quality as accurately as an in-person appraisal	Substitutability	0.02		0.001	
Finding products and information using the Internet requires a lot of exploring (reverse scale)	Navigation	0.01		0.06	**
I buy online because people who are important to me, do it	SN	0.004		0.007	
The information given on the Internet about a product is a good substitute for seeing and touching it	Substitutability	0.0007		0.001	
Online experience will offer knowledge of a product similar to that available from a personal examination	Substitutability	0.0005		0.001	

Notes – significant at p values: *** = 0.001; ** = 0.01; * = 0.05.

The first regional shopping centre in the UK (i.e. with at least 50 000 m² gross retail area) was the Arndale Centre, Poole, opened in 1969 (Guy, 1994b).

12

E-shopping Compared with Shopping Centres

An earlier version of this chapter was published in *Qualitative Market Research: An International Journal* (Dennis et al, 2002c).[1]

Introduction

Despite the dot.com crash of 2000, online shopping is growing in the UK with sales having reached at least £3.3 billion by 2003 (Verdict, 2003). This represents only two percent of all retail sales but the proportion is predicted to rise to five percent within a year or two (BCSC, 2001) and 10 percent by 2009 (Gibson, 1999; Verdict, 2003). Other estimates are even higher. The industry body, the Interactive Media in Retail Group (IMRG, 2003) for example, estimated that e-retail had already reached seven percent of total retail sales. 'Most people' are prepared to buy groceries, books, CDs and even clothes by e-shopping (RICS, 2000). Books, DVDs and software are high on 'factual search' (Shim et al, 2001) and thus natural for e-retailing, but for other categories such as groceries and clothing are also increasing (Figure 12.3). It has been forecast that 94 percent of e-retailing will be at the expense of existing channels (perhaps half of this diverted from catalogue shopping, half from high street retailers – BCSC, 2001), with only 6 percent arising from incremental growth (PreFontayne, 1999). According to IMRG, there are about 4 million people in the UK who spend an average of £3000 to £5000 per year online (IMRG, 2003).

---

[1] Dennis C E, Harris L and Sandhu B (2002c) 'From bricks to clicks: understanding the e-consumer', *Qualitative Market Research: An International Journal*, 5 (4): 281–290.

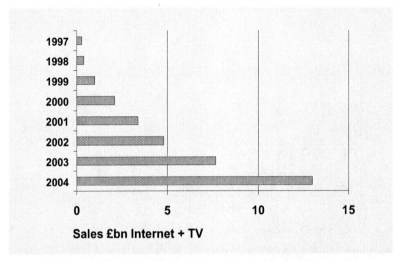

Figure 12.1   The Growth of Online Shopping in the UK: surveys, 1997 to 2003, forecast 2004
Sources: IMRG (2003); Verdict (2003).

Evidence indicates, though, that e-retailers have been failing to deliver the standards of service expected by customers. A survey of 9500 online shoppers by BizRate.com indicated that 55 percent abandoned their carts prior to checkout (Shop.org, 2001). Worldwide, $6 billion per year are being lost through failed purchase attempts (Blank, 2000). A Verdict Research (2000) survey of 2000 people found that 'consumers are being put off shopping online by poor after sales service and unreliable delivery'. Problems cited included lack of weekend/evening delivery and complicated systems for returning unsuitable or unsatisfactory merchandise. More than a quarter 'preferred the reassurance of [the] high street'. The problems are especially acute for the clothing & footwear; and food & drink sectors, where 10 percent and 16 percent of shoppers respectively said that they would not buy on the Internet again, causing an annual loss of sales of around £240 million (Verdict, 2002). Typical comments from customers have included: 'They left it in the garden and didn't even tell me'; 'It's a 24 hour shopping service but 6 hour delivery service'; 'Returning unwanted products is when it goes low tech'; (Consumer surveys from Vincent et al, 2000).

Lunt (2000) carried out 16 focus groups and 42 user trials. The main reasons for eschewing net shopping included: (i) Mismatch between buying on line and handling the products; (ii) 'It's not like shopping –

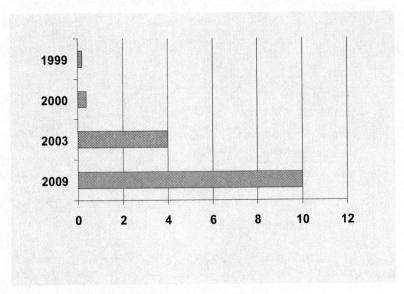

Figure 12.2   E-retailing as percent of UK Shopping
Sources: IMRG (2003); Verdict (2003).

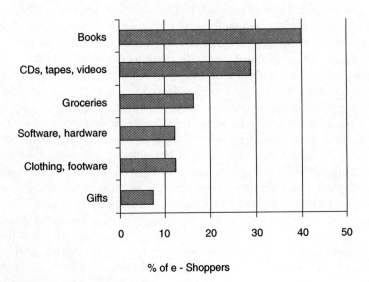

% of e - Shoppers

Figure 12.3   What e-shoppers buy
Sources: Doidge and Higgins, 2000; IMRG, 2003.

more like typing' and (iii) Lacks the experiential aspects of shopping. A consistent picture has emerged of the importance of the interpersonal aspects of shopping, particularly for female shoppers (see Chapters 7 and 10 above and e.g. Dholakia, 1999; Elliot, 1994). A Colliers Conrad Ritblat Erdman survey revealed the top reason for not e-shopping to be 'Prefer personal shopping and seeing the goods', mentioned by half of internet-connected households (Figure 12.4, Doidge and Higgins, 2000).

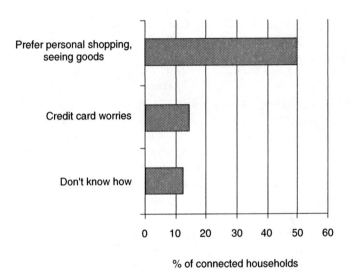

Figure 12.4   Why Internet-connected consumers do not e-shop
Source: Doidge and Higgins, 2000.

The USA picture has been similar. Shim's and associates' (2000) postal survey of 684 respondents concluded that social influences were more important for Internet and 'cross' shoppers than for traditional ones. Childers's et al (2001) experiment with 274 participants found that while instrumental aspects were important 'the more immersive, hedonic aspects of the new media play at least an equal role'. Mathwick and colleagues (2001) questioned whether the Internet channel in its current form lacked 'the ability to deliver aesthetic value (i.e. is it dull and lifeless?)'. According to McCarthy (2000), '63 percent of web site visitors will not buy online until there is more human interaction'. 'Women want ease of navigation and sense of personalised relationship' – helped by 'community' or 'chat' rooms (Harris, 1998). The community site iVillage, hosted by Tesco in the UK, is an example of the more interactive approach. Evans and colleagues (2001) investigated the relatively new consumer to consumer (C2C) 'community' model. Their focus group findings illustrated the importance of the way consumers interact with each other and potentially with marketers. As they pointed out (drawing support from Anderson, 1999), 'social interaction now has a "virtual" version':

> People come together for sexual flirtation, business, idle gossip, spiritual exploration, psychological support, political action, intellectual discourse on all kinds of subjects – the whole range of human interests and needs.
>
> (Anderson, 1999).

Claims that virtual communities are a 'social phenomenon' (Rheingold, 1993) set to become 'big commercial business' (Hagel and Armstrong, 1997) are now being borne out in the marketplace. For example, eBay (auction site), with its emphasis on community interests such as chat rooms and bulletin boards, was one of the few Internet start-up companies to have 'avoided financial pain' in the dot.com crash of 2000 (Reynolds, 2000), and is now one of the one of the most successful sites in terms of sales, time spent on the site and providing enjoyment (Nielsen NetRatings, 2003) (jointly with Amazon, also one of the most interactive sites). In fact, the worldwide success of eBay has made it the biggest e-commerce site in the world (NAMNEWS, 2003).

As with conventional shopping (see Chapters 7 and 10 above) there are differences between the sexes concerning e-shopping behaviour. For example, 77 percent of US women browse online, then buy in store, but only 54 percent of men do this. Men are more purposeful shoppers than women are (Lindquist et al, 2000). In the early days of the Internet, male users heavily outnumbered females, but this has now changed with 50 percent of e-shoppers female in the US (Cyr, 2000; Mathwick et al, 2001) and 42 percent in the UK (Verdict, 2002 – up from 30 percent reported by Pavitt in 1997). Internet shoppers are becoming more mainstream with more e-shoppers coming from the less affluent socio-economic groups and many new sales arising from consumers more representative of the UK population. The profile has moved away from a 'geek' majority (Orton, 1999; Verdict, 2003).

The indications are, then, that e-shopping is growing at the expense of traditional shopping, but that e-shoppers are missing benefits associated with personal interaction. In this chapter we report on exploratory pilot research in West London, UK. The remainder of the chapter proceeds as follows. Firstly, a small study comparing Internet *vs.* an exemplar shopping centre, the West London Shopping Centre (not its real name), and comparing the centre with an 'ideal' centre is reported. In this initial stage, the respondents were sixth form students. Secondly, the results of a further small study are reported with slightly more mature shoppers – university students. Finally, we speculate on the possible future of shopping.

Research questions

This chapter aims to explore two questions:

(i) To compare factors that consumers consider in deciding where to shop and to determine whether they associate them more positively with the Internet or 'bricks' shopping centres.

(ii) To identify the various attributes consumers associate with their ideal image of a shopping centre, and to explore the congruence between this ideal image and the centre studied.

Procedure

In line with an intention to investigate likely future trends in shopping, the initial sample comprised 30 young people aged 16 to 18 – the shoppers of tomorrow – expected to be more web-literate than older age groups. As a pilot investigation, this was a small convenience sample of students at a sixth-form college. In this preliminary phase, structured questionnaire instruments were used to compare shopping perceptions of Internet shopping with the nearby West London Shopping Centre. It is interesting to report that out of 52 of the sixth-form students initially screened, only 22 did **not** shop at both, i.e. 60 percent shopped at both the West London Shopping Centre **and** on the Internet. For Internet shopping, these young people had access to their parents' credit cards. The use of credit by minors raises ethical issues which have been explored further elsewhere (Dennis et al, 2001c). Many of the attributes that shoppers use in deciding choices of shopping centres (See, for example, Chapter 3 above) are not relevant to the Internet – e.g. 'availability of toilets'.

Therefore, for research question (i), comparison of Internet *vs.* the shopping centre was restricted to the six attributes identified by Quelch (1999) on which the Internet and shopping centres could compete head-to-head. A seven-point Likert-type scale was used, ranging from 'strongly agree' (1) to 'strongly disagree' (7) with the statement.

For research question (ii), the image dimensions of the respondents' 'ideal' shopping centre were studied and compared with the ideal centre, using a 2-stage approach. In Step 1, respondents were asked how relevant were each of 50 image dimensions (e.g. Exciting – Calm). The 50 dimensions chosen initially were compiled from image dimensions used in previous studies (Foxall and Goldsmith, 1994; Graeff, 1996; Malhotra, 1989). Again, a seven-point scale was used, this time from 'Not at all' (1) to 'Very much' (7). The 12 image dimensions having a mean score of 4.5 or higher were selected as the relevant dimensions for Step 2. Here, the thirty respondents were asked to indicate where they perceived the ideal image of a shopping centre to be **within** a dimension. For example, for the image dimension 'Exciting – Calm', respondents were asked the extent to which their ideal shopping centre had more of an exciting or calm image. They were then asked to indicate where the West London Shopping Centre would lie on the same scale. Responses were recorded on a 7-point Semantic Differential scale.

In a second stage of the research the survey was extended to young adult respondents – university students – to compare Internet with shopping centre shopping. Unfortunately, terrorist action precluded the exact duplication of the study comparing the West London Shopping Centre. In this second stage, respondents compared Internet shopping with their usual shopping centre. One striking figure is that 57 percent of the sample were e-shoppers – compared with the UK average for all adults of around 15 percent (estimated from NetValue 2001). The average expenditure of the Internet shoppers on e-shopping was £22 per month, compared to £86 per month on conventional shopping. Thus, over half of the student sample shopped on the Internet, spending on average over 20 percent of their non-food shopping by Internet. In order to provide a deeper insight, respondents were invited to add comments on Internet shopping or shopping centres. In total, 278 students were interviewed at different university locations, but for comparison with the first part of the study, the quantitative results reported below refer to a subset of 55 students based at a campus close to the West London Shopping Centre.

Results

Comparing satisfaction ratings of the internet vs. The West London shopping centre

Table 12.1 is the comparison of ratings, illustrated in Figure 12.5. Table 12.1(a) and Figure 12.5(a) are for the sixth-form students, Table 12.1(b) and Figure 12.5(b) refer to the university students. Ratings have been re-scaled for convenience on a 0 to 100 scale, where 100 represents the 'better' end of the scales.

Table 12.1(a) Comparison of ratings (converted to 0 – 100 scales, where 100 = most agreement), Internet vs. the West London Shopping Centre – sixth-form students

	Internet – Mean Score	Shopping Centre – Mean Score
A good **breadth and depth of products** (i.e. range) is offered	93	58
The **price of goods and services** is favourable	98	63
It is a **convenient** way to shop	96	68
There are good quality stores	84	71
There is a high quality of **customer service**	61	90
There is a **positive image** associated with the shopping experience	57	92

Table 12.1(b) Comparison of ratings (converted to 0 – 100 scales where 100 = most agreement), Internet vs. shopping centres – university students

	Internet – Mean Score	Shopping Centre – Mean Score
A good **breadth and depth of products** (i.e. range) is offered	75	75
The **price of goods and services** is favourable	74	67
It is a **convenient** way to shop	78	71
There are good quality stores	70	70
There is a high quality of **customer service**	46	62
There is a **positive image** associated with the shopping experience	61	65

The results indicated that the sixth-form respondents marginally preferred the Internet for the quality of the stores and more emphatically for the breadth and depth of products, although the university students rated the Internet equally with shopping centres on these attributes.

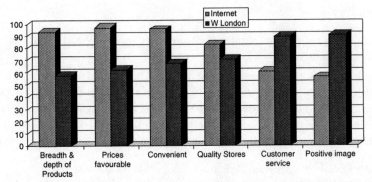

Figure 12.5(a) Comparing ratings – Internet *vs.* West London Shopping Centre – sixth-form students

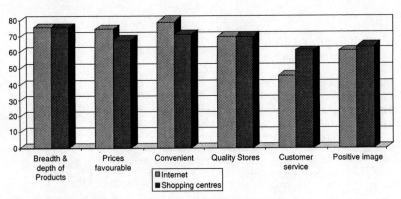

Figure 12.5(b) Comparing ratings – Internet *vs.* shopping centres – university students

Both groups rated Internet shopping higher for favourable prices and convenience. On the other hand, the shopping centre was preferred for its positive image and more emphatically for customer service. This customer service finding is consistent with other work drawing attention to service from e-retailers, outlined earlier. Bearing in mind the size of the Internet, it would seem inevitable that e-shopping provides a bigger range of products. Similarly, it is natural for many shoppers to take advantage of the Internet's convenience (buy where you like, someone else delivers) and lower prices arising from the ease of comparing prices. Given the lead that e-shopping has on these major shopping dimensions, it is perhaps surprising that the shopping centre was ahead on positive image. As discussed above, consumers value the social and experience aspects of shopping which, we contend, contribute to the positive image of the 'bricks' centre.

The sixth-form students were more favourably disposed towards the Internet than were the university students, perhaps reflecting the higher web literacy of the younger respondents.

The ideal shopping centre

The top 12 image dimensions (out of 50) for the ideal shopping centre (sixth-form respondents) were: (i) pleasant/unpleasant; (ii) interesting/dull; (iii) modern/old fashioned; (iv) adventurous/timid; (v) relaxed/tense; (vi) sophisticated/unsophisticated; (vii) clean/dirty; (viii) changeable/stable; (ix) friendly/unfriendly; (x) fun/boring; (xi) comfortable/uncomfortable and (xii) exciting/calm.

Comparing image ratings

In Table 12.2 the image ratings of the West London Shopping Centre have been compared with the sixth-form respondents' ideal ratings. As with the satisfaction ratings, these have been re-scaled for convenience on a 0 to 100 scale, so that for example, the 'Exciting' end of the scale = 100, whereas the 'Calm' end = 0. Those image ratings on which the centre studied was rated close to the ideal image are in Table 12.2(a); those further away in Table 12.2(b), illustrated in Figures 12.6 and 12.7 respectively.

The image ratings on which the West London Shopping Centre performed close to the ideal were: (i) relaxed; (ii) comfortable; (iii) pleasant; (iv) sophisticated; (v) modern and (vi) clean.

Whereas those on which it fell short of the ideal were: (i) exciting; (ii) interesting; (iii) adventurous; (iv) changeable; (v) friendly and (vi) fun.

Table 12.2(a) Comparing image ratings, West London Shopping Centre vs. ideal – dimensions on which the centre rated close to ideal – sixth-form students

	Mean Ideal Shopping Centre image, 0 – 100 scale	*Mean West London Shopping Centre image, 0 – 100 scale*
Relaxed – Tense	95	91
Comfortable – Uncomfortable	99	91
Pleasant – Unpleasant	94	93
Sophisticated – Unsophisticated	91	88
Modern – Old fashioned	87	82
Clean – Dirty	98	93

Table 12.2(b) Comparing image ratings, West London Shopping Centre vs. ideal – dimensions on which the centre rated further from ideal – sixth-form students

	Mean Ideal Shopping Centre image, 0 – 100 scale	Mean West London Shopping Centre image, 0 – 100 scale
Exciting – Calm	95	55
Interesting – Dull	93	48
Adventurous – Timid	87	52
Changeable – Stable	85	47
Friendly – Unfriendly	98	51
Fun – Boring	96	50

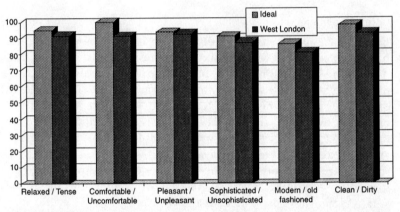

Figure 12.6 Comparing image ratings – ideal shopping centre *vs.* West London shopping centre – dimensions on which the centre was rated close to ideal

The image dimensions on which the West London Shopping Centre was close to the ideal largely concerned 'hygene' or the shopping environment. Poor performance on these might result in a substantial loss of business for a centre, but the good performance is not in itself likely to be a substantial generator of sales. It is postulated that the busiest shopping centres owe much of their success to generating extra patronage through a proactive approach to 'entertainment'. The biggest centres in the world are not situated in areas of great population, but are well known as tourist destinations (West Edmonton Mall and Mall of America, see Chapter 6 above). It is this vital entertainment area which seems to challenge smaller centres and for which the centre did not come close to the ideal.

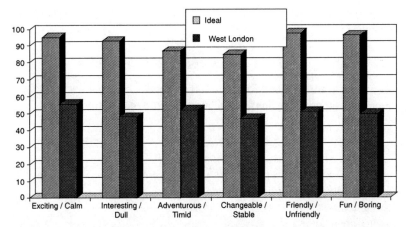

Figure 12.7 Comparing image ratings – ideal shopping centre *vs.* West London shopping centre – dimensions on which the centre was rated further from ideal

Qualitative findings

The comments of shoppers who shop by Internet **and** in shopping centres (from the unstructured part of the questionnaire) were coded manually. The main constructs are listed below.

Prefer to shop in shopping centres – more enjoyable/sociable – 10 respondents. Comments included:

> 'Internet shopping is not a personal experience. You cannot try and see what you're buying'
> 'Internet shopping is convenient but will never replace actual shops. Shopping is not purely to purchase goods/products, but is also a leisure activity and can be very sociable – unlike Internet shopping'.
> 'I would rather use the Internet as a research tool in comparing potential purchases and to search for exclusive products. However, when making purchases, I would rather the physical nature of going into the shop. It is more reliable and the experience is pleasurable'.
> 'If you want to shop for clothes, you are not able to feel and see the quality of the fabrics. Never ends up being as seen on the screen'.

Internet needs more trust – concern for safety of financial transactions and credit cards – 7 respondents. A typical comment was:

> 'Not totally confident about giving credit card details over the Internet yet'.

Three respondents mentioned, though, that Internet security is improving:

'There's more trust than 2 years ago as the bad dot.coms have gone'.

Internet convenient, good for [product] research – 5 respondents made comments along these lines, but all added some reservation, for example:

'Internet shopping is a very convenient channel for shopping, but it's not as time saving as people think, because time spent on searching and comparison takes a couple of hours'.

'Some Internet sites very good, but it is hard to find and to know which sites are reliable'.

Three respondents commented that the Internet was too slow or unreliable.

Refund/exchange problems with Internet – 2 respondents expressed concern, for example:

'Most of them do not have shop-floor support for after sales service, refund/change always takes more time and more troublesome and gives less feeling of secure'.

'Hassle with exchange or refunding. Too much hassle'.

Internet cheaper – mentioned by 5 respondents, but only 2 stated that shopping centres were more expensive in general than the Internet. One considered the Internet cheaper for books and 2 for CDs (one of these also mentioned videos), for example:

'I only buy CDs on line because they are cheaper. I buy everything else in shops'.

The comments from this qualitative work support previous findings that the most important issue affecting Internet shopping is shoppers' preferences for the experience of 'real' shopping. Next in degree of concern is security, although this is becoming less prominent. The Internet is often described as 'convenient' for shopping, but the degree of convenience is subject to considerable reservations such as slowness, unreliability (of both the Internet and the shopping process) and aftercare. Internet shopping has perceived price advantages, but these are not universal.

Conclusions

In drawing inferences from these results, the limitations arising from the small and non-representative nature of the samples must be borne in mind. Nevertheless, if the views of the respondents were in any way typical of young people and the shoppers of the future, the conclusions below could be indicated.

(i) Shopping centres may have difficulty competing on: breadth and depth of products; prices; researching products; and convenience – although shoppers have many reservations about the convenience of e-shopping. Shopping centres could do more to make the shopping experience: exciting; interesting; adventurous; friendly; fun and changeable. These are aspects that e-marketers could be well advised to emphasise when promoting Internet shopping.

(ii) Shoppers are still concerned about the security and payment aspects of buying online. Shopping centres may still have the edge over Internet shopping on customer service, positive image and experiential shopping. A central qualitative finding was that even the young, e-literate web shoppers had a strong preference for shopping in shopping centres rather than online as more enjoyable and sociable. E-retailers need to address these limitations of Internet shopping.

The future of shopping?

If, as forecast, conventional 'bricks' shopping is set to lose substantial business to Internet shopping, how might retailers protect market share? We suggest three possible approaches, the first two of which entail recognition of the wants of the e-consumer of the future: (i) multi-channel retailing; (ii) the Internet shopping centre and (iii) emphasis on leisure, eating and drinking, i.e. services that the e-shopper cannot consume from the web.

Multi-channel retailing

Some commentators speculate that the future of shopping lies in multi-channel retailing. Shim and colleagues (2000), drawing support from an Ernst & Young LLP (2000) report, suggested that, rather than compete with the Internet, conventional shops should incorporate it as part of their retail strategy. Most UK 'bricks' retailers were yet so to do at the time of Doherty and associates' survey (1999), although many of the biggest high street retailers do now also e-retail.

According to a Deloitte & Touche study (reported in Sunday Times Business, 10 September 2000), those e-retailers that are part of traditional, old economy companies will fare best, with 75 percent expected to gain market share. Verdict (2001) forecast that a handful of companies in each online sector will account for over 75 percent of online sales – and these players will all be multi-channel. A British Council of Shopping Centres (BCSC, 2001) survey forecast that stores that integrate e-retailing and a strong high street brand will continue to be successful over the next 5 years. Illustrating this trend, Amazon had a tie-up with Toys R Us in the UK that gave a physical presence to Amazon in Toys R Us stores. There are at least 12 UK-based online malls – but the author is aware of only one 'bricks' shopping centre that also offers 'clicks' shopping. This so-called 'wired lease' (BCSC 2001) approach could represent a growth opportunity for UK shopping centres?

The Internet shopping centre (the Dubai Internet City approach)

Dubai Internet City is a 'bricks' shopping centre devoted solely to the Internet, with tenants including, for example: hardware companies, software suppliers, service providers and Internet cafes – in fact, everything to do with the Internet in a one-stop shopping centre (Scudder, 2000). Whilst not a suitable model for every UK shopping centre, there may be UK potential for some centres of this type.

Emphasis on leisure, eating and drinking (the Easton Town Centre approach)

Coverage in the popular press (e.g. Daily Mail, 15 July 1996: 'Shops Turn Corner In War On Malls'), and anecdotal evidence from both sides of the Atlantic, indicates that many consumers love small traditional town centres with character. Researchers such as Hallsworth (e.g. 2000) have reported the attraction of such (UK) towns and their fight-back from decline. Despite the appeal of the traditional small towns, though, many of us tend to shop for preference at (planned) shopping centres and retail sheds. Easton Town Centre, Columbus, Ohio, is the first of two to date of a new-style centre combining the 'traditional' town centre with shopping centre and 'edge-of-town'. The sales area is approximately one-third shopping, one-third leisure and one-third eating and drinking. The illustrations (Figure 12.8) show a conventional-looking town with streets and a town square – but this is entirely a planned and managed shopping centre. There is even the 'edge of town' Wal-Mart and Home Depot (hardware shed) on the perimeter. The author considers that this new approach illustrates the potential for shopping centres to make the experience more exciting, interesting, adventurous, friendly, fun and changeable. Conversely, e-retailers need to improve their offerings to compete with new style 'bricks' shopping experiences by offering more interaction, entertainment and community activities.

What next?

The work reported in this chapter has been exploratory in nature, but has drawn attention to the need to keep alive the interpersonal and experience aspects of shopping in the Internet age. The final chapter, Chapter 13, rounds up the findings of this book, attempting an integrated framework drawing together the threads of understanding of why people shop where they do in choices of shopping centres.

Figure 12.8 (a)

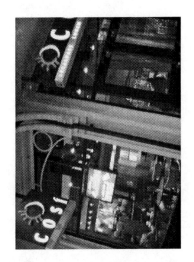

Figure 12.8 (b) Views of Easton Town Centre, Columbus, Ohio, USA
Sources: First five photos courtesy of imedia inc, from the Easton Town Center website: www.eastontowncenter.com. Other three photos Michael Morrison.

*The first out-of-town regional shopping centre in the UK was said to
have been Brent Cross, Hendon, in 1976 (Guy, 1994a).*

13
Conclusions and Implications

Limitations

The empirical work reported in this book has been subject to a number of limitations. Firstly, sample sizes have been small. This has especially been a limitation when studying segments of the samples. Although the results reported have mostly been statistically significant, all samples have been selected on a convenience basis and results cannot therefore be generalised.

Chapter 9 was subject to particular limitations as at the time of writing, the work was still being prepared in 'working paper' format with a view to more extensive publication elsewhere. Therefore, it has not been possible to report quantitative results fully on account of copyright limitations. Similarly, the empirical work reported in Chapter 10 represents a preliminary stage in the search for a suitable method to test a hypothesis. Nevertheless, the nascent work reported in these two chapters is indicative of current research into the still-challenging question of 'Why people shop where they do?'.

Finally (apart from the cross-cultural study in Chapter 10), the empirical work refers only to the UK and more particularly, only to specific locations in the UK selected on a convenience basis.

Theoretical frameworks utilised

This book has attempted to address broad questions of why people shop where they do in terms of choices of shopping centres and whether to e-shop rather than shop in shopping centres. Chapter numbers are indicated on the path diagram in Figure 13.1 as an indication of the overall theoretical structure of the book. A summary of the theoretical approaches taken follows. Firstly, Attitude-behaviour theory has been utilised (Chapter 3) in combination with gravity, spatial interaction and Central Place approaches (Chapters 5 and 6). The attractiveness of shopping centres has been quantified and triangulated using a branding framework (Chapter 4). The importance of branding implies relevance for theories of loyalty and learning, although these have yet to be utilised as theoretical frameworks for studying shopping centre choice. Marketing segmentation has been applied in studying why different segments of shoppers shop where they do (Chapter 7).

The second major framework, suggested by questions of why people act in particular ways, was Motivation (Chapter 8), utilising and adapting classical theories originally developed to explain motivation in the workplace. The particular contribution of motivation theory was in an understanding of the part played by shopping centres in satisfying higher order *vs.* lower order needs.

Thirdly, the study of the extent to which shoppers may be influenced by the shopping environment has been studied using an Environmental Psychology approach (Chapter 9). An important contribution from this approach was the example of a shopping centre manipulating an atmospheric stimulus to influence shoppers' pleasure, image of the shopping centre and, indirectly, 'Approach' variables such as spending.

The deeper 'why' has been addressed with a tentative exploratory use of Evolutionary Psychology, potentially explaining some differences in shopping styles (Chapter 10).

Finally, the reasons for shoppers taking up (or not) e-shopping rather than shopping centre and high street shopping have been studied using a modified Technology Acceptance Model framework together with the Theory of Planned Behaviour (Chapters 11 and 12).

Theoretical postulations supported

Figure 13.1 schematically illustrates the links of association that have been supported by the various exploratory studies reported in this book. As the samples of shoppers and shopping centres differed in different chapters of the book, it has not been possible to apply path weights to this overall model, but all the paths included received at least qualified support in the respective studies.

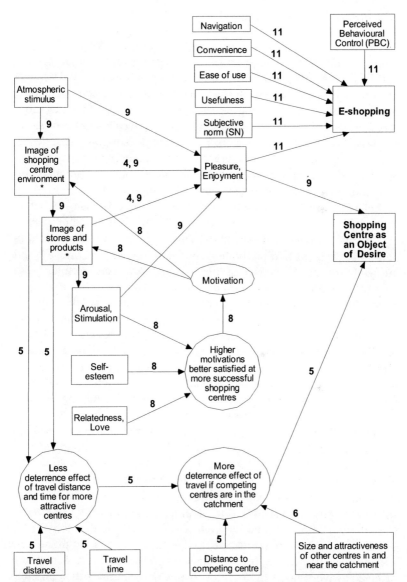

Figure 13.1 Links of association supported in this book – indicating chapter numbers
* Weights different for: (a) segments (Chapter 7) and (b) shopping centres (Chapter 3)
Sources: The author, plus part adapted from Dennis et al, 2004.

Conclusions and implications

Conclusions can be framed around the theoretical paths that have been supported, illustrated in Figure 13.1. The 'pleasure' and 'arousal' parts of the Environmental Psychology 'Pleasure-arousal-dominance' (PAD) model (applied by other researchers to store image) were supported for shopping centres (Chapter 9). Shopping centre 'approach' variables such as shoppers' spending were influenced by shoppers' perceived image of the stores and products in the centre and the pleasure of the shopping experience. Pleasure was influenced by the images of the shopping centre environment and the stores and products. The image of stores and products also acted indirectly to increase pleasure by increasing arousal.

The experimental atmospheric stimulus – in this case a Captive Audience Network of private TV screens (CAN) – had a small but significant effect on increasing spending. This operated by increasing shoppers' pleasure, both directly (e.g. pleasant scenes and music) and indirectly through the image of the shopping centre environment (e.g. by providing useful information on the benefits).

The influence of pleasure and experiential aspects in shopping choices has been a recurring theme. A shopping centre that satisfies shoppers' higher level motivations tends to be more successful than one that concentrates on lower level motivations (Chapter 8). Enjoyment is even one of the main dimensions influencing e-shopping (Chapter 11). The higher level motivations include dimensions that we have named 'Love', 'Self-esteem' and 'Stimulation'. Buying gifts for others is a strong 'Love' motivation that allows shoppers to experience the pleasure of shopping guilt-free. 'Self-esteem' is significant as shoppers want to be thought of as the sort of people who shop at a centre with associations of high class and style. 'Stimulation' includes the relief of boredom, often referred to as 'retail therapy'.

The implications are that shopping centres that concentrate on pleasure, experience and stimulation of shoppers will be more successful than those providing primarily product and price benefits. Many of the components of this shopping centre experience can be manipulated by shopping centre marketing management. One example is the use of CANs (investigated in Chapter 9) but there many other possible controllable stimuli. For example, in Chapter 10, the Evolutionary Psychology approach supported the use of atmospheric stimuli such as natural daylight, water features and greenery.

Shoppers' travel distance and travel time has a deterrent effect on shopping centre patronage (Chapters 5 and 6). The deterrent effect is less, though, for centres that are more attractive. Refurbishing a shopping centre with suitable controllable atmospheric stimuli should not only increase sales patronage from existing customers, but also attract new customers from a wider catchment area.

The deterrence effect of travel time and distance was found to be greater the closer a competing centre is within the catchment area. Although the actions of competitors are not usually within the control of management, this effect should be borne in mind in planning new centres.

The investigation into catchment areas in Chapter 6 illuminated retail hierarchy considerations. Two centres at similar levels in the hierarchy will have a 'break point' in catchment area between them, but a centre at a lower level in the hierarchy can exist within the catchment of a larger, more attractive centre. New centres in the vicinity of other centres should either be smaller, local community centres, or larger centres that will draw in a wider catchment area.

Chapter 7 drew attention to differences in weights of the components of image between different segments of shoppers. For example, males and females were strikingly different, with female shopping behaviour more associated with shopping and experience, males with the centre itself. In Chapter 10, the differences between male and female shopping styles were explored. The conclusion is that shopping centres should continue to satisfy the female-type need for comparison shopping as an end in itself, whilst attempting to make separate provision to satisfy the male more purposeful style. This might be done to utilise the 'mens' creche' idea not just as a waiting room, but also as a means of selling male-type products (e.g. 'boys toys' and gifts for females) fast, e.g. by using a catalogue and delivery type approach.

An important conclusion from Chapter 7 related to the difference between two benefit-motivation segments: 'Experience' and 'Shopping'. Continuing the theme of the importance of the shopping experience, the 'Experience' segment were higher spending than the 'Shopping' segment shoppers. Shopping centres can use data techniques based on this chapter to identify and target the 'Experience' shoppers.

The main findings from Chapter 3 related to the differences between shopping centres in terms of shopper behaviour that were not accounted for by demographic differences between the shoppers. Shopping centres can use techniques based on Chapters 2 and 3 to satisfy shoppers better on a local basis. The differences between centres may be largely accounted for by differences in competing shopping locations.

As e-retailers become more efficient in delivering convenience, ease of use and usefulness benefits, shopping centres will continue to lose market share to e-shopping. E-shopping is even providing pleasure and enjoyment benefits. E-retailing was not part of the main focus of this book on shopping centres, but the results have been useful in directing attention to the need for shopping centres to adapt and improve in order to counter growing competition from e-retailers. Shopping centres need to compete by doing more to make shopping more exciting, interesting, friendly and fun. The experience can be enhanced by for example offering more leisure, eating and drinking facilities. Many large retailers are now also multi-channel e-retailers, but shopping centres seem to be missing out on the opportunity to e-retail *via* wired leases or e-malls.

Future research

As mentioned in the 'Limitations' section of this chapter above, the work reported in this book has all been exploratory in nature and should form the starting point for a larger, more representative project. Further work is recommended to test and develop the ideas presented here across a representative sample of shopping centres and also to explore the extent to which the findings may be generalisable. It is hoped that this book may stimulate other researchers to follow up some of the ideas in other countries and cultures.

The Environmental Psychology approach introduced in Chapter 9 represents a promising area for further research. As mentioned in the 'Conclusions and implications' section of this chapter above, there are many more possible controllable atmospheric stimuli that management might be able to use to improve image and sales. For example, aroma and music (and combinations of those) have been successfully evaluated by previous researchers in store settings. Similar evaluations should be carried out for shopping centres.

A number of traditional consumer behaviour approaches have been omitted from this work and exploratory studies are recommended to evaluate their potential. For example, the psychology of 'Learning' might have value in studying shopper loyalty. Most of the empirical work in this book has confirmed that nearly all shoppers shop at not just one shopping centre, but at least one other shopping location as well. There may therefore be the potential for shopping centres to help shoppers to learn the benefits of shopping more in the specific centre, i.e. increasing shopper loyalty. Chapter 4 included a tantalising glimpse into the 'Personality' of shopping centres. Is congruence between the personalities of shopping centres and shoppers themselves (or perhaps their aspired self-images?) a factor in shopping centre choice? This could be a fruitful area for research, as it is possible that shopping centres might be able to change or adapt their personalities if necessary (for example by varying atmospheric stimuli).

Finally, despite the varied exploratory empirical work carried out for this book, the process of eliciting a deeper understanding into the 'Why' has barely started. The Evolutionary Psychology approach introduced in Chapter 10 has shown initial promise. Further work needs to be carried out to extend the cross-cultural study to many more cultures using many more participant judges. Investigations into the physiology of shopping, neural activity and essential body functions have not even been touched upon here and represent opportunities to utilise developing research techniques to gain a better understanding of shopping as an important part of human psychology.

The first super-regional (at least 100 000 m² gross retail area) out-of-town shopping centre was the MetroCentre, near Gateshead, in 1986; following an extension in 2004, once again the largest shopping centre in Europe (Guy, 1994b).

References

Aaker D A (1991) *Managing Brand Equity*, New York, Free Press.

Aaker J L (1997) 'Dimensions of brand personality', *Journal of Marketing Research*, 24 (August): 347–356.

Achabal D D, Gorr W L and Mahajan V (1982) 'MULTILOC: A multiple store location decision model', *Journal of Retailing*, 58 (2): 5–25.

Adcock D, Bradfield R, Halborg A and Ross C (1998) *Marketing Principles and Practice*, 3rd edition, London, Financial Times Pitman.

Ajzen I (1985) 'From Intention to action: a theory of planned behaviour', in Kuhl J and Beckman J (eds), *Action Control: From Cognitions to Behaviours*, New York, Springer.

Ajzen I (1991) 'The Theory of Planned Behaviour', *Organisational Behaviours and Human Decision Processes*, 50: 179–211.

Ajzen I and Fishbein M (1980) *Understanding Attitudes and Predicting Social Behaviour*, New Jersey, Prentice Hall.

Akehurst G and Alexander N (1995) *The Internationalisation of Retailing*, London, Frank Cass.

Alderfer C P (1972) *Existence, Relatedness and Growth*, New York, Free Press.

Allegra (2002) *Shopping Centres in the UK*, London, Allegra Strategies.

Alt M and Griggs S (1988) 'Can a brand be cheeky?' *31st Annual Conference*, London, Market Research Society: 99–127.

Anderson W T (1999) 'Communities in a world of open systems', *Futures*, 31: 457–463.

Ang S H, Leong S M and Lim J (1997) 'The mediating influence of pleasure and arousal on layout and signage effects', *Journal of Retailing and Consumer Services*, 4 (1): 13–24.

Arburgham A (1979) *Shopping in Style: London from the Restoration to Edwardian Elegance*, London, Thames and Hudson: 18, 21, 24.

Association of Town Centre Management (1994) *The Effectiveness of Town Centre Management – Research Study*, Association of Town Centre Management, London.

Babin B J, Darden W R and Griffin M (1994) 'Work and/or fun: measuring hedonic and utilitarian shopping value', *Journal of Consumer Research*, 20: 644–656.

Bagozzi R P (1985) 'Expectancy-value attitude models: an analysis of critical theoretical issues', *International Journal of Research in Marketing*, 2: 43–60.

Bakewell C and Mitchell V-W (2004) 'Male consumer decision-making styles', *International Review of Retail, Distribution and Consumer Research*, 14 (2): 223–240.

Batty M and Saether A (1972) 'A note on the design of shopping models', *Journal of the Royal Town Planning Institute*, 58: 303–306.

BCSC (2001) 'Future Shock or E-Hype: The Impact of Online Shopping on UK Retail Property, British Council of Shopping Centres', *The College of Estate Management*, London.

Beddington N (1982) *Design for Shopping Centres*, London, Butterworth.

Beddington N (1991) *Shopping Centres: Retail Development, Design and Management*, Oxford, Butterworth.

Benson J and Ugolini L (eds) (2003) *A Nation of Shopkeepers: Five Centuries of British Retailing*, London, Tauris.

Berry L L (1969) 'The components of department store image: a theoretical and empirical analysis', *Journal of Retailing*, 45 (1): 3–20.

Birkin M (1994) 'Assessing brand value', in *Brand Power*, Stebart P (ed.), Basingstoke, Macmillan.

Bitner Mary Jo (1992) 'Servicescapes: the impact of physical surroundings on customers and employees', *Journal of Marketing*, 56 (April), 57–71.

Blank C (2000) 'Study: E-tailers must close more sales', *Marketing News*, 86.

Blanko V M and McCusky S W (1961) *Basic Physics of the Solar System*, Reading, Mass., Addison-Wesley.

Bloch P H, Ridgway N M and Dawson S A (1994) 'The shopping mall as consumer habitat', *Journal of Retailing*, 70 (1): 23–42.

Block J (1978) *The Q-Sort Method in Personality Assessment and Psychiatric Research*, Palo Alto, Consulting Psychologists.

Bodkin C D and Lord J D (1997) 'Attraction of power shopping centres', *The International Review of Retail, Distribution and Consumer Research*, 7 (2): 93–108.

Boedeker M (1995) 'New type and traditional shoppers: a comparison of two major consumer groups', *International Journal of Retail and Distribution Management*, 23(3): 17–26.

Boedeker M and Marjanen H (1993) 'Choice orientation types and their shopping trips: an empirical study of shopping trips to the city centre *vs.* to an edge-of-town retail park', *7th International Conference on Research in the Distributive Trades*, Stirling, University of Stirling, Institute for Retail Studies.

Borden N H (1941) *The Economic Effects of Advertising*, Homewood, Ill., Irwin.

Boulding K E (1956) *The Image*, Ann Arbor, University of Michigan Press.

Brambilla R and Longo G (1977) *For Pedestrians Only*, New York, Watson-Guptill: 99.

Brand Finance (1999) *The Brand Finance Report*, Kingston upon Thames, Brand Finance plc.

Breakwell G M, Hammond S and Fife-Shaw C (2000) *Research Methods in Psychology*, London, Sage.

Breheny M J (1988) 'Practical methods of retail location analysis; a review', in Wrigley, *Store Choice, Store Location and Market Analysis*, London, Routledge, 39–86.

Brown S (1992) *Retail Location: A Micro-Scale Perspective*, Aldershot: Avebury.

Bryman A and Cramer D (1994) *Quantitative Data for Social Scientists*, London, Routledge.

Burns D J and Warren H B (1995) 'Need for uniqueness: shopping mall preference and choice activity', *International Journal of Retail and Distribution Management*, 23 (12).

Bullimore A (1997) *Saved*, Boston, MA, Little Brown.

Butterfield L and Haigh D (1998) *Understanding the Financial Value of Brands*, London, Institute of Practitioners in Advertising.

Buss D N (1989) 'Sex differences in human mate preferences: evolutionary hypotheses tested in 37 cultures', *Behavioural and Brain Sciences*, 12: 1–14.

Buss D M (1999) *Evolutionary psychology*, Needham Heights, MA, Allyn & Bacon.

Buzzell R and Gale B (1987) *The PIMS Principles*, London, Collier Macmillan.

Calantone R J and Sawyer A G (1978) 'The stability of benefit segments', *Journal of Marketing Research*, 15: 395–404.

Capital Shopping Centres PLC *1996 Annual Report and Accounts*, London, Capital Shopping Centres.

Carlson H J (1991) 'The role of the shopping centre in US retailing', *International Journal of Retail and Distribution Management*, 19 (6): 91.

Catton W R (1966) *From Animistic to Naturalistic Sociology*, New York, McGraw Hill.

Cavanaugh T (1996) 'Mall crawl palls', *American Demographics* (Sept).

C B Hillier Parker (2002) *The Development of Shopping Centres in Europe 2002*, London, C B Hillier Parker.

Census of Population (1991) London, HMSO.

Chartered Institute of Marketing (1997) Examiner's report (by John E) *Understanding Customers*, Certificate in Marketing, Cookham, Chartered Institute of Marketing.

Chebat J-C and Michon R (2003) 'Impact of ambient odors on mall shoppers' emotions, cognition and spending: a test of competitive causal theories', *Journal of Business Research*, 56: 529–539.

Chicksand L and Knowles R (2002) 'Selling "look and feel goods" online', *IBM E-Business Conference*, Birmingham University.

Christaller W (1933) *Central Places in Southern Germany*, translated by Baskin C (1966), Englewood Cliffs, Prentice-Hall.

Chignell M H and Patty B W (1987) 'Unidimensional scaling with efficient ranking methods', *Psychological Bulletin*, 101 (2): 304–311.

Childers T L, Carr C L, Peck J and Carson S (2001) 'Hedonic and utilitarian motivations for online retail shopping behaviour', *Journal of Retailing*, 77: 511–535.

Coates D, Doherty N, French A and Kirkup M (1995) 'Neural networks for store performance and forecasting: an empirical comparison with regression techniques', *The International Review of Retail, Distribution and Consumer Research*, 5 (4): 415–432.

Clark D (1982) *Urban Geography*, London, Croom Helm.

Clarke R (2003) 'Question: when is a retailer not a retailer? Answer: when it's a media owner', *The European Retail Digest*, 38: 20–23.

Converse P D (1949) 'New Laws of Retail Gravitation', *Journal of Marketing*, 14: 379–384.

Cooke J (1993) 'The shopping challenge – centres without a future', in Henry Stewart Conference Studies (ed.), *Latest Developments in the Ongoing Marketing and Promotion of Shopping Centres*, London, 29 September: 1–9.

CSC (1996) *1996 Annual Report and Accounts*, London, Capital Shopping Centres PLC.

Cushman & Wakefield/Healey & Baker (2002) *Where People Shop 2002*, London, Cushman & Wakefield/Healey & Baker.

Cyr D (2000) 'Your new consumer', *Catalogue Age*, July: 125–132.

Davies R L (1976) *Marketing Geography, with Special Reference to Retailing*, Corbridge, Retail Planning Associates.

Davies R L and Bennison D J (1979) *British Town Centre Shopping Schemes: a statistical digest. Report U11*. Reading, Unit for Retail Planning Information.

Davis F (1989) 'Perceived usefulness, perceived ease of use acceptance of information technology', *MIS Quarterly*, 13 (3): 319–340.

Dawson J A (1979) *The Marketing Environment*, London, Croom Helm.

Dawson J A (1983) *Shopping Centre Development*. London, Longman.

Dawson S, Bloch P H and Ridgway N M (1990) 'Shopping motives, emotional states and Retail Outcomes', *Journal of Retailing*, 66 (4): 408–427.

De Chernatony L and McDonald M H B (1998) *Creating Powerful Brands in Consumer, Service and Industrial Markets*, Oxford, Butterworth-Heinemann.

Dellaert G C, Arentze T A, Bierlaire M, Borgers W J and Timmermans H J P (1998) '"Investigating consumers" tendency to combine multiple shopping purposes and destinations', *Journal of Marketing Research*, 35 (2): 177–188.

Denison T (2003) 'Men and women arguing when shopping is genetic', *News Shop*, Exeter University, available from www.ex.ac.uk/news/newsshop.htm (accessed 22 September 2003).

Dennis C E, Harris L and Sandhu B (2002c) 'From bricks to clicks: understanding the e-consumer', *Qualitative Market Research: An International Journal*, 5 (4): 281–290.

Dennis C E and Hilton J (2001) '"Shoppers" motivations in choices of shopping centres', *8ᵗʰ International Conference on Recent Advances in Retailing and Services Science*, Vancouver, EIRASS.

Dennis C, Kent A, Harris L and Sandhu B (2001c) 'Ethical Considerations in e-Tailing – work in progress', *CIRM 2001, New Technologies and Retail SMEs*, Manchester Metropolitan University.

Dennis C E, Murphy J, Marsland D, Cockett W and Patel T (2002a) 'Measuring image: shopping centre case studies', *International Review of Retail, Distribution and Consumer Research*, 12 (4): 353–373.

Dennis C E, Marsland D and Cockett W A (1999) 'Why do people shop where they do?', *Recent Advances in Retailing and Services Science, 6ᵗʰ International Conference*, Eindhoven, The Netherlands, The European Institute of Retailing and Services Studies.

Dennis C E, Marsland D and Cockett W (2000a) 'Objects of desire: attraction and distance in shopping centre choice', *International Journal of New Product Development and Innovation Management*, 2 (2): 43–60.

Dennis C E, Marsland D and Cockett W (2001) 'The mystery of consumer behaviour: market segmentation and shoppers' choices of shopping centres', *International Journal of New Product Development and Innovation Management*, 3 (3): 221–237.

Dennis C E, Marsland D and Cockett W (2002b) 'Central place practice: shopping centre attractiveness measures, hinterland boundaries and the UK retail hierarchy', *Journal of Retailing and Consumer Services*, 9 (4): 185–199.

Dennis C E, Newman A, Zaman S, Nicholas R and Grundy A (2004) 'Manipulation of stimuli in a retail setting: a study into the effects of Captive Audience Network screens on shopping centre customers', *British Academy of Management Conference*, Fife, Scotland, University of St Andrews.

Dennis C E and Papamatthaiou E (2003) '"Shoppers" motivations for e-shopping', *10ᵗʰ International Conference on Recent Advances in Retailing and Services Science*, Portland, OR, EIRASS.

Dennis C E, Patel T and Hilton J (2002c) '"Shoppers" motivations in choices of shopping centres, a qualitative study', *9ᵗʰ International Conference on Recent Advances in Retailing and Services Science*, Heidelberg, EIRASS.

Des Rosiers F, Lagana A, Thierault M and Beaudoin M (1996) 'Shopping centres and house values: an empirical investigation', *Journal of Property Valuation and Investment*, 14 (4): 411–62.

Dichter E (1964) *Handbook of Consumer Motivations*, New York, McGraw.

Dholakia R R (1999) 'Going shopping: key determinants of shopping behaviour and motivations', *International Journal of Retail and Distribution Management*, 27 (4–5): 154.

Dholakia R R and Chiang K-P (2003) 'Shoppers in cyberspace: are they from Venus or Mars and does it matter?', *Journal of Consumer Psychology*, 13 (1/2): 171–176.

Dholakia R R, Pedersen B and Hikmet N (1995) 'Married males and shopping: are they sleeping partners?', *International Journal of Retail and Distribution Management*, 23 (3): 27–33.

Dholakia R R and Uusitalo O (2002) 'Switching to electronic stores: consumer characteristics and the perception of shopping benefits', *International Journal of Retail and Distribution Management*, 30 (10): 459–469.

Doherty N F Ellis-Chadwick F and Hart C A (1999) 'Cyber retailing in the UK: the potential of the Internet as a retail channel', *International Journal of Retail and Distribution Management*, 27 (1): 22–36.

Doidge R and Higgins C (2000) *The Big Dot.com Con*, Colliers Conrad Ritblad Erdman.

Donovan R J, Rossiter J R, Marcoolyn G and Nesdale A (1994) 'Store atmosphere and purchasing behavior', *Journal of Retailing*, 70 (3): 283–294.

Doyle P (1989) 'Building Successful Brand: the Strategic Options', *Journal of Marketing Management*, 5 (1): 77–95.

Dubé L and Morin S (2001) 'Background music pleasure and store evaluation: intensity effects and psychological mechanisms', *Journal of Business Research*, 54 (2): 107–113.

Eagly A H and Wood W (2002) 'The origins of sex differences in human behaviour: evolved dispositions versus social roles', *American Psychologist*, 54 (6): 408–423.

East R (1997) *Consumer Behaviour*, Hemel Hempstead, Prentice Hall.

Elliot R (1994) 'Addictive consumption: function and fragmentation in postmodernity', *Journal of Consumer Policy*, 17: 159–179.

English Tourist Board (1989) *Retail Leisure and Tourism*, London, English Tourist Board/James Lang Wootton.

Ernst & Young LLP (2000) *Internet Shopping: an Ernst & Young Special Report*, National Retail Federation, Washington, D.C.

Euromonitor (1987) *Concessions Retailing in the UK*, London, Euromonitor.

Evans L (2001) 'Fanbuzz.com launches mass customisation capability', *Sporting Good Business*, 34 (1).

Evans M J, Moutinho L and Van Raaij W F (1996) *Applied Consumer Behaviour*, Harlow, Addison Wesley.

Evans M, Wedande G, Ralston L and van 't Hul S (2001) 'Consumer interaction in the virtual era: some qualitative insights', *Qualitative Market Research: An International Journal*, 4 (3): 150–159.

Feinberg R, Stanton J, Keen C, Kim I-S, Hokama L and de Ruyter K (2000) 'Attraction as a determinant of mall choice', *7th International Conference on Retailing and Services Science*, Eindhoven, European Institute of Retailing and Services Science.

Fenech T O (2000) 'Attitude and security do count for shopping on the World Wide Web', *Australian and New Zealand Marketing Academy Conference ANZMAC 2000 Visionary Marketing for the 21st Century: Facing the Challenge.* Griffith University, Gold Coast, Queensland, Australia.

Fernie J (1995) 'The coming of the fourth wave: new forms of retail out-of-town development', *International Journal of Retail and Distribution Management,* 23 (1): 4–7.

Fernie J (1998) 'The breaking of the fourth wave: recent out-of-town retail developments in Britain', *International Review of Retail, Distribution and Consumer Research,* 8: 3.

Field C (1997a) *The Future of the Store,* London, Financial Times.

Field M (1997) 'Shopping as a way of life', *Architecture and Design Blueprint,* 135: 28–30.

Finn A (2000) 'Retail entertainment: lessons from the world's first mega-multi-mall', *11th International EARCD Conference on Retail Innovation,* ESADE, Barcelona.

Finn A and Louviere J J (1996) 'Shopping centre image, consideration and choice: anchor store contribution', *Journal of Business Research,* 35: 241–251.

Forshaw A and Bergstrom T (1983) *The Markets of London,* London, Penguin.

Foucault B E and Scheufele D A (2002) 'Web *vs.* campus store? Why students buy textbooks online', *Journal of Consumer Marketing,* 19 (5): 409–423.

Foxall G R and Goldsmith R E (1994) *Consumer Psychology for Marketing,* Routledge, London.

Foxall G and Hackett P (1994) '"Consumers" perceptions of micro-retail location', in Jenkins M and Knox S, *Advances in Consumer Marketing,* London, Kogan Page/Cranfield.

Foxall G R, Goldsmith R E and Brown S (1998) *Consumer Psychology for Marketing,* 2nd edition, London, Thompson Learning.

Fransella F and Bannister P (1977) *A Manual for Repertory Grid Technique,* London, Academic Press.

Frasquet M, Gil I and Molla A (2001) 'Shopping-centre selection modelling: a segmentation approach', *International Review of Retail, Distribution and Consumer Research,* 11 (1): 23–38.

Garreau J (1991) *Edge City: Life on the New Frontier,* New York, Anchor.

Gautschi D A (1981) 'Specification of patronage models for retail center choice', *Journal of Marketing Research,* 18 (May): 162–174.

Geist J F (1983) *Arcades: the History of a Building Type,* London, MIT: 4, 24.

Gentry J W and Burns A C (1977) 'How "important" are evaluative criteria in shopping center patronage?', *Journal of Retailing,* 53 (4): 73–86.

Ghosh A J and McLafferty S (1987) *Location Strategies for Retail Chains,* Lexington, Massachusetts, Heath.

Gibson B (1999) 'Beyond shopping centres – e-commerce', *British Council of Shopping Centres Conference.*

Gilbert D (1999) *Retail Marketing Management,* London, FT Prentice Hall.

Goad Plans/OXIRM (1991) *The New Guide to Shopping Centres of Great Britain,* London, Hillier Parker.

Gosling D and Maitland B (1976) *Design and Planning of Retail Systems,* London, Architectural Press.

Graeff T R (1996) 'Using promotional messages to manage the effects of brand and self image in brand evaluations', *Journal of Consumer Marketing,* 13 (3).

Greensted C S, Jardine A K S and Macfarlane J D (1978) *The Essentials of Statistics in Marketing*, London, Heinemann.

Gribbin J (2002) *Science: A History, 1543–2001*, London, Allen Lane.

Guildford J P (1954) *Psychometric Methods*, New York, McGraw Hill.

Guy C M (1984) 'The urban pattern of retailing: within the UK', in Davies and Rogers (eds) *Store Location and Store Assessment Research*, Chichester: Wiley.

Guy C M (1994a) *The Retail Development Process: location, property and planning*, London, Routledge.

Guy C M (1994b) 'Whatever happened to Regional Shopping Centres', *Geography*, 79 (4) 293–312.

Guy C M (1996) 'Corporate strategies in food retailing and their local impacts: a case study of Cardiff', *Environment and Planning A*, 28, 1575–1602.

Guy C M (1998) 'Classification of retail stores and shopping centres: some methodological issues', *Geojournal*, 45: 255–264.

Guy C M (1999) 'Retail location analysis', in Pacione M (ed.), *Applied Geography: Principles and Practice*, London, Routledge.

Hackett P M W and Foxall G R (1994) 'A factor analytic study of consumers' location specific values: a traditional high street and a modern shopping mall', *Journal of Marketing Management* 10: 163–178.

Hagel J and Armstrong A G (1997) *Net Gain: Expanding Markets through Virtual Communities*, Harvard Business School, Boston, Mass.

Haigh D (2003) 'An introduction to brand equity – how to understand and appreciate brand value and the economic impact of brand investment', *Interactive Marketing*, 5 (1): 21–32.

Haley R I (1968) 'Benefit segmentation: a decision-orientated research tool', *Journal of Marketing*, 32: 30–35.

Hallsworth A G (1988a) 'Repertory grid methodology and the analysis of group perceptions in retailing', *International Journal of Retailing*, 3 (4): 43–54.

Hallsworth A G (1988b) *The Human Impact of Hypermarkets and Superstores*, Aldershot, Avebury.

Hallsworth A (2000) 'Britain's local loyalty cards – an unmanageable revolution', *International Journal of New Product Development & Innovation Management*, 2 (2): 133–144.

Hankinson G and Cowking P (1993) *Branding in Action*, Maidenhead, McGraw-Hill.

Harris K (1998) 'Women on the Net II: the female-friendly site', *Sporting Goods Business*, 31 (13): 16.

Harris K, Davies B J and Baron S (1997) 'Conversations during purchase consideration: sales assistants and customers', *International Review of Retail, Distribution and Consumer Research*, 7 (3): 173–190.

Hartmann G W (1938) 'Immediate and remote goals as political motives', *Journal of Abnormal and Social Psychology*, 33: 87.

Haubl G and Trifts V (2000) 'Consumer decision making in inline shopping environments: the effects of interactive decision aids', *Marketing Science*, 19 (1): 4–21.

Haytko D L and Baker J (2004) 'It's all at the mall: exploring adolescent girls' experiences', *Journal of Retailing*, 80: 67–83.

Hildebrandt L (1988) 'Store image and the prediction of performance in retailing', *Journal of Business Research*, 17: 91–100.

Hillier Parker (1993) *British Shopping Centre Development Master List*, London, Hillier Parker.

Hoel P G and Jesson R J (1982) *Basic Statistics for Business and Economics*, New York, Wiley.

Houston M J and Nevin J R (1980) 'Retail shopping area image: structure and congruency between downtown areas and shopping centers', in Monroe K B (ed., 1980) *Advances in Consumer Research*, Ann Arbor, Association for Consumer Research.

Howard E (ed., 1990) *Leisure and Retailing*, Harlow, Longman/OXIRM.

Howard E (1992) 'Evaluating the success of retail out of town shopping centres', *The International Review of Retail, Distribution and Consumer Research*, 2 (1) 59–80.

Howard E (1993) 'Assessing the impact of shopping centre development: the Meadowhall case', *Journal of Property Research*, 10: 97–119.

Howard E (1995) *Partnerships in Shopping Centres*, Oxford, OXIRM.

Howard E (1997) 'The management of shopping centres: conflict or collaboration?', *The International Review of Retail, Distribution and Consumer Research*, 7(3): 263–286.

Howell R D and Rogers J D (1980) 'Research into shopping mall choice behaviour', in Monroe K B (ed., 1980) *Advances in Consumer Research*, Ann Arbor, Association for Consumer Research.

Huff D L (1963) 'A probabilistic analysis of shopping centre trade areas', *Land Economics*, 39: 81–90.

Huff D L (1964) 'Defining and estimating a trade area', *Journal of Marketing*, 28 (July): 34–38.

Illeris S (1967) 'Functional regions in Denmark about 1960: Theoretical models and empirical observations', *Geografisk Tidsskrift*, 66: 225–51.

IMRG (2003) *Internet Shopping 7% of All Retail in November*, Interactive Media in Retail Group/Forrester Research, London.

James D L, Durand R M and Dreves R A (1976) 'The use of a multi-attribute attitude model in a store image study', *Journal of Retailing*, 52 (2): 24.

Jarratt D E (1996) 'A shopper typology for retail strategy development', *The International Review of Retail Distribution and Consumer Research*, 6 (2): 196–215.

Jary M and Wileman A (1998) 'Managing retail brands', in Hart S and Murphy J (eds), *Brands: the New Wealth Creators*, Basingstoke, Macmillan Business.

Jobber D (1995) *Principles and Practice of Marketing*, London, McGraw-Hill.

Jobber D (2004) *Principles and Practice of Marketing*, 4th edition, London, McGraw Hill.

Jones M A (1999) 'Entertaining shopping experiences: an exploratory investigation', *Journal of Retailing and Consumer Services*, 6: 129–139.

Jones K and Simmons J (1990) *The Retail Environment*, London, Routledge.

Kent A and Omar O (2003) *Retailing*, London, Palgrave.

Kinnear P R and Gray C D (1997) *SPSS for Windows*, Hove, Psychology.

Kelly G A (1955) *The Psychology of Personal Constructs*, Vols. 1–2, New York, Norton.

King S (1991) 'Brand Building in the 1990s', *Journal of Marketing Management*, 7 (1): 3–14.

King T and Dennis C E (2002) 'The investigation of the phenomenon of deshopping using the theory of planned behaviour', *Proceedings of the British Academy of Management Annual Conference*, Middlesex University Business School.

King T and Dennis C E (2003) 'Interviews of deshopping behaviour: an analysis of theory of planned behaviour', *International Journal of Retail and Distribution Management*, 31 (3): 153–163.

Kinnear P R and Gray C D (1997) *SPSS for Windows*, Hove, Psychology.

Kirkup M and Rafiq M (1993) 'An Examination of Occupancy Dynamics in New Shopping Centres', *Marketing Education Group, Proceedings of Annual Conference*, 2: 559–69.

Kirkup M and Rafiq M (1994a) 'Tenancy Development in New Shopping Centres: Implications for Developers and Retailers', *The International Review of Retail Distribution and Consumer Research*, 4 (1): 17–32.

Kirkup M and Rafiq M (1994b) 'Managing Tenant Mix in New Shopping Centres', *International Journal of Retail and Distribution Management*, 22 (6): 29–37.

Kirkup M H and Rafiq M (1999) 'Marketing shopping centres: challenges in the UK context', *Journal of Marketing Practice*, 5 (5): 119–133.

Knowles J (2003) 'Value-based brand measurement and management', *Interactive Marketing*, 5 (1): 40–50.

Kolesar M B and Galbraith R W (2000) 'A services-marketing perspective on e-retailing: implications for e-retailers and directions for further research', *Internet Research: Electronic Networking Applications and Policy*, 10 (5): 424–438.

Lakshmanan T R and Hansen W G (1965) 'A Retail Market Potential Model', *Journal of the American Institute of Planners*, 31: 134–143.

Lang T and Rayner G (eds) (2001) *Why Health is the Key to the Future of Food and Farming, Joint Submission to the Policy Commission on the Future of Farming and Food*, December, www.ukpha.org.uk.

Lazarus R S (1991) *Emotion and Adaptation*, New York, Oxford University Press.

Lee K S and Tan S J (2003) 'E-retailing versus physical retailing: a theoretical model and empirical test of consumer choice', *Journal of Business Research*, 56 (11): 877–885.

LeHew M L A, Burgess B and Wesley S (2002) 'Expanding the loyalty concept to include preference for a shopping mall', *International Review of Retail, Distribution and Consumer Research*, 12 (3): 225–236.

LeHew M L A and Fairhurst A E (2000) 'US shopping mall attributes: an exploratory investigation if their relationship to retail productivity', *International Journal of Retail and Distribution Management*, 28 (6): 261–279.

Lieber C (1981) 'Periodic upgrading is essential', *National Mail Monitor*, 11: 31–36.

Lindquist J D (1974) 'Meaning of image: a survey of empirical and hypothetical evidence', *Journal of Retailing*, 50 (4): 29–38, 116.

Lindquist J D and Kaufman-Scarborough C (2000) 'Browsing and purchasing activity in selected non-store settings: a contrast between female and male shoppers', *Retailing 2000: Launching the New Millennium, Proceedings of the 6th Triennial National Retailing Conference, the Academy of Marketing Science and the American Collegiate Retailing Association*, Hofstra University, Columbus, Ohio.

Lion E (1976) *Shopping Centres Planning Development and Administration*, New York, Wiley, 2.

Lord J D (1985) 'Revitalisation of Shopping Centres', in Dawson J A and Lord J D (eds) *Shopping Centre Development: Policies and Prospects*, London, Croom Helm.

Lorek L (2001) 'Net-wear sells', *Interactive Week*, 8 (22).

Losch A (1940) *The Economics of Location*, translated by Woglam W H and Stolper W F (1954), New Haven, Connecticut, Yale University.

Lowe M S (2000a) 'Britain's regional shopping centres: new urban forms', *Urban Studies*, 37 (2): 261–274.

Lowe M S (2000b) 'Britain's regional shopping centres: new urban forms', *7th International Conference on Retailing and Services Science*, Eindhoven, European Institute of retailing and Services Science.

Luce R D (1959) *Individual Choice Behaviour*, New York, Wiley.

Lunt P (2000) 'The virtual consumer', *Virtual Society? Delivering the Virtual Promise? From Access To Use In The Virtual Society*, ESRC presentation lead by Brunel University, 19 June, London.

McCarthy E J (1960) *Basic Marketing*, Homewood, Ill, Irwin.

McCarthy S (2000) 'Your web site is calling, please hold for your customer', *Call Center Solutions*, 18 (8): 70–73.

McClelland D C (1961) *The Achieving Society*, Van Nostrand Reinhold.

McGoldrick P J (1990) *Retail Marketing*, Maidenhead, McGraw Hill.

McGoldrick P J (2002) *Retail Marketing*, 2nd edition, Maidenhead, McGraw Hill.

McGoldrick P J and Thompson M G (1992a) 'The role of image in the attraction of the out of town Centre', *The International Review of Retail, Distribution and Consumer Research*, 2 (1): 81–98.

McGoldrick P J and Thompson M G (1992b) *Regional Shopping Centres: Out-of-Town versus In-Town*, Aldershot, Avebury.

McGovern (2002) 'Keep your site simple and stable', *Information World Review*, 180.

MacKeith M (1985) *Shopping Arcades: a Gazetteer of Extant British Arcades, 1817–1939*, London, Mansell: vii and 82–83.

McKendrick N, Brewer J and Plumb J H (1982) *The Birth of a Consumer Society: The Commercialisation of Eighteenth-Century England*. Bloomington, Indiana, Indiana University.

Machleit K A and Mantel S P (2001) 'Emotional response and shopping satisfaction: moderating effects of shopper attributions', *Journal of Business Research*, 54: 97–106.

McKendrick N, Brewer J and Plumb J H (1982) *The Birth of a Consumer Society: The Commercialisation of Eighteenth-Century England*. Bloomington, Indiana, Indiana University.

Malhotra N (1989) 'A scale to measure self concepts from concepts, and product concepts, *Journal of Marketing Research*: 18.

Management Horizons (1995) *Index of Shopping Venues*, London, Management Horizon.

Management Horizons (2004) *MHE UK Shopping Index 2003/04*, London: Management Horizons.

Marjanen H (1993) *Store Location Analysis and the Mystery of Consumer Spatial Behaviour: competition between downtown shopping areas and out-of-town shopping centres as a special case*, Turku (Finland), Turku School of Economics and Business Administration.

Marjanen H (1995a) 'A behavioural segmentation approach to out-of-town shopping, *8th International Conference on Research in the Distributive Trades*, Cescom, Centro di studi sul commercio Universita Bocconi.

Marjanen H (1995b) 'Longitudinal study on consumer behaviour with special reference to out-of-town shopping: Experience from Turku, Finland', *Journal of Retailing and Consumer Services*, 2 (4): 163–174.

Marjanen H (1997) *Distance and Store Choice With Special Reference to Out-of-Town Shopping*, Turku (Finland), Turku School of Economics and Business Administration.

Marjanen H (1998) *Staying Alive – Towards a Survival Strategy for Small Shopping Centres in Rural Areas*, Turku (Finland), Turku School of Economics and Business Administration.

Marshall J D (ed., 1967) *Autobiography of William Stout of Lancaster, 1665–1752*, New York, Barnes and Noble.

Martin P G (1982) *Shopping Centre Management*, London, Spon.

Martineau P (1958) 'The personality of the retail store', *Harvard Business Review*, 36 (1): 47–55.

Mathwick C, Malhotra N and Rogdon E (2001) 'Experiential value: conceptualization, measurement and application in the catalog and Internet shopping environment', *Journal of Retailing*, 77 (1): 39–56.

Mattila A S and Wirtz J (2001) 'Congruency of scent and music as a driver of in-store evaluations and behaviour', *Journal of Retailing*, 77 (2): 273–289.

Maslow A H (1943) 'A theory of human motivation', *Psychological Review*, 50, July: 370–396.

Medway D, Alexander A, Bennison D and Warnaby G (1999) '"Retailers" financial support for town centre management', *International Journal of Retail and Distribution Management*, 27 (6–7): 246.

Mehrabian A and Russell J A (1974) *An Approach to Environmental Psychology*, Cambridge (MA), MIT Press.

Michon R and Chebat J-C (2002) 'Cross cultural mall shopping values and habitats: a comparison between English- and French-speaking Canadians', *Journal of Business Research*, 57 (8): 883–892.

Miller D (1998) *A theory of shopping*, Ithaca, NY, Cornell University.

Miller D, Jackson P, Thrift N, Holbrook B and Rowlands M (1998) *Shopping, Place and Identity*, London, Routledge.

Miller G (2001) *The Mating Mind: How Sexual Choice Shaped the Evolution of Human Nature*, Vintage.

Mintel (1997) *Shopping Centres*, London, Mintel.

Mitchell V-W and Kiral H R (1999) 'Risk positioning of UK multiple retailers', *The International Review of Retail, Distribution and Consumer Research*, 9 (1): 17–39.

Mui H-C and Mui L H (1989) *Shops and Shopkeeping in Eighteenth-Century England*, Montreal, McGill-Queens University: 8–18 and 226.

Murphy J (1989) *Brand Valuation: Establishing a True and Fair View*, London, Business Books.

Murphy J (1998) 'What is branding', in Hart S and Murphy J (eds), *Brands: the New Wealth Creators*, Basingstoke, Macmillan Business.

Murray H A (1938) *Explorations in Personality*, New York, Oxford.

Myers J H (1976) 'Benefit structure analysis – a new tool for product planning', *Journal of Marketing*, 32: 30–55.

Nakanishi M and Cooper L G (1974) 'Parameter estimation for a multiplicative interaction model – least squares approach', *Journal of Marketing Research*, 11 (3): 303–311.

NAMNEWS (2003) 'US: eBay tells analysts growth can be sustained', *NAMNEWS The Original Newsletter for Key Account Managers*, EMR-NAMNEWS, London, www.kamcity.com/namnews.

NetValue (2001) *Home Internet Use Continues to Grow in the UK*, London, NetValue, www.netvalue.com.

Newman A J (2002/3) 'Some manipulable elements of the service setting and their impact on company image and reputation', *International Journal of New Product Development and Innovation Management*, 4 (3): 287–304.

Newman A J and Foxall G R (2003) 'In-store customer behaviour in the fashion sector: some emerging methodological and theoretical directions', *International Journal of Retail and Distribution Management*, 31 (11): 591–600.

Newman A J and Patel D (2004) 'The Marketing directions of two fashion retailers', *European Journal of Marketing* (special issue: Fashion Retailing) 38 (7/8) pp.

Newton Sir I (1687) *Philosophiae Naturalis Principia Mathematica*, London, Juffu Societas Regia ac Typis.

Nielsen NetRatings (2003) www.nielsen-netratings.com Accessed August.

Nishikawa T (1989) 'New product planning at Hitachi', *Long Range Planning*, 22 (4): 20–24.

Novak T P, Hoffman D L and Yung Y-F 'Measuring the customer experience in online environments: a structural modelling approach, *Marketing Science*, 19 (1): 22–42.

O'Brien L and Harris F (1991) *Retailing: Shopping, Society, Space*, London, David Fulton.

Opacic S and Potter R B (1986) 'Grocery store cognitions of disadvantaged consumer groups: a Reading case study', *Tijdschrift voor Econ. en Soc. Geografie*, 77 (4): 288–298.

Openshaw S (1973) 'Insoluble problems in shopping model calibration when the trip pattern is not known', *Regional Studies*, 7: 367–371.

Oppewal H, Louviere J J and Timmermans H J P (1994) 'Modeling hierarchical conjoint processes with integrated choice experiments', *Journal of Marketing Research*, XXXI (February): 92–105.

Oppewal H and Timmermans H (1997) 'Retailer Self-perceived Store Image and Competitive Position', *International Review of Retail, Distribution and Consumer Research*, 7 (3): 41–59.

Oppewal H and Timmermans H (1999) 'Modelling consumer perception of public space in shopping centres', *Environment and Behaviour*, 31 (1): 45.

Oppenheim A N (1992) *Questionnaire Design, Interviewing and Attitude Measurement*, London, Pinter.

Orians G (1980) 'Habitat selection: general theory and applications to human behaviour', in Lockard J S (ed.), *The Evolution of Human Social Behaviour*: 49–66, Chicago, Elsevier.

Orians G (1986) 'An ecological and evolutionary approach to landscape aesthetics', in Penning-Rowsell E C and Lowenthal D (eds), *Landscape Meaning and Values*, 3–25, London, Allen & Unwin.

Orton D C (1999) 'Internet News', *Science, Technology and Innovation*, October (5): 12.

Osgood G E, Suci G J and Tannenbaum P M (1957) *The Measurement of Meaning*, Urbana, Illinois, University of Illinois.

Otnes C and McGrath M A (2001) 'Perceptions and realities of male shopping behaviour', *Journal of Retailing*, 77: 111–137.

OXIRM (1993) *The Shopping Centre Industry 1993: 30 Years of Growth*, British Council of Shopping Centres.

Parsons A G (2003) 'Assessing the effectiveness of shopping mall promotions: customer analysis', *International Journal of Retail and Distribution Management*, 31 (2): 74–79.

Pavitt D (1997) 'Retailing and the high street: the future of the electronic home shopping industry', *International Journal of Retail and Distribution Management*, 25 (1): 38–43.

Phipps R and Simmons C (1996) *Understanding Customers*, Oxford, Butterworth-Heinemann.

PreFontayne M (1999) 'Beyond shopping centres – e-commerce', *British Council of Shopping Centres Conference*.

Pung G and Stewart D (1983) 'Cluster analysis in marketing research: review and suggestions for application', *Journal of Marketing Research*, 20: 134–148.

Quelch J (1999) 'Retailing – confronting the challenges that face bricks and mortar', *Harvard Business Review*, 77 (4–July/August): 159.

Randall G (1997) *Branding*, London, Kogan Page.

Redstone L G (1973) *New Dimensions in Shopping Centres and Stores*, New York, McGraw Hill: xvii.

Reilly W J (1929) 'Methods for the study of retail relationships', *University of Texas Bulletin*, 2944.

Reilly W J (1931) *The Law of Gravitation*, New York, Knickerbocker Press.

Reimers V and Clulow V (2004) 'Retail concentration: a comparison of spatial convenience in shopping strips and shopping centres', *Journal of Retailing and Consumer Services*, 11 (4): 207–221.

Retail (1989) 'No fears at Sears', *Retail*, 6 (4): 16–24.

Reynolds J (1992) 'Generic Models of European Shopping Centre Development', *European Journal of Marketing*, 26 (8/9): 48–60.

Reynolds J (1993) 'The proliferation of the planned shopping centre' in Bromley D F and Thomas C J (eds), *Retail Change Contemporary Issues*, London, UCL.

Reynolds J and Schiller R (1992) 'A new classification of shopping centres in Great Britain using multiple branch numbers', *Journal of Property Research*, 9: 122–160.

Rheingold H (1993) *Virtual Community: homesteading on the Electronic Frontier*, Addison Wesley, Reading, Mass.

Reynolds J (1993) 'The proliferation of the planned shopping centre' in Bromley D F and Thomas C J (eds), *Retail Change Contemporary Issues*, London, UCL.

Reynolds J (2000) 'Pricing dynamics and European retailing: direct and indirect impacts of eCommerce', *Proceedings of the International EARCD Conference on Retail Innovation* (CD-ROM), ESADE, European Association for Education and Research in Commercial Distribution, Barcelona.

Rogers D S (1984) 'Modern methods of sales forecasting' in Davies and Rogers, *Store Location and Store Assessment Research*, Chichester, Wiley: 319–331.

Rogers E M (1995) *The Diffusion of Innovations*, 4th edition, Free Press, New York.

Rhodes T and Whitaker R (1967) 'Forecasting shopping demand', *JTPI*, May: 188–192.

RICS Foundation (2000) *20:20 Visions of the Future*, Royal Institute of Chartered Surveyors.

Rohm A J and Swaminathan V (2004) 'A typology of online shoppers based on shopping motivations,' *Journal of Business Research*, 57 (7): 748–757.

Routemaster (~1998) SK 6801, St Albans, Pan Star.

Roy A (1994) 'Correlates of mall visit frequency', *Journal of Retailing*, 70 (2): 139–161.

Rudgley R (2000) *The Secrets of the Stone Age*, Evergreen, CO, USA, Century.

Ruiz J-P, Chebat J-C and Hansen P (2005 forthcoming) *Journal of Retailing and Consumer Services*.

Russell J A and Pratt G (1980) 'A description of the affective quality attributed to environments', *Journal of Personality and Social Psychology*, 38 (2), pp. 311–322.

Schiller R and Jarrett A (1985) 'A ranking of shopping centres using multiple branch numbers', *Journal of Property Research*, 9: 122–160.

Scott N K (1991) *Shopping Centre Design*, London, Spon: 156.

Scott P (1970) *Geography and Retailing*, London, Hutchinson.

Scudder B (2000) 'Dubai comes of e-age', *Gulf Marketing Review*, November: 86–87.

SERPLAN (1987) Retail Monitoring Working Party. Regional shopping centres around London: background papers, London, SERPLAN.

Severin V, Louviere J J and Finn A (2001) 'The stability of retail shopping choices over time and across countries', *Journal of Retailing*, 77 (2): 185–202.

Sherman E and Smith R B (1987) 'Mood states of shoppers and store image: promising interactions and possible behavioural effect', *Advances in Consumer Research*, 14 (1): 251–254.

Sheth J N, Mittal B and Newman B I (1999) *Customer Behaviour: Consumer Behaviour and Beyond*, Fort Worth, Dryden.

Shim S and Eastlick M A (1998) 'The hierarchical influence of personal values on mall shopping attitude and behaviour', *Journal of Retailing*, 74 (1, Spring): 139–160.

Shim S, Eastlick M A and Lotz S (2000) 'Assessing the impact of Internet Shopping on Store shopping among mall shoppers and Internet users', *Journal of Shopping Center Research*.

Shim S, Eastlick M A, Lotz S L and Warrington P (2001) 'An online prepurchase intentions model: the role of intention to search', *Journal of Retailing*, 77: 397–416.

Shop.org (2001) *Shop.org Press Room*, National Retail Federation, Washington D.C.: www.shop.org.

Simkin L P (1996) 'Tackling barriers to effective implementation of modelling in retail marketing applications', *The International Review of Retail, Distribution and Consumer Research*, 6 (3): 225–241.

Sinha P K and Uniyal D P (forthcoming 2005) 'Using observational research for behavioural segmentation of shoppers', *Journal of Retailing and Consumer Services*.

Sirgy M J and Cocksun S A (1989) 'The store loyalty concept: dimensions and measurement', in Cocksun S A (ed.), *Retail Marketing Strategy*, New York, quorum.

Sit J, Merrilees W and Birch D (2003) 'Entertainment-seeking shopping centre patrons: the missing segments', *International Journal of Retail and Distribution Management*, 31 (2): 80–94.

Smith P and Burns D J (1996) 'Atmospherics and retail environments: the case for the "power aisle"', *International Journal of Retail and Distribution management*, 24 (1): 7–14.

Smith R B and Sherman E (1993) 'Effects of store image and mood on consumer behaviour: a theoretical and empirical analysis', *Advances in Consumer Research*, 20 (1): 631.

Spies K, Hesse F and Loesch K (1997) 'Store atmosphere, mood and purchasing behaviour', *International Journal of Research in Marketing*, 14: 1–17.

Sternlieb G W and Hughes J H (1981) 'Introduction: the uncertain future of shopping centres', in Sternlieb G W and Hughes J H (eds), *Shopping Centres USA*, Rutgers, State University of New Jersey: 1–18.

Suarez A, Rodriguez del Bosque I, Rodriguez-Poo J M and Moral I (2004) 'Accounting for heterogeneity in shopping centre choice models', *Journal of Retailing and Consumer Services*, 11: 119–129.

Swinyard W R (1992) 'An opportunity based model of customer service', *The International Review of Retail, Distribution and Consumer Research*, 2 (1): 1–12.

Tang E and Ingene C (2000) 'Determinants of Consumer Shopping Productivity', *7th International Conference on Retailing and Services Science*, Eindhoven, European Institute of Retailing and Services Science.

Tauber E M (1972) 'Marketing notes and communications: Why do people shop?' *Journal of Marketing*, 36, October: 46–59.

Timmermans H, Van Der Heijden R and Westerfield H (1982) 'Cognition of urban retailing structures: a Dutch case study', *Tijdschrift voor Econ. en Soc. Geografie*, 1: 2–12.

Turchiano F (1990) 'Farewell field of dreams: 'Build it and they will come' era ends for shopping centres', *Retail Issues Newsletter*, 2 (9): 1–4.

Turley L W and Chebat J-C (2002) 'Linking retail strategy, atmospheric design and shopping behaviour', *Journal of Marketing Management*, 18: 125–144.

Turley L W and Milliman R E (2000) 'Atmospheric effects on shopping behaviour: a review of the experimental evidence', *Journal of Business Research*, 49 (2): 193–211.

Thomke S (2003) 'R&D comes to services', *Harvard Business Review*, April: 3–11.

Uncles M D (1996) 'Classifying shoppers by their shopping-trip behaviour: a polythetic-divisive method', *Marketing Intelligence and Planning*, 14 (1): 35–44.

Underhill P (1999) *Why We Buy*, London, Orion.

Vallerand R J (1997) 'Toward a hierarchical model of intrinsic and extrinsic motivation', *Advances in Experimental Social Psychology*, 29: 271–360.

Van den Poel D and Leunis J (1999) 'Customer-orientated conceptual model of repeat direct-mail patronage behavior', *10th International Conference on Research in the Distributive Trades*, Stirling, Institute for Retail Studies.

Verdict (2000) *Verdict on Electronic Shopping 2000*, Verdict Research, London.

Verdict (2001) *Verdict on Electronic Shopping 2001*, Verdict Research, London.

Verdict (2002) *Verdict on Electronic Shopping 2002*, Verdict Research, London.

Verdict (2003) *Verdict on Electronic Shopping 2003*, Verdict Research, London.

Victoria Centre (~1987) *Victoria Centre Information Pack*, Capital Shopping Centres.

Vincent A, Clark H and English A (2000) 'Retail distribution: a multi-channel traffic jam', *International Journal of New Product Development & Innovation Management*, 2 (2): 179–196.

Vrechopoulos A P (2001) *Virtual Store Atmosphere in Internet Retailing: Measuring Virtual Retail Store Layout Effects on Consumer Buying Behaviour*, Brunel University, unpublished PhD thesis.

Vrechopoulos A P, O'Keefe R M, Doukidis G I and Siomkos G J (2004) 'Virtual store layout: an experimental comparison in the context of grocery retail', *Journal of Retailing*, 80 (1): 13–22.

Vrechopoulos A P, Papamichail G and Doukidis G I (2002) 'Identifying patterns in Internet retail store layouts' in Pardalos P and Tsitiringos V (eds) *Financial Engineering, E-Commerce and Supply Chain*, Kluwer Academic Publishers.

Wahba M A and Bridwell L G (1976) 'Maslow reconsidered: a review of the research on the need hierarchy theory', *Organizational Behaviour and Human Performance*, 15: 212–240.

Wakefield K L and Baker J (1998) 'Excitement at the mall: determinants and effects on shopping response', *Journal of Retailing*, 74 (4): 515.

Waller M (2000) *1700: Scenes from London Life*, London, Hodder and Stoughton.

Walsh C (2003a) 'Social meaning and social place in the shopping galleries of early modern London', in Benson J and Ugolini L (eds), *A Nation of Shopkeepers: Five Centuries of British Retailing*, London, Tauris.

Walsh C (2003b) 'The shopping galaries of early modern London in Benson J and Ugolini (eds), *A Nation of Shopkeepers: Five Centuries of British Retailing*, London, Tauris.

Warnaby G and Davies B J (1997) 'Commentary: cities as service factories? Using the Servuction system for marketing cities as shopping destinations', *International Journal of Retail and Distribution Management*, 25 (6–7): 204–210.

Warnaby G (1998) 'Marketing UK cities as shopping destinations: problems and prospects', *Journal of Retailing and Consumer Services*, 5 (1): 55–58.

Warnaby G and Medway D (2000) 'Competitive Responses by Town Centres to Off-Centre Retail Developments', *The Planning and Management of Retail Locations, Annual Manchester Conference for Contemporary Issues in Retail Marketing*, Manchester Metropolitan University.

Wensley R (1994) 'Strategic marketing: a review', in Baker (1994).

Westbrook R A (1980) 'Intrapersonal affective influences upon consumer satisfaction', *Journal of Consumer Research*, 7 (June): 49–54.

Westbrook R A and Black W C (1985) 'A motivation-based shopper typology', *Journal of Retailing*, 61 (1): 78–103.

Wilke W L (1970) *An Empirical Analysis of Alternative Bases for Market Segmentation*, doctoral dissertation, Stanford, Stanford University.

Wilson A G (1971) 'A family of spatial interaction models and associated development', *Environment and Planning*, 3: 1–32 and Batty M (1971) 'Exploratory calibration of a retail locational model using search by golden section', *Environment and Planning*, 3: 411–432.

Wong G K M, Lu Y and Yuan L L (2001) 'SCATTR: an instrument for measuring shopping centre attractiveness', *International Journal of Retail and Distribution Management*, 29 (2): 76–86.

Worthington S (1999) 'A classic example of a misnomer: the loyalty card', *Journal of Targeting, Measurement and Analysis for Marketing*, 8 (3): 222–234.

Worthington S and Hallsworth A (1999) 'Cards in context – the comparative development of local loyalty schemes', *International Journal of Retail and Distribution Management*, 27 (10): 420–428.

Yankelovich D (1964) 'New criteria for market segmentation', *Harvard Business Review*, 42: 83–90.

Yoo C, Park J and NacUnnis D J (1998) 'Effects of store characteristics and in-store emotional experiences on store attitude', *Journal of Business Research*, 42 (3): 253–263.

Young R A (1985) 'Suburban Growth Poles' in Dawson J A and Lord J D (eds), *Shopping Centre Development: Policies and Prospects*, London, Croom Helm.

Young W (1975) 'Distance decay values and shopping centre size', *Professional Geographer*, 27: 304–309.

Winston R (2002) *Human Instinct*, London, Bantam.

www.nielsen-netratings.com *Property Level, UK at Home and Work Combined, March 2002–March 2003*, Nielson/NetRating, accessed June 2003.

Russia is now the largest growth market for super-regional centres (C B Hillier Parker, 2002).

Index